THEORIES OF DEVELOPMENT

CLASS, STATE, & DEVELOPMENT

Series Editor:
DALE L. JOHNSON
Department of Sociology, Rutgers University

Class, State, & Development intends to provide class analysis perspectives on questions of the state and of development. Volumes will emphasize critical and Marxist approaches to the class structure and class relations of advanced capitalist societies, the social basis of contemporary states—both democratic and authoritarian—and the social and economic development of Latin America, Asia, Africa, and the Middle East. The series is published in cooperation with the Department of Sociology, Rutgers University.

Volumes in this series:
1. *CLASS & SOCIAL DEVELOPMENT*
2. *THEORIES OF DEVELOPMENT*
(other titles in preparation)

THEORIES OF DEVELOPMENT

MODE OF PRODUCTION OR DEPENDENCY?

EDITED BY

RONALD H. CHILCOTE
AND
DALE L. JOHNSON

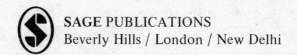

SAGE PUBLICATIONS
Beverly Hills / London / New Delhi

For information address:

SAGE Publications, Inc.
275 South Beverly Drive
Beverly Hills, California 90212

SAGE Publications India Pvt. Ltd.
C-236 Defence Colony
New Delhi 110 024, India

SAGE Publications Ltd
28 Banner Street
London EC1Y 8QE, England

Printed in the United States of America

Library of Congress Cataloging in Publication Data

Main entry under title:

Theories of development.

  (Class, state, and development ; v. 2)
  Bibliography: p.
  1. Capitalism—Addresses, essays, lectures.
2. Dependency—Addresses, essays, lectures.   3. Imperialism—Addresses, essays, lectures.   4. Marxian economics—Addresses, essays, lectures.   5. Underdeveloped areas—Addresses, essays, lectures.   I. Chilcote, Ronald H.
II. Johnson, Dale L.   III. Series.
HB501.M689   1982   330.12'2   82-19141
ISBN 0-8039-1925-5
ISBN 0-8039-1926-3 (pbk.)

FIRST PRINTING

Contents

Preface

In the intense international climate of the 1960s and early 1970s a conceptual revolution in thinking about development and underdevelopment exploded in intellectual and political spheres. "Dependency theory" achieved a certain theoretical and ideological hegemony among academics and reformist and revolutionary thinkers. However, it did not go unnoticed that dependency formulations represented a considerable "revisionist" challenge to traditional Marxism. And numerous Marxists in Europe, Latin America, and throughout the world took up the challenge. By the mid-1970s, critical dissection of dependency views incited serious questioning of the adequacy of the entire framework. A new approach to development, underdevelopment, and imperialism emerged to rival dependency theory. "Mode of production" analysis, while it is more faithful to traditional Marxist principles, is not a resurrected orthodoxy; its origins are largely traceable to a relatively new theoretical current, European "Marxist structuralism."

This volume plunges deeply into the theoretical and political controversies surrounding dependency and modes of production. Its immediate origins are in papers (here greatly revised) presented at a July 1979 panel of the Congress of Americanists in Vancouver, British Columbia. The well-attended feature panel of the congress was scheduled from 9:00 a.m. to noon. At 1:00 p.m. we broke for lunch. An even larger crowd appeared for the afternoon dialogue. Discussion raged among the panelists, between members of the audience and the panelists, and within the audience, becoming ever more heated. At about 4:00 p.m. an indignant person jumped onto his chair, denounced André Gunder Frank, and led a walkout of some of the audience. At 5:00 p.m. I put down my now useless gavel and left. Some of the intellectual and political excitement of that moment is

7

undoubtedly subdued in the present, more formal form of book chapters. We do expect, though, that this book will contribute to, and serve to continue, a serious search for an understanding of development, underdevelopment, imperialism, and dependency.

Dale Johnson

Chesapeake Center

Ronald H. Chilcote:

Introduction: Dependency or Mode of Production? Theoretical Issues

During the past generation various lines of thinking have evolved around questions of large-scale economic and social change. The literature has emphasized the themes of development and under-development, beginning with the idea of modernization, then turning to dependency in the less advanced areas of the world, and more recently examining precapitalist and capitalist modes of production. In particular, the challenge to earlier models of modernization and imperialism emanated in the thought of Latin American social scientists. Today the major debates revolve around interpretations of dependency or modes of production. The present volume includes essays that reflect these positions.

My introductory essay identifies these positions, debates, and questions and is organized around three concerns: first, to trace the major lines of thinking; second, to discuss contending issues in the literature; and third, to present the essays that follow. As a basis for discussion, Figure 1.1 offers a graphic representation of much of the thinking about development.

Theories of modernization assumed the evolution of capitalist development along a linear path toward modernization. The idea of modernization seems to have originated in the nineteenth-century belief that the Western world would civilize other backward areas by spreading Western values, capital, and technology. Underdeveloped areas would evolve into developed, modern nations along paths charted

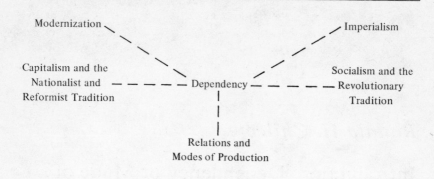

FIGURE 1.1 **Approaches to Study of Capitalist Development**

in the West. Modernization theory often was associated with the practices of Western democracy: constitutionalism, electoral participation, and competitive politics. Sometimes this theory was tied to nationalism and the emergence of the nation-state, first in the experience of Europe and later the Third World. Then too, modernization implied industrialization. The economic and political bases of modernization theory were contained in the writings of two Americans. Economic historian Walt W. Rostow (1960) outlined stages of economic growth through which societies tend to pass. Political scientist Samuel Huntington (1968), leaving many of the earlier democratic biases of modernization aside, emphasized authority and control over rapid social and economic change so as to avoid political decay that might ensue and bring instability and violence. While still in fashionable use today, these theories are criticized by many for their ethnocentrism in favor of the model of Anglo-American society and their assumption of a continuous progression through stages of development. They also have been rejected by some for their emphasis on the national society and lack of attention to the international order (Valenzuela and Valenzuela, 1978).

Modernization reflected the conservative intellectual tradition. On the critical side a theory of imperialism evolved. Imperialism can be traced to the Greek and Roman empires, but it finds its modern form in the mercantilism of the sixteenth and seventeenth centuries. At that time Portugal, in an expansionist phase, gained control of major trading points along the African coast, thereby ensuring its hold over African exports of gold and ivory as well as control over routes to the

Far East. Perry Anderson (1962) called this exchange imperialism and characterized a later phase, when the Portuguese penetrated the interior of Africa and established hegemony over the source of these raw materials, as extraction imperialism. Later, with the rise of industrialization and the rapid expansion of manufacturing in Europe, there was a need not only to control raw materials but to establish markets for the products of the new industrialization. This period dates to about 1870 and is often called the "new" imperialism in contrast to the old or classical forms (Magdoff, 1969).

Contemporary theories of imperialism tend to focus on the rise of monopoly capital in advanced capitalist countries and the push to expand markets to other areas in order to mitigate the problem of overproduction at home. This approach was first offered in 1902 by the English liberal, E. J. Hobson, who condemned British imperialism and urged an increase in domestic consumption to stem the drive of capital to expand into foreign markets. Lenin was influenced by Hobson in his treatment of imperialism as the highest stage of capitalism, and also by Hilferding in his emphasis on the exploitive role of finance capital. Two lines of thinking emanate from the literature thereafter. Followers of Hobson and later Schumpeter (1955) adopted the liberal line and the idea that imperialism would wither away through an increase of domestic consumption, the progression of capitalism itself, or peaceful processes designed to mitigate military expansionism and international conflict in the interests of the capitalist class as a whole. A Marxist line in the tradition of Lenin, Bukharin, and Rosa Luxemburg focused on imperialism as the inevitable expansion of capital everywhere. While finance capital was seen as the motor force of this imperialism during the early twentieth century, later observers such as Baran and Sweezy (1966) attempted to update and revise the theory by emphasizing the surplus capital of large monopolies. Complementing this work was the attention by Barnet and Muller (1974) to the rise of multinational corporations after World War II, a phase Ernest Mandel (1975) called "late capitalism." These views of imperialism tended to focus on capitalism in the advanced countries. This concern with the imperial center and the failure to analyze the impact of monopoly capital on internal dominant classes in colonized areas prompted some writers to turn their attention to the effects of imperialism in what came to be called the "periphery." Galtung (1971), for example, applied a model of center and periphery to a theory of imperialism. His structural approach was similar to interpretations that emphasized the negative consequences of capitalism in the less developed parts of the world. Thus an alternative view of imperialism turned to the periphery.

The concern with underdevelopment and dependency evolved from the earlier work on imperialism and concern with its effects. Relationships of dependency and descriptions of exploitation and deformation were mentioned in the writings of Marx, Lenin, and Trotsky, but no full theory had been elaborated. Third World writers also noted that the writing on imperialism overlooked internal structure and suffered from a lack of class analysis. Their work attempted to shift analysis from external to internal considerations.

Two traditions emerged. A nationalist-developmentalist view was concerned with the prospects for reforming capitalism in the periphery, given the rise of nationalism and a tendency for nations to resist outside influence and to try to develop their economies along more autonomous lines. The other tradition not only opposed outside influence but urged revolutionary means to overcome imperialism and transform underdevelopment.

After World War II nationalist sentiment in the periphery was accompanied by an outcry against imperialism, demands that national resources be preserved, and insistence that the domestic economy be transformed through state-guided national capitalism. Theoretically, these ideas were manifested through the writings of the United Nations Economic Commission for Latin America and its chief economist, Raúl Prebisch. Prebisch divided the world into two parts, a center of industrialized countries and a periphery of underdeveloped countries. Prebisch demonstrated that there had been a deterioration in the terms of trade for the periphery, the result of distortions in international commodity markets; this impeded development because of a decline in exchange earnings. The solution to this disparity was industrialization promoted through the building of an infrastructure along with tariff protection against high-cost imports that could be produced domestically. Prebisch believed that the state must play a major role in coordinating private and public enterprise to overcome obstacles to development and contradictions between center and periphery. Government intervention in the form of subsidy, tariff protection, and import substitution would allow the periphery to counter the hegemonic centers and move toward an autonomous capitalist solution (see Prebisch, 1980, for an update on his views).

The Prebisch approach influenced other thinkers, such as Chilean economist Osvaldo Sunkel, who believed that dependency links the development of the international capitalist system to the local processes of development and underdevelopment within a society; he saw underdevelopment and development as simultaneous processes representing two facets in the evolution of capitalism. He was particularly concerned about denationalization and inequality in the periphery (Sunkel, 1972). Brazilian economist Celso Furtado illustrated these consequences in his historical overview of Portuguese commercial influence in Brazil (1963). His book included an underlying explanation of development and underdevelopment through Brazilian history, and he considered underdevelopment the consequence of external dependence. Furtado and Sunkel emphasized the need for reforms and state planning in the drive for autonomous national development. They also recognized the deforming character of outside capital as well as the limitations of a capitalism that is unable to reproduce itself in the periphery and serve the needs of the majority of people.

Fernando Henrique Cardoso, the Brazilian sociologist, and Pablo González Casanova, the Mexican political sociologist, presented differing versions of the autonomous capitalist approach. Cardoso emphasized a structural perspective but wrote about situations of dependency rather than dependency theory; he suggested that "associated dependent development" in some situations might permit some local participation in production and yield growth (see Cardoso, 1973; and Cardoso and Faletto, 1979). González Casanova (1970) believed that imperialism was somewhat contained in Mexico but that an internal colonialism, similar to the colonialist relationship between nations, was evident. A marginal society of Indians was exploited and dependent on the dominant society ruled from Mexico City, so that in this dualist relationship, one society dominates and exploits the other. The solution would be a democratic revolution and a class alliance of the masses with the bourgeoisie to oppose imperialism and support capitalist democracy and peaceful development. Thus a national bourgeoisie could be expected to emerge as a unifying force. Both González Casanova and Cardoso envisaged an eventual socialist society, but they believed that a progressive capitalism would make an impact.

While all these views incorporated notions of nationalism and autonomy to counter the exploitive tendencies of the world market and multinational firms, a quite different perspective also was evident after World War II. Revolutionary in outlook and oriented toward socialism, this view opposed imperialism and saw capitalism as a negative force in the periphery. Among those advocating this stance were Silvio Frondizi, Sergio Bagú, and Caio Prado Júnior in an early period and writers such as Theotonio dos Santos and Ruy Mauro Marini in more recent times. Briefly, I want to locate their work and ideas in this revolutionary tradition.

Frondizi, an Argentine Marxist influential in leftist intellectual circles, was one of the first to focus on questions of underdevelopment and dependency. An essay published in 1947 identified two imperialisms, British commercial imperialism and U.S. industrial imperialism. He linked imperialism with the national bourgeoisie in Argentina and attacked the notion of a dual society, arguing that capitalism in its various forms, not feudalism, was responsible for the underdevelopment and dependency on world capitalism (Frondizi, 1947, 1957). This line of thinking was adopted by another Argentine Trotskyist, Luis Vitale (1968), known for his writing on capitalist underdevelopment and dependency in Chile.

Sergio Bagú (1949), an Argentine historian, developed similar ideas about the relationship of the advanced capitalist nations to backward colonial areas. As early as 1944, while lecturing in the United States, he elaborated on the economic structure of the Spanish and Portuguese colonial regimes in Latin America. Bagú argued that capitalism appeared very early in the area and that the international market had shaped the structure of the colonial economies. He believed that while feudal-like institutions appeared during the colonial period, they were not the cause of underdevelopment, nor did the feudal cycle of the Iberian Peninsula reproduce itself in the colonies. Important, however, were accumulation of capital, financial capital, production for markets, and commerce.

Caio Prado Júnior (1967) analyzed the consequences of capitalism in Brazil since the colonial period. He argued that Brazilian relations with the outside world involved dependence on Portugal and ties to an international market. Further, the Brazilian economy was characterized by a cyclical pattern of successive periods of prosperity and decline, a consequence of the reliance on international trade. Prado believed that feudalism was of no importance in Brazil, and he attacked the idea that nationalism and a national bourgeoisie could stand up to imperialism. Socialism achieved through revolutionary means would be the only course (Prado Júnior, 1966).

Two other Brazilians, Theotonio dos Santos (1970) and Ruy Mauro Marini, also advocated revolution and socialism. Dos Santos adopted the notion of new dependency to explain the rise of the multinational corporations in the period following World War II. He also accepted the premise that expansion of imperialist centers accompanies their domination over the world economy. He emphasized the

unequal and combined nature of development, concepts drawn from
the writing of Trotsky and his followers, but he was also apparently
influenced by Paul Baran, who had insisted that monopolistic control
at the center results in transfers of surplus from dependent to dominant countries. Thus, he showed the compatibility of theories of
dependency and imperialism, and he pushed for revolutionary action
as a way out of dependency (Dos Santos, 1978). Marini politically
aligned himself to a position favoring revolution, and he attempted to
locate his analysis in the process of capitalist production rather than
circulation. Dependent capitalism, he believed, was unable to reproduce itself through the process of accumulation. He offered the thesis
of subimperialism to explain the outward expansion of Brazil in
search of new markets, especially in Latin America, as a means of
coping with the failure of Brazilian industrial capital to create new
domestic markets and increased productivity. Subimperialism was
accompanied by impoverishment of Brazilian workers, and consequently their response should be armed struggle (see Marini, 1969,
1973).

The theories of André Gunder Frank received widespread recep-
tion by students and scholars of underdevelopment during the 1960s,
and since that time critics have identified a number of weaknesses in
this writing. Frank also assumed a revolutionary position, arguing
that capitalism, not feudalism, had been dominant in Latin America
since the colonial period and attacking the notion that the national
bourgeoisie was a progressive force for change. He also advocated
the thesis of capitalist development of underdevelopment, and, influenced by Paul Baran, emphasized the appropriation by the center of
economic surplus in the periphery (Frank, 1966, 1967). Partly in response to his critics, Frank later moved from a theory of underdevelopment and dependency to analyses of the world capitalist
system.

The debates on the usefulness of theories of dependency and underdevelopment have persisted for some time. Some of the useful reviews
of these themes are Chilcote (1974), O'Brien (1975), and Munck
(1981), while the most comprehensive treatment is in Anthony
Brewer (1980, especially Part III). Among the issues emanating from
these debates are the question of external versus internal determinations, whether the national bourgeoisie can be a viable force for
change, and concern over the emphasis on unequal exchange and production relations. This latter issue particularly concerned John Taylor
(1979) in his critical overview, *From Modernization to Modes of
Production: A Critique of the Sociologies of Development and*

Underdevelopment. Taylor attacked both bourgeois and Marxist efforts to elaborate theories of development and underdevelopment in the periphery, and he advocated modes of production analysis as a means for understanding noncapitalist social formations. His work, however, was but one contribution among many in the debate over mode of production to which I now turn.

Historically, Marxism has focused on modes of production as successive stages, each stage marked by a transition in which the old mode is undermined by new forms of organization. In the European experience the transition from feudalism to capitalism was of particular importance and was accompanied by a revolutionary process that swept away the feudal mode of production. Marx emphasized the structural or stage view of this process in his *Preface to the Critique of Political Economy,* although the determinism implied in his treatment was not characteristic of his writings in general. Lenin wrote of the transition from feudalism to capitalism in *The Development of Capitalism in Russia,* in which he focused on the transition of a backward country to a new social formation; his treatment was similar to writers who examine the transition in the contemporary underdeveloped world. Trotsky, with his emphasis on combined and uneven development, was able to recognize the importance of backward societies that could not necessarily advance from stage to stage in progressive fashion.

In recent times the debate over the transition from feudalism to capitalism was renewed vigorously in a series of articles originally published in the journal *Science and Society.* Contributors to this debate included Maurice Dobb, Paul Sweezy, Kokarchiro Takahashi, Christopher Hill, and Rodney Hilton; attention focused on the exchange between Dobb and Sweezy in particular (see Hilton, 1978). There has been much concern about the nature of feudalism and precapitalist modes of production. Thus, Eric Hobsbawm introduced some of Marx's important writing in *Pre-Capitalist Economic Formations* (1946), while the French structuralists Louis Althusser and Etienne Balibar set forth their own formulations in *Reading Capital* (1970). Their work in turn was criticized by Barry Hindess and Paul Hirst (1975, 1977), while the question of the transition was discussed in a different way by Immanuel Wallerstein (1976) in his work on emerging capitalism in Europe.

In Latin America attention to analysis of modes of production appeared with disenchantment over dependency theory and, after the death of Ché Guevara, with "ultra-leftist" efforts to bring about change through revolutionary guerrilla movements and armed struggle.

One of the early criticisms was Ernesto Laclau's attack (1971) on André Gunder Frank's thesis that capitalism had dominated in Latin America since the sixteenth century. However, the theoretical works of Western European Marxists such as Althusser and Balibar, along with Nicos Poulantzas, Pierre-Philippe Rey, Maurice Godelier, and Emmanuel Terray, were to have a special impact on Latin American intellectuals who desired to return to texts of "classical Marxism." Roger Bartra and Rodrigo Montoya were two scholars who combined this classical orientation with new empirical investigation, especially in the agrarian sector, on precapitalist and capitalist modes of production. (For a comprehensive review of these developments, see Richard Harris, 1979.) Many writers began not only to research the classical modes of production but to suggest new modes relevant to the non-European experience. The concept of colonial mode of production, for example, was applied to some situations in the Third World. Such efforts at new terminology were called dangerous by Domenico Sindico (1977) in his assessment of the new left theories on the mode of production.

Given the variety of approaches to the investigation of backwardness in the periphery, one must ask what theoretical direction is most useful. Ronaldo Munck has suggested a synthesis of dependency and modes of production analysis. He argues that while dependency analysis effectively broke the hegemony of modernization theory in the field of development studies, it did not "constitute a rounded theoretical alternative as such, it was more of an 'approach' than a theory." While mode of production analysis appeared as a rigorous theoretical formulation to take the place of vague and indeterminate dependency theory, it must not be used as "a structural grid along which history moves in a logical progression." He concluded that dependency and modes of production analysis must be employed "simultaneously, in dialectical combination. . . . However, it is only when a modes of production analysis is inserted *within* the problematic of dependency that it escapes the tendency towards structuralism." He believed that class struggle rather than modes of production serves as the "motor of history" and that it is the uneven and combined development of capitalism that unites an analysis of class and class struggle throughout periods of history (Munch, 1980:61, 65).

My own position is that both dependency and modes of production analyses can lead to useful understanding of concrete situations. Dependency analysis served two purposes. On the one hand, it offered an alternative explanation to the sterile and dogmatic Stalinist analysis emanating from the pro-Soviet communist parties in the period after World War II. On the other hand, it undermined the hegemony of modernization theory in the field of developmental studies. Attention to dependency theory raised new questions, placed old issues in new perspective; and while the concept led to no unified theory, it allowed for reformulation of analysis on imperialism and class struggle. Attention to modes of production analysis opened the way to in-depth research on modes and relations of production and understanding of concrete situations rather than unsubstantiated theory and abstract analysis.

Contrasting Essays

The essays in this volume are drawn from the symposium, "Theories of Imperialism and Dependence Reconsidered," which was organized by the co-editors at the July 1979 Vancouver meetings of the Congress of Americanists. The structure of the symposium roughly corresponded to the organization of the present volume. Introductory comments were presented by Ronald Chilcote while Norma Chinchilla, André Gunder Frank, and Carlos Johnson presented papers, and a concluding critical commentary was provided by Dale Johnson. In addition, there were papers by Aníbal Quijano and Henry Veltmeyer, who were unable to attend the proceedings.

Among the initial concerns of the symposium was analysis of theories of imperialism and dependency during the twentieth century. Liberals such as Hobson and Schumpeter influenced one line of thinking, while Marxists such as Bukharin and Lenin conceptualized imperialism as monopoly capitalism. Marx, Lenin, and Trotsky all referred to dependency in their writings, but the recent formulations of dependency varied from those evolved by radical and Marxist intellectuals to the *desarrollista* or developmental theses of the Economic Commission for Latin America. Additionally, there were the issues of the relationship of dependency theory to Marxism and the idea that dependency had opened new questions and areas of investigation in Latin America and influenced study of Africa and Asia as well. Dependency writing had also stimulated a multitude of criticisms, ranging from confusion over terminology to fixation on markets and relations of exchange, whereas, it was argued, Marxism places emphasis on relations of production. So the symposium attempted to focus on the relationship of theories of dependency and imperialism to Marxist theory and to examine, in particular, patterns of circulation, markets, and production relations.

The participants dealt with these questions from a variety of theoretical perspectives. Carlos Johnson argued that most theories of dependency and imperialism are obscured in idealist and ideological thinking, a problem that could be resolved by utilizing a dialectical and materialist analysis in the tradition of Marx and Lenin. Norma Chinchilla mainly agreed with the criticism of Johnson but attempted to break new theoretical ground by applying an analysis focused on modes of production to the relatively unknown case of Guatemala. André Gunder Frank focused on the thesis of capitalist development of underdevelopment as well as on world-systems theory. He addressed the issues of economic crisis and the role of the state in the Third World and at the same time initiated a rebuttal to the criticism of Carlos Johnson. In a summary critique, Dale Johnson analyzed the contributions of dependency writings and took a critical view of the mode of production approach. Johnson acknowledged weaknesses in the past dependency literature, but argued that it had established itself as a viable paradigm; modes of productionist critiques of dependency offered little substantive research to support their own assumptions and tended toward theoretical dogmatism.

Since the Vancouver Congress all the essays have been substantially revised and placed into the present framework. The contribution of Aijaz Ahmad has been added. To assist the reader, it may be helpful to summarize the content and direction of each essay, while identifying critical issues and concerns that are essential to the debate on how best to understand issues of development and underdevelopment in the periphery.

The first two chapters contain the critical views of Carlos Johnson and Aijaz Ahmad; Part II includes interpretation and application of theory by Norma Chinchilla to Guatemala and Aníbal Quijano to Peru; finally, there are theoretical reflections by Henry Veltmeyer, André Gunder Frank, and Dale Johnson, who examine such issues as the relationship of a class analysis to the dependency and modes of production approaches and the weight of world-system-level forces.

Carlos Johnson launches a devastating attack on dependency thinking. He takes a strong position in support of using fundamentals of dialectical materialist historical Marxism and Leninism to analyze the contemporary world. He opposes any revision to these fundamentals, arguing that this would promote idealist and ideological notions which are counterrevolutionary and supportive of dominant classes. He is not interested in the ideas and debates generated by new or revisionist work or the intellectual stirrings and endeavors in the face of a stagnant social science which pervades the academic arena.

He also condemns as adventurist efforts by intellectuals to break from tradition and find solution through revolutionary means such as guerrilla warfare.

At the outset of his paper he attacks the common usage of the terms "dependency" and "imperialism" by showing that they are not new concepts and, in fact, were fashionable before Lenin and were used by bourgeois political economists. He feels that these terms have been exaggerated through their incorporation into useless theoretical constructs; and they are words which may be used only if accompanied by materialist explanations of social relations. Carlos Johnson identifies a theory of imperialism by focusing on the theses elaborated by Lenin and showing how these ideas were drawn from bourgeois, liberal, and socialist political economists. He also identifies the theses of dependency, breaking these into socioeconomic and political components. The socioeconomic theses tend to be idealist and ideological, a tendency illustrated in the work of Ruy Mauro Marini who attempted to relate dependency and imperialism through the concept of subimperialism. Johnson argues that Marini is led to the position that capitalism is not possible in Latin America and only dependency is reproduced; thus Marini overlooks the impact of monopoly capital "that creates itself again and again in the form of imperialism, out of the economic rises of capitalism and the concentration and centralization of capital." Dependency tends to reflect the critical manifestations of nationalism and anti-imperialism but does not always assume an anti-capitalist stance; ideologically it is supportive of local dominant classes even if its proponents argue that they oppose the national bourgeoisie and favor revolution and socialism. Johnson believes that the dependency theses are easy to comprehend because they consist of simplistic postulates. The political theses attack national bourgeoisies and local capital which sometimes have a role in national liberation movements, thus isolating the proletariat from a potential ally. Also the criticisms of Frank and others of the communist parties was counterproductive to the proletariat, while the support of dependentistas to intellectuals who turned to guerrilla warfare simply isolated them from the true revolutionary process. Johnson is critical of the Dos Santos "reformist" theses which encourage renegotiation of terms of trade and exchange of surplus value in order to mitigate the impact of dependency and work toward autonomous capitalist development. In summary, he argues that the dependency theses call for a nationalist articulation of the needs of competitive capital in the face of monopoly capital. The socioeconomic theses do not deal with relations of production of monopoly capital. The political theses of dependency attack the local dominant classes, isolating them from the workers, on the one hand, while the petty bourgeois intellectuals turn to guerrilla struggle and in turn also become isolated from the workers. The dependency theses, he feels, also obscure or ignore the impact of imperialist capitalist penetration in Latin America. Finally, he suggests that the more recent work in world-systems theory is molded in the traditions of idealist theory of the dependentistas.

Carlos Johnson calls for a return to a more orthodox Marxism. This call is echoed among many European theorists but often modified by new forms of theory. One such variant is represented in the work of Bill Warren. In confronting the stance of Warren in his *Imperialism: Pioneer of Capitalism,* Aijaz Ahmad also attacks the Marxist orthodoxy of authors like Carlos Johnson.

Warren argued that capitalism as an agent of social and economic progress must be considered in analyses of dependency and imperialism and that capitalism is a prerequisite to socialism. Further, he believed Lenin had distorted the Marxist assumption that capitalism could advance in precapitalist economies; Lenin's theory of imperialism had served the "underdevelopment fiction." Warren insisted that contrary to some current Marxist views, the prospects are good for capitalist development in underdeveloped peripheral areas.

Ahmad examines these views in relation to the outlook by Marx and Lenin on colonialism. He concludes that Warren adopted a traditional view in support of the proposition that Marx equated colonialism with progress—that is, colonialism serves to break down precapitalism and usher in industrial capitalism. Ahmad counters by identifying the context of two articles by Marx that served as the basis for Warren's argument—they offered "great insights, mingled with ideological blinders and fanciful fiction." Further, he attempts to show that Marx went beyond the traditional view to argue, in contradictory fashion, that revolution was necessary to counter "progressive" colonialism and capitalism. This was particularly evident in Marx's writings throughout the 1850s and up to the 1880s, a period he characterized as a "bleeding process" that foreshadowed the imperialism in Lenin's writing.

Lenin dealt with the period 1880 to 1920, and Ahmad refers to Lenin's own dissatisfaction with his *Imperialism* and his conviction that under the new conditions, the prospects for revolution had shifted from the metropoles to the colonies; there nationalism and anti-colonialism characterized the struggle for national liberation and self-determination. According to Ahmad, Lenin's support for national liberation in the colonies related to his expectation that the working class, although weak, might emerge as the hegemonic class in the colonial formation, whether under capitalism or precapitalism.

Ahmad criticizes Warren for his "highly tendencious reading" of Marx and Lenin and accuses him of ignoring the negative impact of capitalism. He also indicts Warren for assuming that capitalism will bring democracy to the periphery; he claims that there is a negative tie between capitalism and democracy so that the more countries of the Third World are integrated into global capitalism, the more despotic they become. Ahmad goes on to show how Warren's extremist position relates to current theoretical debates in Europe and thus must be taken seriously.

Norma Chinchilla reviews the research on Guatemala and finds that dependency theorists have concentrated on relations of exchange and circulation and at the same time have experienced difficulty in relating their theory to concrete situations, thereby tending to emphasize abstract propositions to the neglect of an empirical analysis. While much work on Guatemala has followed this direction, there have been some recent efforts to examine modes and relations of production. Such research was a response to the inadequacies of modernization, evolutionary Marxism, and most dependency analysis and to the debates generated by dependentistas who argued that Latin America has been capitalist since colonial times, that feudalism was never implanted in the area due to its demise in the Iberian Peninsula at the time of the conquest, and that backwardness was the consequence of capitalist penetration into the countryside and not attributable to precapitalist conditions there.

Chinchilla attempts to apply these recent theoretical formulations to a relatively unknown case study of Guatemala. It is her intention to move theoretically beyond the limitations of dependency theory by examining the relationship of external and internal factors in the development of modes of production in colonialized societies. Her central thesis is that the feudal mode of production in Guatemala was primarily the result of the Spanish conquest, an external phenomenon, but that once the mode of production established itself, its development must be explained by such internal considerations as class structure and its corresponding forms of accumulation and the state.

Aníbal Quijano attempts to transcend the debates around dependency and to locate the structural dependency of Peru within an analysis of imperialism as a stage in the process of production and reproduction of capital. He does this through discussion of Latin America in general and Peru in particular, with attention to the 1890-1930 period. The focus on Peru examines the role of capital, especially the historical conditions for the penetration by imperialist capital. This penetration involved semicolonial accumulation, a mixture of monopoly capitalism and precapitalism. This articulation of precapitalist and capitalist relations of production was influenced by the participation of U.S. and British firms. Semicolonial accumulation was characterized by the lack of an internal circuit of accumulation and by the enclave nature of the economy. Quijano shows that monopoly capital during the period 1890-1925 was concentrated in the sectors of the economy such as mining, oil, and agriculture rather than in finance, commerce, and transportation. Consequently, manufacturing was weak, including the textile industry, which came under control of foreign capital, and its development was effectively contained. The extraction of surplus value by monopoly capital and the weakness of national capital resulted in the structurally dependent nature of the capitalism that was established in Peru. Monopoly capital thus was concentrated in the primary areas of production, giving the Peruvian economy its "enclave" character. Production in these enclaves was destined for markets outside Peru.

The appearance of a dual structure in Peru, one capitalist and the other precapitalist, was in reality one combined structure which showed both its complementary and contradictory nature. This thesis permits Quijano to analyze class relations in Peruvian society. He emphasizes the rise and decline of the national bourgeoisie in the face of imperialism and the imperialist bourgeoisie. He shows how the imperialist hegemony prevailed as the landowning class integrated itself with the expansion of mercantilism. This in turn affected Indian communities, resulting in a series of peasant uprisings in the early decades of the twentieth century. Quijano goes on to show the influences of the imperialist hegemony on the formation of the rural and urban proletariat and the formation of intermediate strata. For example, he explains how the small merchant bourgeoisie was pushed toward proletarianization as the economy changed from a mercantile to its capitalist base. Finally, he analyzes class relations in terms of the Peruvian state.

Henry Veltmeyer attempts to locate his analysis in the process of capital accumulation as it affects class relations and class struggle. He demonstrates that in a peripheral area like Latin America such analysis is complex and subject to intense debate around questions of the transition to capitalism and the conversion of direct producers into wage workers. Specifically, he focuses on class formation in the periphery, and he addresses the issue of whether peripheral societies have reached an early stage of capitalist development along lines identified by Marx or whether such development assumes a new form and different class structure. Some studies suggest that such a form might comprise a mode of production based on colonialism, whereas other studies emphasize the extension of the capitalist market into the world-system and examine the relationship of classes to the structure of economic dependence rather than to productive relations; other studies stress the lack of capitalist development, especially in agriculture, and the persistence of precapitalist relations and merchant capital in the periphery. In addition to these three approaches, attention has focused on structures that combine several modes of production within a social formation. Veltmeyer assess these studies from the perspective of an appreciation of class formation.

In particular, Veltmeyer looks at the penetration of capitalism into agriculture in the periphery and the extent to which direct producers are dispossessed from their means of production and form a surplus population or labor reserve. He notes several features of the peripheral social formation: the incomplete nature of rural proletarianization; the degree to which peasant producers function as a class of independent commodity producers integrated into the market economy; and the subordination of the peasantry to the dominant mode of production. He believes that only pockets of a real peasantry exist, in the sense that peasants are insulated from capitalist society. These might consist of those who maintain land through family ties, tenancy, sharecropping, and other precapitalist relationships. He also refers to a semiproletariat of dispossessed peasants as well as those who combine subsistence and petty commodity production with seasonal or casual wage labor.

Semiproletarianization, he suggests, serves capital as a means of cheap surplus labor, especially among casual workers in the agro-export sector and the working class in the urban centers. Veltmeyer relates the existence of this work force to the general law of capital accumulation whereby expanding capital results in an increase of surplus population at lower wage rates, and he analyzes this phenomenon in light of published research. He shows how conditions lead to "superexploitation" or the "forcible reduction of wages below the value of labor power." Thus, peripheral accumulation creates a large class of persons struggling for survival. It also results in structural divisions within the proletariat of the periphery, such as the semi-proletarianized peasantry, rural migrants, women, and other forms of the surplus population.

Frank reiterates some long-standing themes in his writing on the theory of the world-system of the past 500 years, and he examines past and present world economic crises. He discusses the prospects for autonomous socialist development—that is, the breaking or "delinking" from dependent capitalist development that has shaped the processes of development and underdevelopment in many parts of the world. He envisages a single world economic system of many unequal parts, including a developed North and an underdeveloped South, as well as a capitalist West and a socialist East; within this system there are precapitalist, capitalist, and postcapitalist relations of production.

Frank focuses on periods of crisis throughout Western history and shows that a crisis is the consequence of expansion that cannot continue. Thus costs of production must be reduced through the lowering of wages, employment of cheaper labor, and technological change. He examines such crises in the past, identifies periods of expansion and stagnation, and shows that the present crisis of stagnation since the 1960s followed a period of expansion after World War II. He notes the shift of the metropolitan center from Great Britain to the United States, as well as the impact of imperialism on India and other parts of the Third World. Thus, the single world-system consists of unequal parts affected by a continuously uneven process of development and by periodic crises.

The dimensions of the present world crisis are examined. Frank compares the period since 1967 to the crises of 1914-1945 and 1873-1896. He looks at rates of productivity, growth, unemployment, investment, and rate of profit and demonstrates that in the present crisis the international financial system applies economic policies designed to repress labor and to reduce or keep wages low in the third World. This objective was linked to the wave of repression that has swept the Third World in recent years.

Finally, Frank discusses the prospects for delinking from dependent capitalism and for revolutionary strategy. He reviews situations where there was a transfer of power, popular participation, and an attempt at delinking but concludes that they were failures. He argues that external delinking and internal participation must be combined with social and political mobilization to bring about rapid structural change; in the capitalist West the only countries able to accomplish this objective were socialist, whereas in the Socialist East the tendency of many countries was to "relink" into the "capitalist international division of labor, not only through trade but also through production." The socialist countries, he argues, were able to meet basic needs of people, but they were not successful in increasing productivity. As socialism is undergoing these changes the capitalist system is entering a deep transformation, involving the lowering of production costs and a reorganization of the world economy so as to create the conditions for a subsequent period of renewed capitalist expansion.

The essay by Dale Johnson offers a concluding evaluation of the theoretical disputes at issue and critical commentary on the contributions to this volume. He criticizes the dependency perspective for its economism, excessive determinism, and lack of attention to class relations, criticisms shared with mode of productionists. Nevertheless, Johnson concludes that questions of development and underdevelopment are best addressed through modification and extension of dependency theory, not by discarding it. Mode of productionists have made a contribution by pointing to the deficiencies of dependency thinking, but Johnson suggests that modes of production falls short as an adequate alternative framework.

Johnson proposes a historical-structural method that poses a dialectic of the "general" and "proximate" determinants of the historical condition of dependency and underdevelopment. General determinants are the processes of internationalized accumulation and class formation operating at the level of the world-system. Proximate determinants are those class relations that are rooted in territorial units of the world-system. Johnson utilizes this approach to focus on class formation and polarization in the Latin American region.

Conclusion

The various approaches to dependency theory can be viewed within a dichotomy of perspectives, one combining dependency and capitalism in the periphery with nationalist orientations and reformist traditions, and the other linking dependency to socialism and revolutionary traditions. It is clear that the recent literature on dependency served to raise questions about diffusionist, developmentalist, and modernizationist explanations; yet no formal unified theory has evolved, nor are the assessments of concrete situations of dependency fully satisfactory. The focus on dependency also has served to direct critical attention to the prospects for a national bourgeoisie in Latin America and in other peripheral areas. Experience seems to have demonstrated that alliances of the bourgeoisie and working class are doomed to failure, but posing the problem of class alliances has opened the way for analysis of class relations. Yet after years of calling for analysis of class and class struggle, very little empirical work is available to us. While dependency theory has questioned old and static formulations, it has not provided concrete or consistent guidelines to transforming society. It is for this reason that despite their different perspectives, all the contributors to this volume seek to transcend the limitations of past work on dependency and to turn to analysis of either the relations of production or of the articulation of modes of production.

In summary, five considerations appear paramount in the essays contained here. First, there is the concern, expressed by many contributors, that a dialectical and historical materialist approach be applied to analysis of the contemporary world. Whether this framework must rest with theory in the original writings of Marx, as Carlos Johnson insists, or be updated and revised, as Dale Johnson and others would urge, is in dispute. Second, there is attention to the ideological implications of work on dependency and imperialism. Carlos Johnson argues that the current theory simply reproduces the ideological mystification of past bourgeois and petty bourgeois radical perceptions. Ahmad looks carefully at contradictory understandings in the writing of Marx and Lenin to expose what he considers a serious political error in Western Marxism. Chinchilla and Quijano attempt to transcend the early work of Marx and Lenin as well as the recent writings on dependency and mode of production to move in new directions. Veltmeyer looks at a variety of approaches in order to understand the lack of capitalist development and the persistence of precapitalism in the periphery. While Frank leaves aside his earlier emphasis on dependency, he extends some of his original ideas to an overview of the world-system. Third, there are differences over whether capitalism is progressive or regressive in the periphery. Writers like Bill Warren argued for a progressive capitalism, a view endorsed by Carlos Johnson, while other contributors tend to see capitalism as both progressive and regressive, depending on conditions and particular situations. Ahmad carefully bases this position on the thought of Marx and Lenin; Chinchilla and Quijano call for study of the articulation of various modes of production in combination; while Frank and Dale Johnson continue to emphasize the negative consequences of capitalism; and Veltmeyer attributes these consequences to superexploitation of labor in the periphery. Fourth, the contributors differ over what kinds of economic formations exist in the periphery. Are they precapitalist or capitalist, or some combination of both? In general, the contributors move away from the position that capitalism alone has been the root of backwardness and underdevelopment, as suggested by Paul Baran and Frank many years ago. Veltmeyer refers to semiproletarianization and Quijano mentions semicolonial accumulation as ways of explaining the failure of capitalism to reproduce itself on an expanding basis in the periphery. Finally, the majority of essays stress the nature of class relations and class struggle. Chinchilla, Quijano, Veltmeyer, and Dale Johnson all move in this direction. It is clear that despite the diversity in perspectives among the contributors, there is desire not only to ensure familiarity with and base analysis on the classical Marxist theories and writings on precapitalist and capitalist accumulation but to continue the search for new formulations and ideas about relations and modes of production, ties of class to state, and the impact of international capital.

References

Althusser, Louis and Etienne Balibar
  1970   Reading Capital. London: New Left Books.
Anderson, Perry
  1962   "Portugal and the end of ultra-colonialism." New Left Review 15 (May-June): 89-102; 16 (July-August): 88-123; 17 (Winter): 85-114.
Bagú, Sergio
  1949   Economía de la sociedad colonial. Buenos Aires: Librería "El Ateneo."
Baran, Paul and Paul Sweezy
  1966   Monopoly Capitalism. New York: Monthly Review Press.
Barnet, Richard J. and Ronald E. Muller
  1974   Global Reach: The Power of the Multinational Corporations. New York: Simon & Schuster.
Brewer, Anthony
  1980   Theories of Imperialism. London: Routledge and Kegan Paul. (Includes chapters on "Amin," pp. 233-257; "Frank, Wallerstein and the Dependency 'Theorists,'" pp. 158-181.)
Cardoso, Fernando Henrique
  1973   "Associated-dependent development: theoretical and practical implications," pp. 142-176 in Alfred Stepan (ed.) Authoritarian Brazil: Origins, Policies, and Future. New Haven: Yale University Press.
Cardoso, Fernando Henrique and Enzo Faletto
  1979   Dependency and Development (Marjory Mattingly Urquidi, trans.). Berkeley: University of California Press.
Chilcote, Ronald H.
  1974   "Dependency: a critical synthesis of the literature." Latin American Perspectives 1 (Fall): 4-29.
Dos Santos, Theotonio
  1970   "The structure of dependence." American Economic Review 60 (May): 231-236.

1978   Imperialismo y dependencia. Mexico City: Ediciones Era.

Frank, André Gunder
1966   "The development of underdevelopment." Monthly Review 28 (September): 17-31.
1967   Capitalism and Underdevelopment in Latin America: Historical Studies of Chile and Brazil. New York: Monthly Review Press.

Frondizi, Silvio
1954   La integración mundial, última etapa del capitalismo (respuesta a una crítica) (1947). Buenos Aires: Praxis.
1957   La realidad argentina: ensayo de interpretación sociológica (2 vols.). Buenos Aires: Praxis.

Furtado, Celso
1963   The Economic Growth of Brazil: A Survey from Colonial to Modern Times. (Ricardo W. de Aguiar and Eric Charles Drysdale, trans.). Berkeley: University of California Press.

Galtung, Johan
1971   "A structural theory of imperialism." Journal of Peace Research, 8, 2: 81-117.

González Casanova, Pablo
1970   Democracy in Mexico (Danielle Salti, trans.). New York: Oxford University Press. Originally published as La democracia en México, (Mexico City: Ediciones Era, 1965.)

Harris, Richard
1979   "The influence of Marxist structuralism on the intellectual left in Latin America." Insurgent Sociologist (Summer): 62-73.

Hilton, Rodney (ed.)
1978   Feudalism or Capitalism. London: Verso.

Hindess, Barry and Paul Hirst
1975   Pre-Capitalist Modes of Production. London: Routledge & Kegan Paul.
1977   Mode of Production and Social Formation: An Auto-Critique of Pre-Capitalist Modes of Production. New York: Macmillan.

Huntington, Samuel P.
1968   Political Order in Changing Societies. New Haven: Yale University Press.

Laclau, Ernesto
1971   "Feudalism and capitalism in Latin America." New Left Review 67 (May-June): 19-38.

Lenin, V. I.
1967   "Imperialism: the highest stage of capitalism," in Selected Works, Vol. 1. Moscow: Progress Books.

Magdoff, Harry
1969   The Age of Imperialism: The Economics of U.S. Foreign Policy. New York: Monthly Review Press.

Mandel, Ernest
1975   Late Capitalism. London: New Left Books.

Marini, Ruy Mauro
1969   Subdesarrollo y revolución. Mexico City: Siglo Vientiuno Editores.
1973   Dialéctica de la dependencia. Mexico City: Ediciones Era.

Marx, Karl
  1946   Pre-Capitalist Economic Formations (introduction by Eric J. Hobsbawm). New York: International Publishers.
Munck, Ronaldo
  1980   Development and Politics in the Third World. Unpublished manuscript, Ulster, Northern Ireland.
  1981   "Imperialism and dependency: recent debates and old dead-ends." Latin American Perspectives 8 (Summer-Fall): 162-179.
O'Brien, Philip L.
  1975   "A critique of Latin American theories of dependency," pp. 7-27 in Ivar Oxaal, Tony Barnett, and David Booth (eds.) Beyond the Sociology of Development. London: Routledge & Kegan Paul.
Prado Júnior, Caio
  1966   A revolução brasileira. São Paulo: Editora Brasiliense.
  1967   The Colonial Background of Modern Brazil (Suzette Macedo, trans.). Berkeley: University of California Press.
Prebisch, Raúl
  1980   "The dynamics of peripheral capitalism," pp. 21-27 in Louis Lefeber and Liisa L. North (eds.) Democracy and Development in Latin America. Toronto: Studies on the Political Economy, Society and Culture of Latin America and the Caribbean (1).
Rostow, Walt W.
  1960   The Stages of Economic Growth: A Non-Communist Manifesto. Cambridge: Cambridge University Press.
Schumpeter, Joseph
  1955   Imperialism. Social Classes. New York: Meridian Books.
Sindico, Domenico
  1977   "New left theories on the mode of production." Studies in Marxism 1: 95-102.
Sunkel, Osvaldo
  1972   "Big business and 'dependencia.'" Foreign Affairs 50 (April): 517-531.
Taylor, John G.
  1979   From Modernization to Modes of Production: A Critique of the Sociologies of Development and Underdevelopment. New York: Macmillan.
Valenzuela, J. Samuel and Arturo Valenzuela
  1978   "Modernization and dependency. Alternative perspectives in the study of Latin American underdevelopment." Comparative Politics 10 (July): 535-557.
Vitale, Luis
  1968   "Latin America: feudal or capitalist?" pp. 32-43 in James Petras and Maurice Zeitlin (eds.) Latin America: Reform or Revolution? Greenwich, CT: Fawcett.
Wallerstein, Immanuel
  1976   "From feudalism to capitalism: transition or transitions." Social Forces 55 (December): 273-283.

Part One: Critical Perspectives

Aijaz Ahmad: Imperialism and Progress

My point of departure in this article is *Imperialism: Pioneer of Capitalism,* (1980) a book by the influential British writer, Bill Warren, who argues, in painstaking Marxist terms, in favor of the well-known thesis that imperialism is good for the human race, and especially good for its victims. One undoubtedly prefers, for the most part, to ignore such prognoses. The present case is, however, quite exceptional, thanks to the remarkable conjunction of author, publisher, and the wider theoretical configuration within which this argument is now being revived within Western Marxism.[1]

Since his article of almost a decade ago, "Imperialism and Capitalist Industrialisation," (1973) which came to us with the prestige of *New Left Review* attached to it and which has so far gone largely unanswered, Warren has commanded substantial influence in left-wing circles, especially in England. The purpose of that article was, as is now well known, to prepare an elaborate defense of imperialism as a progressive agency of industrialization and technological advance in the backward periphery of the global capitalist system; in both explicit and implicit ways, Warren's argument then was, and still is, radically opposed to a number of currents in modern Marxism, including the Leninist current, where imperialism has been viewed as a particularly "rapacious" stage in the history of capitalism which intensifies the exploitation of the imperialized formations while augmenting the process of accumulation by the more advanced bourgeoisies of the imperialist countries. The present book is in some basic ways an elaboration of that earlier text, and the argument, on both theoretical and empirical levels, is now much more ambitious and far less compromising; Warren now sets out to debunk every aspect of the theory of imperialism and to show that Leninism is nothing less than a wholesale "reversal" of Marxism. These elaborations have again come to us through the agency of New Left Books, possibly the most prestigious publisher of Marxist books in English. That alone should guarantee that the book will gain wide currency. Moreover, far from being a case of lone eccentricity, Warren's book is wholly of a piece with, and in some respects a point of culmination for, tendencies that have been ascendant among Eurocommunist parties as well as particular left-wing intellectuals on both sides of the Atlantic.

The general context of the book—the political field that requires yet another attack on Leninism from inside the "Marxist" positions, as well as the theoretical work of the past decade that has facilitated Warren's own defense of imperialism—will be examined in the concluding section of our text. In summary, however, one should note at the outset that it has become rather common on the Left over the past decade or so to portray Marx as an enthusiast of colonialism and "modernization"; colonialism itself as having been only of marginal importance in the development of the capitalist mode of production; and modern imperialism as being at least unnecessary for the process of accumulation in the metropolitan countries and, at worst, a mere figment of the imagination of those who are disparagingly called "third-worldists." Inter alia, colonialism is also presented in these discourses as a force of robust social transformation and technological advance in the colonies. Thus, for example, Shlomo Avineri's (1968) well-known selection of Marx's writings on colonialism portrays him as a theorist of "modernization," and his own book on Marx (1968) presents the standard view that Marx had nothing but faltering admiration for the transplantation of "Western civilization" in "barbaric Asia." Aidan Foster-Carter's more recent (1978) and rather lengthy reflections on the famous Sweezy-Dobb debate further postulate that the transformation of the relations of production in Northern Europe is sufficient explanation for the original transition to capitalism, while assigning only marginal and wholly secondary importance to the accumulation of capital from the colonies as well as to the acquisition of markets abroad. Meanwhile, Szymanski (1977) has lengthily argued that what one ordinarily calls imperialism is quite unnecessary for the accumulation of capital, and that if any exploitation of the periphery still occurs, that exploitation can be renounced, simply as a matter of a series of changes in policy, with no detrimental effect on the process of accumulation as such. And there are a number of other authors, from Robert Brenner (1977) to John Weeks and

Elizabeth Dore (1977), who dismiss the theorists of dependency and unequal exchange as mere "neo-Smithians" and argue that the system of international exchanges that occurs within capitalism's global structure is neither unequal nor contributive to the backwardness of the peripheral formations; the explaination of their backwardness is that they are backward. In addition, there are many other explicit and implicit ways in which the whole phenomenon of imperialism is being relegated to a position of irrelevance in several debates regarding the nature of modern capitalism and the lines of political struggle. For example, the famous Poulantzas-Miliband-Laclau debate on the nature of the capitalist state nowhere acknowledges that the state, which is being postulated as the state of the capitalist formation inside Europe, is also—both from the perspective of its internal organization as well as its effectivity and responsibility on the global scale—an imperialist state, with very concrete and highly repressive functions in the military, economic, and social fields.[2] Meanwhile, the idea that the leading European countries, such as France, are themselves imperialist countries and that any program of genuine socialist transformation must include concrete measures to dismantle the structure of imperialism within these state formations has completely disappeared from the programmatical pronouncements of the leading Eurocommunist parties.

I will return to all this presently. Suffice to say that Warren's particular dispositions have arisen from a much wider theoretical conjuncture. His own thinking is surely less subtle and more one-sided than many of the authors cited above, and many would surely not associate themselves with the totality of his propostions. However, the complacency and even the extremism of his rhetoric comes, it would seem, from the fact that the sum of ideas to which he subscribes have now gained, in one form or another, considerable popularity within several currents of contemporary Western Marxism. By the same token, my critique also has a wider object: to examine a set of ideas which Warren presents with exceptional clarity but which are held quite widely and are therefore symptomatic of a broader drift.

Warren's Argument

It is just as well, then, to start with a passage that sets the tone and defines the purpose of the entire polemic. The book begins:

The concept of imperialism has become the dominant political dogma of our era . . . It embodies a set of quite specific (albeit often vaguely articulated) theses about the domination of imperialism in the affairs of the human race as a whole and in particular about the past and present economic, political, and cultural disaster imperialism has allegedly inflicted and continues to inflict on the great majority of mankind . . . Its effect has been toward a transmutation of Western liberalism from a philosophy of forward-looking improvement based upon the past achievements of capitalism to a philosophy of guilt and shame . . . If to this we add the literature of the masochistic modern version of the White Man's Burden, more or less directly inspired by the view of imperialism as uniformly disastrous, then Marxism can record the greatest publication and propaganda triumph in its history . . . Marxism's involvement in and theoretical characterisation of the anti-imperialist movement has disarmed the working classes of much of Asia, Africa and Latin America.

The polemic thus knows no bounds. The concept of imperialism is sheer propaganda and dogma; that imperialism might have done harm to its victims is mere allegation; Western liberalism must be restored to preeminence as a "forward-looking" philosophy; Marxism is a misfortune for the working class. However, Warren is no ordinary theorist of modernization. He locates himself emphatically within what he takes to be a Marxist framework, constructs a certain version of the famous "theory of the productive forces," and charges Leninism with being "utopian" on the one hand and collaborating on the other, with nationalism, populism, anticolonialism, and all other "retrogressive" ideologies of the Third World which obstruct foreign investment and thereby also obstruct capitalism, the development of the productive forces, and hence the world revolution itself.

Underneath the broad sweep of this generalized polemic, one can identify two special objects of Warren's thought. First, he seeks to examine and debunk that whole theory of imperialism, originating in the famous texts of Bukharin and Lenin but reaching fullest elaboration only since World War II, which is normally regarded as "Marxist" but which Warren takes to be wholly at variance both with Marx's own thought as well as with the facts, as he sees them, of global capitalism over roughly the past one hundred years. Second, Warren sets out to prove (a) that the age of imperialism is virtually ended, (b) that the historic contribution of imperialism to the forward march of humanity has been that it laid "increasingly vigorous" foundations for industrialization in the Third World, and (c) that the modern, transnational capitalism is based on a salutary logic, leading to immense development of the productive forces on the global scale, which will inevitably wipe out—and is in fact wiping out—the gap between rich and poor countries. Somalia, by this logic, will soon catch up with Sweden, and all our children, white, black and yellow, will live equally happily in corporate bliss. The struggle for socialism may then, presumably, begin.

In keeping with these basic propositions, the book is divided into two parts. After a "Schematic outline of the Arguments" (pp. 7-10), from which I will quote presently, Part One begins with a somewhat lengthy and stirring defense of colonialism and imperialism as globally progressive forces (pp. 11-47). As it turns out, this "theory" is based almost entirely on the two most anthologized of Marx's journalistic articles on India, ignoring much else that both Marx and Engels wrote on the subject of colonialism. The theoretical work of the past one hundred years is to be judged, we are told, by the standards set by Marx's rather offhand and highly problematic remarks in those two pieces. We are also told that Marx "correctly" believed colonialism to be necessary for human progress and that this "scientific view" remained altogether universal in the international revolutionary movement until the unfortunate ascendancy of Bolshevism. A lengthly second section (pp. 48-109) is then devoted to a refutation of Lenin, "who initiated the ideological process" based on "the reversal of Marx's own view of the progressive character of imperialism." Warren then goes on to argue that it was under the influence of Lenin's "utopian" thought on imperialism and the national and colonial questions that the Comintern adopted "the underdevelopment fiction," "sacrificing" Marxist analysis "to the requirements of bourgeois anti-imperialist propaganda and, indirectly, to what were thought to be the security requirements of the encircled Soviet state." The errors of the more recent theorists, such as André Gunder Frank and Samir Amin, are then traced back to the earlier, compounded errors of Lenin and the Comintern (pp. 110-121).

Two themes are then interwoven in Part Two. One is the ideological concern to construct a wholesale rejection of all the strands that have been dominant in more modern theories of imperialism, namely the theory of unequal exchange, unequal development, dependency, underdevelopment and backwardness of the periphery. The list of enemies is truly long: Baran, Sweezy, the Soviet scholarship, all the dependentistas, Arghiri Emmanual, Poulantzas, Samir Amin, Teresa Hayter, the Economic Commission on Latin America, Laclau, Gunnar Myrdal, Meillasoux, and so on. Anyone who as much as suggests that colonialism might have done damage to the productive forces in the colonies, or that imperialist domination might impede or distort the process of accumulation and coherent development in the periphery, is dismissed as an "anti-Marxist" propagandist of "nationalist mythology." By contrast, we are told, "*Direct colonialism,* far from having retarded or distorted indigenous capitalist development that might otherwise have occurred, *acted as a powerful engine for progressive social change.* . . . Indeed, although introduced into the Third World externally, capitalism has struck deep roots there and developed its own *increasingly vigorous logic*" (italics added). In the postcolonial period, we are also advised, "the policy of 'imperialist' countries . . . favours the industrialisation and economic development" of the underdeveloped countries, so that "the distribution of politico-economic power within the capitalist world is thereby growing less uneven" and we are now living "in an era of declining imperialism and advancing capitalism." In support of the latter hypothesis, Warren sets out to prove that terms of trade are in fact favorable to the Third World, that manufacturing now accounts for more or less the same percentage of output in the periphery as in the metropolis, and that the *rate* of industrial expansion is quicker at the periphery; hence the notion of a uniformly capitalist world on the verge of absolishing inequality between rich and poor countries.

Throughout the book, Warren returns again and again to "the unique achievements of capitalism, both cultural and material." The enormous violence that has accompanied the globalization of the capitalist mode of production is dismissed, literally, as a "technical by-product" of the development of the productive forces; the destruction of Vietnam by the Americans must be seen, we are told, in the perspective of the advances of science and technology. In a lower register, Warren also makes emphatic claims for the contribution of imperialism to education, health, social welfare, cultural development, and overall well-being of the imperialized peoples, while positing that "there is an important connection between capitalism and parliamentary (bourgeois) democracy," presumably on the global scale.

The political line that derives from all this is also quite unmistakable. Anti-imperialism is nationalist hogwash; in becoming the vehicle of this propaganda, Marxism has duped the working classes. Imperialism must be affirmed as a progressive force, and the working classes must abandon their "utopian opposition" to multinational capital. The future of the world lies in a collaborative relationship between the working classes of the Third World and the multinational corporation, in a common pursuit of a more perfect capitalism.

This is extraordinary stuff. The wonder of it is that it is actually published and is having considerable influence on the Left. My own space in this chapter is so limited, and the literature that documents the exploitation of the colonies is so very voluminous, that with regard to the sheer economic pillage alone, I can neither develop my own argument nor attempt even an adequate citation of the relevant literature.[3] This question will be taken up, therefore, only in a supplementary fashion. Instead, I begin by raising some questions about Warren's method of analysis and his approach to the subject as such. Then I will try to clarify four other questions that are manifestly of considerable significance. First, I should like to examine afresh Marx's views on colonialism, as well as the question of Lenin's "reversal." Second, I will examine in some detail Warren's stupefying fascination with capitalism as such, since this fascination accounts both for his tendentious reading of Marx and Lenin and for his unstinting defense of imperialism. In particular, I will offer some comments on the alleged "cultural and material" contributions of colonialism to the colony, and the "connection between capitalism and democracy." This will help us locate his work within the larger framework of contemporary tendencies within Western Marxism, in the sense that Warren, of course, goes far beyond the general drift of Western Marxist discourses. Edifying texts on the virtues of capitalist democracy have nevertheless become the norm in recent years, to the extent that the past and present history of the global *contradiction* between capitalism and democracy has been revised to a considerable degree. This will raise, in conclusion, the question of the overall politico-theoretical conjuncture in which Warren's particular attack on Leninism has taken shape, especially with reference to the question of imperialism which has been either suppressed or posed in highly problematic terms in the works of some of the most influential Western

Marxists as well as in the programmatical pronouncements and daily practices of the leading Eurocommunist parties.

Warren's Method and the Question of "Third World Industrialization"

The chief problem with Warren's general method is that he takes little care in defining the object of his research, remains rather indifferent to specificity of historical period or determinate social formation, makes a number of assertions that can be supported neither theoretically nor empirically, and operates at a level of polemic and generalization which makes nonsense even of those propositions that might have had a degree of validity if applied with precision and care.

Take, for example, his use of the term "the Third World." Now, the chief flaw of dependency theory, as we all know, has been that colonialism and imperialism are viewed as uniform, worldwide processes with essentially the same line of action everywhere, while the colonized/imperialized world is seen as a mere object of external determinations, and not as variegated system of historically constituted and very real social formations. The consequence of course is that the indigenous ruling classes are viewed as bogus creations, victims, or agents of metropolitan capital, and not as real historical subjects who make decisions and alliances in order to defend, consolidate, and enlarge specific class interests. Analysis is then usually forcused on the processes and quantums of the extraction/distribution of surplus; metropolitan capital is shown to have made all the profits and the indigenous formation is shown to have suffered.

Warren's conclusions are entirely different, but his procedure is exactly the same. He uses the term "Third World" much in the same manner as many of his opponents do, as a uniform category of analysis, as if all social formations of this Third World were undergoing the same historical experience and the same kind of social transformation, paying no attention to the important tasks of periodization and making no real distinctions between differents regions and even among particular countries. Colonialism/imperialism again appears as a uniform, worldwide process said to have obtained uniform results throughout the word in a linear pattern that encompasses a hundred or so years. For Warren, the pattern is one of "development," "progress," "growth," "industrialisation," and "cultural and material" benefits. Acting on this assumption, he can then take data, selectively, from certain countries such as Korea or Brazil, where considerable industrialization has indeed taken place over the past two decades, and have us believe that his analysis applies to the whole of this Third World. Likewise, he can adopt industrialization as sufficient and even exclusive index of "the development of the productive forces," with a kind of singleminded obsessiveness that one may justifiably call "factory fetishism," without caring to analyze the type of industrialization that has occurred, the social relations it has engendered, and the altogether novel and intense forms of dependence that have accompanied this industrialization in the fields of finance, technology, transport and communications, consumption patterns, and even the export markets for products, including factory-made products, which are produced in the peripheral countries for consumption strictly in the metropolitan centers. Furthermore, he can take facts of recent industrialization, and instead of analyzing them as phenomena specific to the recent changes in the process of the internationalization of capital, he presents these as evidence of the "progressive character" of the whole colonial/imperialist process. (Parenthetically, one should note also that Warren uses the terms "colonialism" and "imperialism" interchangeably, rejecting both the Leninist distinction between the two as well as the modern Marxist consensus that imperialism is an existing phenomenon today.)

Colonialism was by no means a uniform process, and the proposition that it laid the basis for industrialization of the Third World is mere myth. The level of industrialization in Africa during the 1950s, when decolonization began, was about as high as the level of industrialization in Latin America at the time of decolonization there, in the 1820s. In the Portuguese possessions, the oldest colonies in the world, there was no industrialization whatever. And, as I will argue presently, it is virtually impossible to say that countries like India, where considerable industrialization occurred during the colonial period, might not have achieved the same, or perhaps higher, levels of industrialization in the absence of colonialism. As regards the more recent period, it is surely true that a number of countries, from Singapore to India to Brazil, have experienced considerable industrialization. But imperialism is not necessarily the agent of industrialization everywhere. Rates of industrialization are, if anything, higher in North Korea than in the South. Egypt is relatively the most industrialized Arab country, and yet the rate of industrialization there was much higher during the Nasser period, when imperialist capital was barred, banking and large-scale manufacturing were nationalized, and technology was imported predominantly from the Soviet bloc,

than it has been in the decade of "open door" policy for foreign capital
and local private investment.

One encounters a similar difficulty with Warren's emphatic assertion that the productive forces of the Third World experienced greater
development under colonialism than they might have otherwise. There
is, of course, no way to prove that he is wrong; but it is equally impossible to say that he is right. There is simply no theoretical method that
can prove what *might* have happened if the history of the past five
hundred years were different; nor is it possible to even speculate
about such matters if one speaks at a level of abstraction that applies
to the whole of the Third World. However, there *is* evidence, of an
empirical character, which suggests that Warren's unquestioning
faith in colonialist developmentalism might be somewhat unwar-
ranted. We *know,* for example, that the productive forces of a number
of Asian and African formations, from the Malay regions to the East
Africa coast, were, by *any* criterion, more advanced on the eve of
colonization than they were at any subsequent point up to the moment
of decolonization; we don't know much about the early history of,
say, Indonesia or Mozambique, but we do know that much. Or, take
the case of the principal Asian countries: China, India, Japan. We
know that India was colonized, that China's exploitation as semicolony
was legendary, and that Japan managed to resist the colonial powers;
only then was Japan able to make a full-fledged transition to industrial capitalism, thanks to the Meiji Revolution, which occurred in
Japan soon after the British conquest of India was completed and at
approximately the same time as the Opium Wars which ended China's
autonomy. We also know that as of the turn of the eighteenth century,
before colonialism won the decisive battles in India and before India's
own internal crisis of state formations set in, the "productive forces"
in India were much more advanced than in Japan; that India possessed historically constituted, socially stable, and numerous classes
that were involved in manufacturing and commerce; and that India
had by then acquired a highly efficient system of trade and transport,
comprising internal navigation and extensive roadworks, leading to
large movements of bulk goods and increasing homogenization of the
domestic market; a relatively high level of urbanization; highly developed systems of uniform currencies; financial houses that were able
to make large-scale investments for long-term maturity; a coun-
trywide system of credit and banking; joint-stock companies; and a
multitudinous work force, dispersed in all major regions of the country, with exceptionally advanced levels of skills in nonagricultural
production, from metalworks to textiles and from mining to ship-

building. In other words, the "productive forces" were doubtless more "mature" in India than in Japan, and there is no theory that can prove, a priori, that, lacking British occupation, India would or could not have had its own equivalent of the Meiji Revolution. In fact, if we are to accept Warren's propositions—his altogether economistic fetishization of the productive forces and his celebration of colonialism as the necessary agency of industry and civilization—the transition should have come logically not in Japan but in India, considering that India was colonized and Japan was not. But history took a different turn, and now it is impossible (even useless) to speculate as to what might have been. Warren, at any rate, is surely careless and probably ignorant of the facts when he postulates that colonialism was historically necessary for the development of the productive forces everywhere in Asia, Africa, and Latin America.

He displays the same kind of carelessness in lumping together rather too casually all those whom he opposes. Some people, especially of the Maoist tendency, have surely asserted that no industrialization or development takes place under imperialist domination; that is, as Warren justly argues, manifest nonsense. But there are many who have not argued *that*. Writers like Frank or Amin, for example, whom Warren castigates for the worst of ills, have always acknowledged and even underscored the fact of industrialization and capitalization in many Third World countries. Like Warren himself, they, too, argue that colonialism and imperialism have had the effect of making the capitalist mode of production universally dominant; Amin even speaks of *a* working class of this universal mode which is global in composition and which has the majority of its members and the most oppressed of its strata located in the Third World. What distinguishes them from Warren is not a dispute about the extent of industrialization or the dominance of the capitalist mode. Rather, they are concerned with the manner in which the capitalist mode in the periphery is articulated to and conditions the subordinate noncapitalist modes; the way the globalization of capitalism augments the process of accumulation in the metropolises; the historical process that accounts for the variegated locations of the different social formations in the international division of labor; the logic whereby the deepening internationalization of the industrial production process locates different branches of industry and whole types of technology in different parts of the capitalist system; and the modalities of what Amin, in particular, calls "peripheral capitalism." It is surely the case that Frank has often been wrong and that many of his prescriptive analyses, especially in his early writings, lead to little more than the idealized

forms of an impossible autarchy. Likewise, Amin's theoretical involvement in some versions of the Maoist "Three Worlds Theory," not to
mention his practical involvement in the bourgeois reformism of
UNCTAD, leads him often in the direction of what Warren rightly
calls "nationalist mythology." These are valid criticisms. However,
the approach that goes beyond the number of factories built and the
quantums of capitalist commodities produced, and one which seeks
to analyze the actual social relations of production engendered by
this industrialization, is surely more valid than the one Warren adopts,
with its abstract and wholly quantitative emphasis on the share of
manufacturing in national income as an index of development, while
conveniently ignoring that majority of Third World formations where
development has not occurred or has been astonishingly sluggish
even by this one index, of industrialization.

If one speaks strictly of the mode of production and of industrialization as its chief indicator, as Warren does, the Third World today
would appear by no means a uniform category; there is little that is
common, by this criterion, between Costa Rica and Saudi Arabia,
Chad and Singapore, Burma and Brazil. One should then speak of
specific social formations or of comparative cases. What *is* common
among these different countries is not the fact of their mode of production internally but their common dependence on the metropolitan
countries: for technology in all cases, for finance in the majority of
cases, and for market relationships which always favor metropolitan
capital, even where the local money-capital is abundant, as in the
case of the OPEC countries. There is also the fact of political dependence; witness, for example, the case of the oil-producing Arab countries which are unable to defend the one cause they call their own—the
Palestinian cause. Likewise, the *fact* of industrialization proves nothing. It applies, first of all, to some countries but not to others. More
important, this fact helps to prove, at best, that the capitalist mode is
globally dominant—hardly a novel proposition at this late stage of the
debate.

Moreover, by isolating industrialization as the predominant indicator
in the supposed leveling of the gap between the metropolitan and the
peripheral countries, Warren obscures the degree of dependence that
is generated by the process of industrialization itself. The majority of
countries in the Third World are now prisoners of the international
credit system, dominated as it is by the metropolitan states and their
banks. Ample evidence exists to demonstrate that financial depend-

ence has *increased constantly* over the past two decades both in absolute quantities and in the *rate* of debt formation; some of the most alarming cases are precisely of those countries, like Brazil and South Korea, which Warren, following the World Bank, celebrates the most. The dependence for markets is again an increasingly difficult problem. As import-substitution is followed by export-oriented industrialization, the industrializing peripheral countries tend increasingly to compete with each other for markets in the metropolitan countries; and if demand relative to supply shrinks, they simply do not have alternative markets for their exports. Moreover, much of this industrialization is simply transitional; metropolitan capital builds factories in pursuit of tax benefits, cheap and captive labor, and the incentives it receives from local despots; profits are quick, and in case the despots begin to fall, disinvestment can be rapid. Some countries, like the Philippines, are beginning to show the evolving pattern. As for technology, very few of the Third World countries have even begun to produce their own means of production, and in any case the higher layers of technology, which constitute the backbone of the international production system, remain exclusive preserves of the metropolitan bourgeoisies. If anything, the real technological gap is widening, and even those few countries of the Third World that have experienced substantial industrialization in recent years, such as the several countries of East Asia, have become enclaves of those lower branches of industry, composed essentially of consumers' goods, from textiles to transistors and automobile assembly, whose location in the metropolitan countries is becoming increasingly redundant owing to the increasing concentration in the metropoles of those branches which are technologically more advanced.

All this involves altogether novel trends and strains in the composition and employment of labor on the global scale, but it does not imply that the gap, either technological or financial, between the imperialist and the imperialized countries is narrowing, as Warren asserts. And there is not an iota of evidence for his contention that the terms of trade for the Third World are really not unfavorable. What we are witnessing, though, is constant restructuring of the international division of labor wherein some countries of the capitalist periphery, such as Singapore and Saudi Arabia, are being privileged, more or less temporarily, owing to their unique positions in the financial networks and raw materials markets, over other countries of the periphery. But two aspects of this relative privileging ought to be noted. One is simply that the privilege is extended to a small number of countries, so that the gap is widening not only between the metropolitan and the peripheral countries but among countries of the Third World as well; in the process, the relative positions of the majority of Third World countries has been worsening constantly. The second aspect is that one can never be sure that the privilege a particular country gains, owing to this or that particularity at a given time, will last very long. Take, for example the cases of such diverse countries as Pakistan, Brazil, and Iran. Each was celebrated, at one time or another within the past two decades, as a model of development, but each has stagnated for one reason or another. In each case, we find a massive failure to transform the real structure of social classes, though a degree of industrialization has been foisted from above. In some cases, as in Brazil, we find the mode of industrialization itself being strained largely by the workings of international credit and finance. In other cases, such as Iran, where finance was theoretically abundant, we have witnessed the model of "modernization" being blown to pieces in the process of a social upheaval generated by the modalities and contradictions of the capitalist development itself.

This brings us to our next point—namely, Warren's overwhelming fascination with numbers and quantities, as well as his wholly economistic view of history. What links his thought to the theorists of modernization, despite his strident references to the purity of (some) texts of Marx, is above all an astonishing absence of class analysis and his naive belief, which he takes to be the kernel of Marxism, that all is well so long as factories are being built. The working class appears in his analysis very sparingly, as an inert category, strictly as the aggregate number of employees in factory production. For him, the means of production are everything, the relations of production nothing. And because the key link for him is not class struggle but the building of factories, there is an equally astonishing lack of discussion of politics and ideology. He never examines the manifest disjuncture, in the so-called industrializing countries, between the industrialization of the means of production and the increasing despotism of regimes and ruling classes, nor does he ask himself what his disjuncture means for the future of these countries. Thus, he speaks admiringly of the supposed "connection between capitalism and democracy," and he speaks of the Third World as having become wholly capitalist, but he never asks himself why is it that it is precisely in the countries where multinational capital is the strongest, from Chile to South Korea, that we have the worst kinds of military regimes and counterinsurgency states. As for the modernization theorists, development for him too is essentially a technical proposition, referring to the administration of things, not an integral social process involving relations among persons.

All this has been brought to us in the name of Marx, who is portrayed as an outright enthusiast of colonialism, like Warren himself. It is therefore useful to comment, however briefly, on Marx's views about colonialism.

Marx, Colonialism, and "The Bleeding Process"

Warren constructs his "Marxist" theory of imperialism, as opposed to the Leninist theory, on the most predictable of grounds: a quick reference to Mexico, a passage on Algeria from one of Engels's letters, and, of course, lengthy quotations from two of Marx's most anthologized articles which he wrote for the *Herald Tribune:* "The British Role In India" and "The Future Results of British Rule In India." He draws unsurprising conclusions: that Marx equated colonialism with progress. This is the traditional view, and Warren in no way indicates any awareness that Marx and Engels wrote much else which contradicts this one-sided view. His only innovation is that he musters immense enthusiasm for this colonialism/progress equation.

For a more complex sense of Marx's thinking on colonialism, we need to keep several things in mind. First, Marx never composed a full-bodied text on the question of colonialism, and it is unfair to derive a global theory from a couple of journalistic pieces. Second, the journalism dates back to the 1850s, when the colonization of India was just being completed, the Opium Wars were still a matter of the future, and fully twenty-five years before the Berlin Conference consolidated the occupation and partition of Africa. Conversely, European capitalism at that stage was entirely of a different order than what it was to become from the 1880s onward. The proper thing to do, then, is not to apply those texts as settled truths but to ask whether or not Marx's tentative predictions of that period have stood the test of time. Third, before adopting Marx's characterizations of the Asian formations, specifically of India, one should inquire into the rudimentary state of knowledge and ideology prevailing at that time, to find out whether the empirical data on which Marx based his observations correspond in any way to the reality of those Asian for-

mations. Fourth, one needs to read the two famous pieces in relation
to a number of other strands which are also present in Marx's writings
on the same subject and which suggest that, far from holding a uniform
view of colonialism as being altogether "progressive," Marx and
Engels register various shifts and even a certain evolution in their
reflections on the subject, which culminate in a view of European
colonialism ultimately as "a bleeding process." Finally, it is legitimate to question and criticize the Eurocentric semantics of "Western civilization" and "Asian barbarism" which is surely present in
Marx's remarks and which Warren simply takes over as "science."

   It has been well established by now, one should have thought, that
the sweeping generalizations in which Marx summarized his picture
of mid-nineteenth-century India in those two articles correspond little to the actual reality of Indian society, and that the predictions he
made regarding the prospects of industrialization in India were not
even remotely realized in subsequent decades. The empirical misin-
formation which underlies the generalities of "The Future Results . . ."
is connected, moreover, with the dominant European ideologies of
the period, and hence with the actual grounding of the intellectual
outlooks of Marx and Engels.[4] The binary opposition between a
"civilized" Europe and a "barbaric" East was a time-honored tradition in European thought, ranging from Aristotle to Hobbes, and from
Machiavelli to Hegel and Montesquieu. By the middle of the nineteenth century, "civilization" had come to mean, among other things,
dynamism, "progress," decency, legality, and rationality; "barbarism" meant the lack of all these, and instead, tyranny and despotism at the top, and a stagnating, "vegetative existence" at the
bottom. Marx inherited this outlook. Thus, it is simply a matter of
record that he had lifted, without citation but almost verbatim, his
whole description of the so-called Indian Village Community from
Hegel's *The Philosophy of History;* Marx did not care to cite the
source because Hegel's was the *agreed* European view. And if that
was the agreed view, then the formulations of "The Future Results"
would undoubtedly follow—that is, the railways, the telegraph, the
beneficence of European capital in general were necessary in order to
break the savage repose of that vegetative existence, regardless of the
cruelty involved in that breakage. Marx could applaud the "destruc-
tive" side of British colonialism because the colonial encounter was
itself conceptualized within a discourse premised on ideas of "civilization," "barbarism" and "progress" whereby the elimination of
barbarism was deemed cruel but necessary.

That was one side of the argument. The other, which applauded the "constructive" side of colonialism, was based on the hope that British capital, particularly the construction of railways, would lead to industrialization in India. As everyone knows, almost exactly the opposite happened. The railways, far from becoming the motivating force for industrialization in India, did not prove to be, at that stage and from the Indian point of view, even a sound economic investment; as of 1921, sixty or so years after Marx had formulated his hopes, more labor was employed on Indian tea plantations, in conditions resembling American slavery, than in all the factories on Indian soil. Moreover, the railways trapped India in a huge debt to British capitalists and functioned, meanwhile, mainly as rapid transport for British soldiery and as a means for hauling raw materials from the interior to the seaports, for utilization in the metropoles.

In short, the two articles Warren selects as the basis for his own version of the Marxist theory are, in fact, a mixed bag: great insights mingled with ideological blinders and fanciful fictions. For Marx, it could perhaps not be otherwise, given the existing conditions of knowledge and ideology. One is more than puzzled, however, when Warren, a modern theorist, picks up the same bag, fails to scrutinize those projections in the light of later researches and developments, elevates the most questionable parts of those theses to the status of a theory that is said to refute Lenin's later contributions, and in the process exhibits even less knowledge and perception.

And Warren does show less knowledge, less subtlety of perception, less commitment to practices of resistance and insurrection than did Marx and Engels, especially if one goes beyond the two articles Warren quotes so copiously. Here we come to our second point: the contradictory character of, and even a certain evolution in, their views on colonialism. Thus, in his more mature writings, such as *Capital,* Marx characterizes the period of primary accumulation as a *two-pronged* process based on the dispossession and horrific exploitation of the direct producers within Europe on the one hand and, on the other, the entombment, enslavement, and general pauperization of the people of Asia, Africa, Latin America. The same kind of dialectic is emphasized in several of the shorter, more agitational writings, such as the *Communist Manifesto,* where the conquest of the globe is viewed as an integral part—even a precondition— in the process of the maturation of the capitalist mode of production as such. Neither in *Capital* nor in the *Manifesto* do we find a characterization of colonialism as an altogether progressive phenomenon. The emphasis placed by the mode of the production theorists on the European transformation is thus wholly in accordance with Marx's thought; the ability to exploit the colonies presupposes that dynamic transformation. But the theory of imperialism, which emphasizes the pillage of the colonies, is not thereby negated; the extent and the rate of accumulation in the metropoles, not to mention the actual modalities of industrialization there, presupposes in like fashion the colossal transfers of value from the colonies, through the exploitation of cheap and unpaid labor by millions of direct producers, through the monopolistic appropriation of raw materials, through the wholesale destruction of the precolonial production systems and the creation, instead, of extensive colonial markets for metropolitan products, and so on. Both views are correct, and in Marx's own writings there is a dialectical correlation between the two. The problem arises when the two views are counterposed against each other and one is forwarded at the expense of the other, as many of the present-day mode of production theorists (such as Warren and Brennen) tend to do. Indeed, there have been the opposite tendencies as well, among many of the dependency theorists, where metropolitan development is seen simply as an effect of the pillage of the colonies. That estimation is equally excessive, and one must restore that original vision of Marx where the European transition and the pillage of the colonies are seen as inextricable links in a dialectical, global process, each reinforcing the other.

Moreover, researches that were not available to Marx but which are now available to us show in extensive detail that the precolonial non-European formations, especially in that world-system which extended from Canton to Zanzibar and from Indonesia to the East Mediterranean, were not nearly as backward as Marx and his contemporaries had supposed: India was not a cluster of "village communities," nor were its cities mere "military encampments"; transportation and communication systems were far more developed in the sixteenth century prior to their destruction by colonialism than they were at the end of the nineteenth century, after three hundred or more years of colonial hegemony; surplus was not produced for mere consumption of local chieftains but was accumulated for brisk networks of trade, giving merchant's capital a vigorous position in the social formations and enhancing the incentive for technical revolutions in the means and processes of production; and so on. In the event, and after colonial destruction, industrial capitalism was surely introduced externally by the metropolitan bourgeoisie. But the idea, which Marx surely held and which Warren repeats with such blind insistence, that the transition could not have occurred without colonial intervention needs to be examined in light of not only Marx's journalistic prediction but, much more important, of more recent researches. Nor can the question be settled on the level of theory alone. If it can be demonstrated that the historical evidence on which the theoretical conjecturing was based was altogether inaccurate, then the validity of that conjecturing itself becomes very much the issue.

Nor is it possible to assume, as Warren emphatically does, that even the journalist writings and the private correspondence of Marx and Engles give us a singleminded view of colonialism as having been uniformally "progressive." There are constant shifts and contradictions, and the main paradox within the structure of their thought appears to be this: Whenever they reflect on colonialism in a general way, in the shape of broad conceptual generalizations, they seem to be on balance on the side of progress and civilization, but in every article that either of them wrote about an actual insurrection or even sporadic acts of resistance in the colony, both speak in the lyrical cadences of revolutionaries: The Chinese Coolie suddenly becomes as admirable as a Parisian Communard, and those who equate colonialism with progress are then derided—in Engels's superb phrase—as "civilizationmongers." And instead of hoping for the triumph of progressive colonialism, they often characterize the acts of resistence as part of a war of national liberation, celebrating the mass character and the continental proportions of the anticolonial movement. Take, for example, the *tone* of the following passage from Engels (*Persia and China,* 1857):

There is evidently a different spirit among the Chinese now... The mass of the people take an active, nay, a fanatical part in the struggle against the foreigners. They poison the bread of the European community at Hongkong by wholesale, and with the coolest meditation... They go with hidden arms on board trading steamers and, when on the journey, massacre the crew and European passengers and seize the boat.... The very coolies emigrating to foreign countries rise in mutiny, and as if by concert, on board every emigrant ship, fight for its possession.... Civilizationmongers who throw hot shell on a defenceless city and add rape to murder, may call the system cowardly, barbarous, atrocious; but what matter it to the Chinese if it be but successful? . . . We had better recognise that this is a war *pro aris et focis,* a popular war for the maintenance of Chinese nationality.

Marx, in somewhat more analytic terms ("The Revolt in the Indian Army," 1857) said:

How far that native army can be relied upon is clearly shown by its recent mutinies, breaking out as soon as the war with Persia had almost denuded the Presidency of Bengal of its European soldiers. . . It is the first time that sepoy regiments have murdered their European officers: that Mussalmans and Hindus, renouncing their mutual antipathies, have combined against their common masters. . . The revolt in the Anglo-Indian Army has coincided with a general dissatisfaction exhibited against British supremacy on the part of the great Asiatic nations, the revolt of the Bengal Army being, beyond doubt, intimately connected with the Persian and Chinese wars.

Finally, on the question as to whether or not Marx thought of colonialism as altogether a "progressive" process, the following from a letter (to F. Danielson, 1881), which he wrote toward the end of his life should suffice:

In India serious complications, if not a general outbreak, are in store for the British government. What the British take from them annually in the form of rent, dividends for railways useless for the Hindoos, pensions for the military and civil servicemen, for Afghanistan and other wars, etc, etc.,—what they take from them *without any equivalent* and *quite apart* from what they appropriate to themselves annually *within* India,—speaking only of *the value of the commodities* and Indians have gratuitously and annually to *send over* to England—it amounts to *more than the total sum of income of the 60 million of agricultural and industrial labourers of India.* This is a bleeding process with a vengeance [italics in original].

When one encounters passages such as these, as one frequently does if one goes beyond the two most anthologized articles and reads Marx's writings on colonialism in their entirety, it becomes altogether difficult to argue that Marx never modified his initial view of colonialism as being "progressive" for the colony. For the "bleeding process" which, in his view, might well have led to a "general outbreak" was, in his own very graphic terms, a process whereby immense quantities of value that were produced in the periphery were accumulated nevertheless in the metropolis, while the colony itself was bearing the costs of being colonized, so that the railways, once expected to be the motor for industrialization, could then be recognized as "useless to the Hindoo." In the process, India was undoubtedly pauperized. But what about the metropolis? I quote and then comment on a somewhat enigmatic but highly suggestive text of 1858 (Letter to Engels):

> The specific task of bourgeois society is the establishment of a world market. As the world is round, this seems to have been completed. . . . The difficult question for us is this: on the Continent the revolution is imminent and will immediately assume a socialist character. Is it not bound to be crushed in this little corner, considering that in a far greater territory the movement of bourgeois society is still in the ascendant?

Some of the ideas Lenin developed later are here, though in embryonic form: the idea that the historical task of capitalism—namely the creation of the world market—is completed already and capitalism is therefore *ripe* in its places of origin for a revolutionary overthrow; as well as the idea that world accumulation might nevertheless give the European bourgeoisies the material means to crush the revolution inside Europe. Yet, Marx seems unable to think these thoughts in exactly that way. This was the period, one may recall, when Marx himself was witnessing tremendous capitalist growth in North America, and he was wondering if the same might not happen in countries like China and India as well. This is at least how I interpret his idea of the movement of bourgeois society being in the ascendant outside Europe. It was only after he lost faith in the industrializing mission of colonial capital that colonialism could be declared, unequivocally, a bleeding process.

One can draw three conclusions from this necessarily brief sketch. First, Marx's views on the long-range consequences of colonialism remained highly contradictory throughout the 1850s. Second, as he witnessed the process, during the three decades leading up to the 1880s, whereby colonialism transformed itself into a fully fledged imperialism, he came to speak of it as (a) a bleeding process, which already foreshadowed Lenin's characterization of it as "parasitic" and "rapacious," and (b) a process that was likely to be highly detrimental to the development of the socialist revolution inside Europe, again an idea that Lenin was to develop greatly. Third, far from being a "reversal" of Marx's thinking, Lenin's (and Bukharin's) theory of imperialism is a development of some of the ideas that had remained ambiguous and rudimentary in Marx.

From Marx to Lenin

The "economics" of Lenin's theory of imperialism is well enough known, and this is at any rate hardly the place to delve into it. But it is necessary to specify briefly what is referred to when speaking of Lenin's theory of imperialism, and to specify also the *political* context that gave rise to this theory.

The problem with conceptualizing the unity of Lenin's theory of imperialism is that it is composed of a series of occasional texts which are, moreover, mutually discontinuous. I am referring here to that thread which connects his pamphlet, *Imperialism: The Highest Stage of Capitalism,* with several texts on the colonial and national questions, and all these with those other texts where the strategic concept of "the weakest link" is elaborated. Together, these writings constitute a whole, though unfortunately a discontinuous one, hence lacking somewhat in rigorous connection between parts. Lenin's own dissatisfaction with *Imperialism,* especially his pointed regret that it deals only with the economic aspects and that the presentation is much distorted owing to the existence of czarist dictatorship, should be better known. In any case, Lenin's profound sense that imperialist capital had become, so far as the colonies were concerned, altogether "rapacious" was intimately connected with (a) his political commitment to the right of national self-determination in the colonies, (b) his emphasis on broad alliances in the colonies so that national contradictions might be incorporated in practices of class struggle, and (c) his sense also that under the new conditions, much of the dynamic of revolution had shifted to the colonies, so that the imperialist chain was likely to break first not in the metropolises ("backward Europe") but in the weakest links (the periphery, "advanced Asia"). The theory is thus not only an economic one (monopolies, capital exports, etc.) but also political (national liberation, the politics of alliances, the weakest link). And regardless of the discontinuity between texts, the connection between the economic and political aspects of the theory was not schematic but conjunctural. Not only had imperialism organized a different kind of world-economy, it had also given rise to a different kind of political conjuncture on the global scale. At least one aspect of this new conjuncture bears some comment here.

What is remarkable about the period under consideration—roughly from the 1880s to the 1920s—is the connection, the almost exact contemporaneity, of two dialectically linked phenomena that had come about, in part, as a consequence of global imperialism: a general drift of the working-class movements in Northwestern Europe toward social democracy (i.e., toward parliamentarism, gradualism, social chauvanism, etc.), combined with the defeat of the revolutionary working class in Germany, and the rise of anticolonialism and revolutionary nationalism in the imperialized countries. Some dates can be given.

For the imperialized countries, this era began, schematically speaking, with the courageous bid in 1898 by Filipino nationalists to establish an independant republic; and the history of the era would include, at the very least, the Irani revolution of 1905-1911, the Mexican revolution of 1910, the Chinese revolution of 1911, the Egyptian revolution of 1919, the coming to power of Amir Amanullah Khan in Afghanistan (also 1919), the Kemalist revolution in Turkey (1923), and a whole history of variegated resistances and struggles for national independence that one cannot begin to catalogue here. Nor was this a sudden flare, without prehistory or future. Rather, the period symbolized a *growth,* a qualitative development, a reconstruction of earlier memories, a revenge for past defeats: the liquidation of that prolonged moment of the national will in Paraguay (1814–1840), when independent development had seemed possible; the suppression of the Great Revolt in India (1857) and parallel resistances in Iran and China throughout the 1850s and beyond; the defeat of Abdel Kader's revolt in Algeria (1871-1872); the Occupation of Egypt (1882); the fall of Hanoi, after bitter war of ten years (also 1882). Throughout the nineteenth century, the peoples of the colonized world—the "backward" peoples of what, after decolonization, came to be called the Third World—had fought hard and lost. The period that began, roughly speaking, in 1898 and spanned the next quarter-century and which also happened to be the period when Lenin's own thought matured and exploded on the world, was one when the dynamic of the nationalist revolution in the imperialized countries had seemed to be on the upswing. While it was none too clear that the anticolonial revolution would indeed develop an anticapitalist content, it seemed at least reasonable to work toward such an eventuality. In any event, imperialism surely reversed most of those gains, and most national bourgeoisies became, especially after World War II, mere conduits and adjuncts of metropolitan capital. However, one should not too easily forget that the few revolutions that did occur over the next few decades—such as the Chinese, Cuban, Vietnamese, and Mozambiquan—owed a great deal to the revolutionary transformation of nationalism and anticolonialism.

As regards the growth of social democracy in Northwestern Europe, the case of the German party is well known, as are Lenin's polemics against Bernstein and Kautsky. Less well known is the fact that it was a period of a *general* drift toward parliamentarism and gradualism in a host of countries, and that the drift, alongside the extension of suffrage which accompanied it, was *characteristic* of the workers' movement in those countries during the opening decades of modern imperialism. Thus, for example, the Belgian party's electoral strength grew from 13.2 percent in 1894 to 39.4 percent in 1925; the strength of the party in the Netherlands grew from 3 percent in 1896 to 18.5 percent in 1913; the Norwegian party's strength grew from a paltry 0.6 percent in 1897 to 32.1 percent in 1915; the Swedish party jumped from 3.5 percent in 1902 to 36.4 percent in 1914; in Finland, the social democrats had already won a plurality in 1907, getting 37 percent of the vote; the Austrian party gained 27 percent in 1907 and then a plurality, of 40.8 percent, in 1919. As for England, Engels had himself occasionally spoken of "the supine character" of the workers' movement there, and more modern commentators would characterize the practices of British social democracy, quite justifiably, as "Labour imperialism."

The opening decades of the imperialist era thus witnessed a crucial conjunction of facts: unprecedented acceleration of colonial conquest, accompanied by the growth of nationalism and anticolonialism in the periphery; and equally unprecedented capitalist prosperity in the metropolitan countries, accompanied by incorporation of vast segments of the European working class into bourgeois parliamentarism via the agency of social democracy. The latter development, the incorporation of the European working class, was by no means inevitable; but that is what happened. Lenin's theory of imperialism, fragmentary as it is in some respects, attempts to define political practices appropriate to this conjuncture. As regards the colonies, his unequivocal support for national liberation was based not only on the theoretical affirmation of the right of national self-determination, but also on his perception of the actual strategic possibilities in the colonies. On the one hand, the parasitic character of imperialist capital was already obstructing the process of indigenous accumulation (thanks to the bleeding process), so that political independence was in any case expected to strengthen the development of the productive forces, whether in the capitalist or the noncapitalist framework. On the other hand, since *all* modern classes in the colony (the bourgeoisie as much as the proletariat) were relatively undeveloped, it was at least possible that the working class, although numerically weak and socially backward, might nonetheless emerge as the hegemonic class in the colonial formation, provided that it was able to create a political framework of practice commensurate with the tasks of national liberation. What was at stake, then, was not the question of socialist revolution as such, but the question of class hegemony. The imperialist parasite had already made the anticolonial struggle historically inevitable, for *all* classes in the colony, and the political hegemony of the working class could only be constructed in the course of *that* struggle—hence the key link in Lenin's writing between class struggle in the colony and the colonial question per se, the idealist discourses on the "progressive" character of capitalism notwithstanding.

The Myth of "Progressive" Capitalism

Assuming, as one in fairness should, that Warren had read more of Marx than he cared to cite, the only possible explanation for his highly tendentious reading lies in his own quite inordinate admiration for capitalism. This admiration is, in fact, a matter of considerable import: all the faults, sins, and brutalities of the system are forgiven in the name of progress.

There is, for example, the overwhelming question of the sheer human costs, the manifestly barbaric slaughters, which constitute a necessary aspect of the construction of capitalism on a global scale. Warren accounts for these in two ways. First, he brushes them aside by drawing a strident distinction between the "moral" and the "historical-materialist" outlooks; the latter, he says, occupies itself with questions of progress and excludes the questions of morality. His second line of argument, which contradicts the first but runs parallel with it, is to the effect that (a) human society has always been cruel but (b) no one in the past much cared about it because precapitalist societies, barbaric as they were, had no sense of morality in any case, and (c) the whole question of cruelty arose only in capitalist societies because (d) only capitalist societies are moral. In this latter line of argument, a higher sense of morality becomes a specifically bourgeois attribute and a gift of Europe to the rest of the world. Pages 21-24 of the book make remarkable reading on this score. Let me give an example or two.

"The slaughter of the First World War, the Nazi concentration camps, the Vietnam War" are, for Warren, "relatively equivalent" to, for example, "the Golden Horde and the Thirty Year War." The difference is merely numerical, and "if the technical advances of capitalism have brought the world horrors on an unprecedented scale, this is essentially a technical by-product." The Nazi camps, he says, were no different than any other manifestation of racism. What *was* new, he emphasizes, was the sense of moral outrage which accompanied this no-greater-than-usual cruelty; moreover, the outrage itself was a product of a morality peculiar to the humanistic civilization of capitalism. In other words, cruelty is transhistorical: Morality is specifically bourgeois. Warren is emphatic on this point and returns to it over and over again, from different angles. "Equality, justice, generosity" and "opposition to cruelty" are said to be unique features of the bourgeois outlook which "emerge early in the cultural history of capitalism." We are also told that "the humanistic side of capitalist culture emerged very early in the development of capitalism in the first industrial society, Britain, and profoundly affected the working of the capitalist productive apparatus from the beginning." In his excitement over capitalist—particularly British—humanism, Warren chooses to forget Marx's unforgettable treatment of the horrors of primitive accumulation, not to speak of Engels's detailed examination of the conditions of the working class in England in the mid-nineteenth century. Anything that even begins to challenge the notions of bourgeois liberalism is dismissed out of hand; the whole of "the modern radical women's liberation movement" is declared to be "revanchist, inward-looking, and backward" compared with the "humanist and progressive" John Stuart Mill. Finally, Warren postulates that there can be no real difference between bourgeois morality and socialist morality, because all industrialized societies must have the same morality, while "the cultural and moral differences between modern industrial societies and pre-industrial societies and cultures are far more fundamental than between the industrial societies themselves." Presumably, inculcating a higher sense of morality is part of the civilizing mission of ITT and Exxon in the Third World, while the socialist society of tomorrow will be not much different, in moral and cultural terms, than the society of today's fetishized universal markets.

Capitalism and Democracy

"Capitalism and democracy are," Warren says, "linked virtually as Siamese twins." Elsewhere we are told that imperialism not only leads to "industrialisation and general economic development" in the Third World, but the "cultural and material achievements" of capitalism, including "the important connection between capitalism and democracy," are equally beneficent for the social and moral uplift of backward peoples. The assumption, of course, is that capitalism will bring democracy to the Third World. This question of capitalist democracy deserves some comment because, unlike his peculiar ideas on capitalist morality, Warren's enthusiasm for capitalist democracy would seem to be widely shared in Western Marxism.

That the working class needs democracy is surely beyond doubt. That there is an "important connection" between capitalism and democracy is perhaps also obvious, though it might have been altogether possible to lose sight of this "connection" if you were an English woman trying to elect a Member of Parliament in 1913, or a German communist trying to raise your voice in 1933, or an Afro-American trying, in 1953, to buy a cup of coffee across most counters in the lovely Carolinas, North or South. In other words, there *is* a connection between metropolitan capitalism and metropolitan democracy, though even that connection seems to have worked, through most of the history of capital, only for those who were male, white, and Tory.

But what of the periphery? Capitalism arrived on our shores, in the shape of its guns and slavers and merchants, roughly five hundred years ago. I cannot think of five countries in the imperialized periphery today where parliamentary democracy can be said to have become the stable political form of bourgeois rule. I will go further: There is a *negative* connection between capitalism and democracy in the periphery. The more these countries are integrated into global capitalism, the more despotic their state systems have become. The fascist, the Bonapartist, the military-dictatorial may be, as is said in Western Marxism,[5] the "exceptional" forms of the state in the metropoles; in the periphery, these are the normal, the generalized forms. Moreover, these new varieties of despotism are manifestations not of the backwardness of the periphery but of the progress of the metropoles: The instruments of torture are usually imported, and those who administer the torture are by and large also either imported from or trained in the metropoles. Not that the local owners of capital are less murderous in their intent; their ability to perpetrate genocides comes nevertheless mostly from the metropoles.

I will go even further. Up to the advent of modern imperialism (1880s or so), parliamentary democracy remained an exceptional, beleaguered, tenuous, and limited form of bourgeois rule even in Europe; it existed in some of the European countries, for some of the time, for some sections of the population. Far from being a "Siamese twin" of capitalism, bourgeois democracy, based on universal suffrage and functioning as a generalized and stable form of the bourgeois state, is, even in the metropoles, a rather recent phenomenon, dating at the most to the aftermath of World War II; in the less privileged parts of the Continent—Spain, Greece, Turkey, and so on—this form is neither generalized nor stable. Even in some of the richer countries, such as West Germany and Italy, the economic prosperity of the past thirty years has been the indispensable foundation for political democracy. Will Italian democracy, for example, survive if economic prosperity is profoundly threatened? One hopes, but only a fool would take a bet one way or the other. And even if we grant, for the sake of argument, that Western democracy is now irreversible, this experience of thirty-five years in a small corner of global capitalism is insufficient to postulate a fundamental connection between capitalism and democracy as such, for the quintessential experience of capitalism even in the present generation is this: Democracy for the metropoles, dictatorship for the periphery; the drug of ideology and protein here, the perfection of despotism there.

I am speaking not of two systems, the civilized and the savage, one capitalist and the other precapitalist, but of one system, the imperialist. And imperialism is not simply a matter of the so-called productive forces, nor is it merely an economic system of unequal exchanges between autonomous national economies. Imperialism is simultaneously a world-economy as well as a global political system. The metropolitan/democratic state and the peripheral/despotic state constitute a dialectical unity in that system, because each is necessary, in its own space, for maximization of the accumulation process. And it is not very difficult to fathom why the typical peripheral state must be despotic.

A *permanent* army of the unemployed; *increased* pauperization for the majority as a consequence of the concentration of the means of production in a few hands; for the *majority* of the proletariat, a wage scale that gives it no more than is absolutely necessary for the reproduction of its own labor power; the common *ruination* of the landless, the small producers, the craftspeople; an *unlimited* supply of wage labor; coercion, pillage, disease, death. These are among the fundamental laws of capitalism, and no reading of *Capital* is possible without this recognition. These laws seem to have disappeared from the vocabulary of Western Marxism because it thinks of capitalism, by and large, in terms of metropolitan states. On the contrary, as soon as one breaks away from Eurocentric nationalisms and thinks of capitalism as a world-system—or, more accurately, imperialism—one immediately recognizes that these laws *are* operative, very much so, though now not merely on the scale of a France or the British Isles but on a global scale. It is in the conditions of existence of the direct producers and the unemployed populations of the periphery—that vast majority of the world's working class which lives in the majority of today's capitalist states—that capitalism continues to reveal itself as a system of political autocracy and economic destitution. As a result, the politics of these classes cannot but be essentially and permanently insurrectionary. Conversely, the open, permanent, overwhelming violence of the typical peripheral state corresponds fairly precisely to this dialectic of destitution and insurrection. The power of capital comes today, as it has always come, out of the barrel of a gun.

Colonialism, Hunger, and Education

Even aside from democracy, colonialism in Warren's discourse is credited with bringing to the colony a host of other social and cultural benefits, especially in the area of education, health, and nutrition. "The colonial record," we are told, "was remarkably free of brutality" (p. 128). Again, "the epochal imperialist sweep was indeed a titanic step toward human unity (on the basis of the greatest cultural and material achievements so far attained by humanity)" (p. 137). These are obviously statements rather contrary to facts. It is doubtful, for example that the indigenous populations of the Americas, whose entombment was the prime condition for capitalist progress in their lands, could have thought that the process of their own demise was "free of brutality." Nor is it at all clear that the enslaved populations of West Africa could have considered the slave trade a "titanic step toward human unity." These matters concern, moreover, not only the remote past but also our own living present. No one who has lived through the period of the Vietnam war could, while in possession of his senses, speak of the "imperialist sweep" as an expression of humanity's greatest achievements. And even setting aside the countless millions who died or were maimed for life in the process of this sweep, what about the ones who survived? Warren makes much of imperialism's contributions to health, education, and nutrition in the colonies. This again seems doubtful. It is perhaps in the history of Latin America, in the annals of Portugese colonialism in Africa, and in those maps of modern hunger which stretch from the Sahel to Kenya and from Somalia to the Bantustans, that one could best see the colonial and imperialist achievements in this regard. But since India is very much the country in question, from Marx to our own more modern author, it is best to give some examples from the past and present history of that "jewel" of the British empire.

Here, too, it is difficult to muster much enthusiasm for these achievements. When one finds, for example, that roughly 80 percent of the population of Bangladesh, one of the earliest beneficiaries of colonialism in the subcontinent, is now eating fewer calories than what is considered minimally necessary even for paupers, one wonders about progress in health and nutrition, especially if one knows that the ratio between food prices and urban incomes is much worse today, in each of the three countries of the subcontinent, than it was in the days of Akbar (the Mughal king, a contemporary of Elizabeth Ist, whose name Warren continually misspells). Nor is this a new development. This ratio, as well as the general food intake, has declined constantly since the advent of colonialism. In this, as in so many other respects, the histories of the metropoles and the peripheries present us with a stark contrast, whereby capitalism has harvested food for the winners, hunger for the losers:

> Only in the course of the last two hundred years, since the Industrial Revolution, has an adequate diet come to be assured to most of that third of mankind living in the rich countries of North America, Western Europe, Eastern Europe, Japan and Australia [Brown and Finterbush, 1972: 7].

By contrast, as Gail Omvedt puts it:

> Whereas capitalist development in the centers of capitalism meant the end of famine as a common feature in human history, it seems to have resulted in intensification of famine elsewhere. The figures are grim. India, the longest fully colonised society, had the worst record: 10 million dead (a third of the population) in Bengal in 1796-70, only a decade after the initial conquest and plunder of that region. . .; one million dead in 1866, again in the east; one and a half million dead in 1869 in Rajasthan; five million dead in 1876-78; one million in 1899-1900. The population of colonial India was literally ravaged by death and disease. China too had major famines beginning about the middle of the 19th century . . . with between nine and thirteen million dead in North China in 1876-79, and two million dead in Hunan in 1929. . . The only major famine in Europe in this period was in its 'white' colony: two to three million dead in the potato famine in Ireland in 1846-47 [Omvedt, 1975].[6]

Except for limitations of space, one could document in virtually inexhaustible detail the declining rate of calorie consumption in the subcontinent, as in much of the periphery; the growing food dependence of the Third World on the surplus-producing metropoles; the manner in which the new technologies of food production have increased the power of the multinational corporations over the peripheral national economies, and how the American ruling class, through the agency of its state, uses and is determined to use food not as a step toward "human unity," as Warren claims, but as a weapon, like the Marines and the nuclear bomb.

I do not have the space. So, I will make some random observations regarding education, again with reference only to India. Britain's long march toward the conquest of India had started much earlier, and the decisive point had been reached already with the Battle of Plassey and the subsequent subjugation of Bengal in 1757. As regards education, however, the customary British practice for the next sixty years or more was to allot millions of rupees to this item in the budget, and then to spend only small portions of it, mostly on schools designed to teach the vernacular to the British themselves. This state of affairs lasted until about the 1820s, although the more farsighted among the colonizing intelligentsia were well aware of the benefits of the teaching of English for the colonial enterprise. It was in the 1830s, when the administration of India was becoming of direct concern to the British Crown, that the question of education, along with a host of other such administrative questions, came to be posed in earnest. Lord Macauley, who traveled to India in 1834 to campaign personally for the teaching of English, summarized the objective quite succinctly:

> We must do our best to form a class who may be interpreters between us and the millions who we govern . . . a class of persons, Indian in blood and color, but English in tastes, in opinions, in morals, and in intellect.

Macauley's brother-in-law, Sir Charles Travelyan, was even more far-sighted and could already foresee the main requirements of what we today call the postcolonial society, for as early as 1838 he wrote in his book, *On the Education of the Peoples of India:*

> No effort of policy can prevent the nations from regaining their independence. English education will achieve by gradual reform what any other method will do by revolution. The nations will not rise against us because we shall stoop to raise them. . . *We shall exchange profitable subjects for even more profitable allies* . . and establish a strict commercial union between the first manufacturing country and the first producing country in the world [italics added].

That just such a "commercial union" was consummated, and that India was given its fill of the gentlemen who were Indian in blood and color but English in tastes and morals, is indeed beyond doubt. But aside from the Anglicized elite, who else benefited? In 1882, half a century after Macauley's tour of duty, the British were spending six dollars for colonial education for every hundred they spent on the colonial Army; forty years after that, in 1921-1922, the ratio was still one to ten. By this latter date, the British were spending an average of sixty-seven cents per annum per school-age child. But even these averages are bogus; most of this money was spent on a handfull of classy outfits which devoted themselves to the reproduction of the colonial elite. The upshot was that literacy rates in India remained almost constant for a century of British rule, from 1835 to 1931, rising for adults from 4.4 percent to 6 percent and for five-year-olds from 5.8 percent to 7 percent. Even the little industrialization that did take place seems to have produced no cultural benefits for the working class: among the Mahars, Holis, and Dheds, the three castes most identified with industrial employment in Central India, the literacy rate in 1921 was found to be a mere 1.5 percent (Buchanan, 1966: 297).

Conclusion: Imperialism and Western Marxism

If Warren's book is really as shallow and wrong-headed as I take it to be, such lengthy commentary on it might seem rather excessive. And one would have surely preferred to have ignored it if it were an expression of lone eccentricity. But as I argued in the beginning, the discussion is made imperative by the much wider context of the theoretical productions and political practices that have contributed to the currency and prestige of the book; it will have its weight, regardless of worth. This context is especially difficult to define because no particular political party, no singular line of political or theoretical argument, no one towering personality can be said to have shaped the entire conjuncture; there are enormous differences of outlook, ability, political preference, object of research, and so on. However, as one surveys the broad range of those recent debates that have dominated first the Continental and now, increasingly, the Anglo-American variants of Marxist theory, three aspects stand out in special relief: a distance from, and even repudiation of, Lenin; an analysis of the transition to capitalism as one that was internal to Europe, and of contemporary capitalism in which the imperalized countries are taken to be essentially irrelevant; and a distance also from politics as such, in the name of culture, or philosophy and epistemology, or economics. Warren's own drawback is that he operates at a low level of intellectual sophistication, and both the intensity and the sweep of his invective is likely to offend most readers. He is nevertheless enormously attractive for several tendencies in contemporary Western Marxism because he *combines* all three elements I cited above in highly pronounced terms: He attacks that part of Lenin's thought—namely the theory of imperialism—that has been the hardest to combat; he makes the case that the benefits of colonialism went not to the colonizer but to the colonized; and, in the name of a wholly economistic "theory of the productive forces," he rejects altogether the very ideas of any political struggle against imperialism.

These are not minor or accidental matters. There have been developing over more than a decade in the theoretical constructions of independant Marxists as well as in the programmatic formulations of the leading European communist parties, powerful tendencies that

have diverse origins but are nonetheless united in seeking to challenge
and refute Lenin's three basic contributions to Marxist theory: his
theory of the capitalist state (as a structure primarily of force, as a dictatorship of the bourgeoisie); his theory of revolutionary politics
(party of the revolutionary vanguard, the politics of insurrection, the
destruction of the bourgeois state, the "dictatorship of the proletariat"); and his theory of imperialism (as "rapacious" and "decay-
ing" capitalism, and as a global system of monopoly capital, which
begins to disintegrate first not in the centers but in its "weakest
links"). Over the past decade or so, the contrary tendencies in Western Marxism have concentrated on the first two of these theories: the
state and revolutionary politics. This was necessary because the
incorporation of the Eurocommunist parties into the modalities of
bourgeois parliamentarism was impossible without considerable repudiation of Leninism. And revision in this direction seemed possible
(a) because a very extensive body of anti-Leninist argument could be
taken over, with certain modifications, from a host of earlier debates
(Bernstein and Kautsky on the one hand; parts of Gramsci on the
other), to be made serviceable for the new conjuncture, and (b)
because there already was the towering and immensely repugnant
fact of Stalinism which could be, with some rearrangement of facts,
collapsed into the *theories* of Lenin, so that the "existing socialisms"
of the Soviet bloc could be read off as incarnations of Lenin's
texts.

The matter of imperialism seemed less pressing and harder to handle, less pressing because, at first glance, it seemed not to conflict
with the practical applications of Eurocommunism: NATO, and
Fiat, and French troops in a dozen African countries, and the French
Communist Party's racist attacks on migrant workers inside France,
could all be tolerated, ignored, filed away, as long as one got enough
votes in Naples and Marseilles. It was a difficult question because, as
Warren rightly points out, there had never been, over the past sixty or
so years, a major Marxist challenge to Lenin's characterization of
imperialism as "rapacious" capitalism. The most important challenge to Lenin's and Bukharin's theories, the one that came from
Rosa Luxemberg, had been argued on a different terrain: the role and
potentialities/limits of the world market, the transformation of values
into prices and the process of their accumulation on the world scale,
and so on. The other big challenge, from Kautsky and his theory of
ultraimperialism, whereby the Western imperialist countries were to
form a benign syndicate for mutually profitable exploitation of the

globe, never gained much currency among communists, due to the sheer persistence of imperialist wars and war machines. It was difficult, then, to suddenly start expounding on the beneficence of imperialism until a lot else had changed in Western Marxism. That Warren can now deliver that much-delayed discourse is a measure of these changes.

In other words, after the rule of the bourgeoisie had been theorized as being based not on force but on consent; after the capitalist state had been theorized not as class dictatorship but in terms of its electoral forms, its bureaucratic structures, and its managerial functions; after revolutionary politics had been conceptualized afresh as politics of the "historic compromise"; after the state of the socialist transition was likewise conceptualized as not the class hegemony (that is, dictatorship) of the proletariat but as greater "perfection" of the parliamentary form and a "reconstruction of the national economy"; after the relationship of the metropoles and the periphery had itself been defined (in the term Enrico Berlinguer had borrowed from Exxon) as "interdependence"; after all that—it had become possible, and perhaps even necessary, to eradicate the theory of imperialism from the vocabulary of Western Marxism, just as the concept of the dictatorship of the proletariat had been purged, by official decree, from the vocabulary of the Eurocommunist parties.

Warren's attack on the Leninist theory of imperialism is voluble and explicit. Analogous ideas were nonetheless present, implicitly and/or partially, in the presuppositions of a number of other, slightly earlier debates. Thus, for example, the Miliband-Poulantzas-Laclau debate presents itself as a theoretical discussion on the general category of "the capitalist state," with none of the participants being aware even to a slight degree that the object of their analysis was not the state of the capitalist mode of production—there perhaps can be no global theory at this level of generality—but a type of state formation which is specific to the metropolitan countries, in the era of imperialism and at a particular juncture in history. Besides, they proceed in their debate with the presupposition that the effectiveness of this type of state is enclosed within the territorial frontiers of the nation-state, with little regard for the obvious fact that the creation and exercise of military might, of historically unprecedented ferocity and wholly commensurate with the requirements of global rapacious accumulation, is a specific task of this state, hence absorbing much of its revenues and accounting for much of the power of its personnel; and that, even in the field of ideology, which is the preferred field of our theorists, the contemporary metroplitan/capitalist state directly generates imperalist and racist ideologies within the metropolitan countries, and intervenes directly and in full force, even with great military force, in the dominant ideological production in the imperial-ized formations; and that the likes of Reagan and Thatcher, the chief executives of such states, are, as a rule, rabid imperialists and racists. This relative neglect of the question of imperialism in much of the contemporary debate on the theory of the state could hardly be an oversight. It attests, rather, to an ideology which looks at the history of Europe as an autonomous history that may have passed through the "aberration" of colonialism, much as it also passed through the "aberration" of fascism (the "exceptional" form), but whose secular history can be theorized adequately within the predicates of its own internal dynamic, so that the aberration in no substantial way con-tributes to, or detracts from, Europe's essential splendor, isolation, and difference.

This view of capitalism also appears in what has come to be known as the mode of production debate—not so much in the original exchange between Sweezy and Dobb, as in the more recent recapitulations of it. As I remarked earlier, the wholesale expropriation of the direct pro-ducers inside Europe and the colossal appropriation of the values produced in Asia, Africa, and Latin America had been, for Marx, two aspects of a *single* global process since that very early stage of capitalism which he calls the stage of primary, or primitive, accum-ulation. As the more modern debate progressed, however, the dialec-tical unity of the original conception was increasingly subjected to an either/or choice, so that there could be only *one* primary source for the transition (the famous prime mover). In the course of this search for a unitary source, the complex historicity of the capitalist mode came to be reduced increasingly to a relation of expropriation between the direct producer and his direct exploiter; in order to understand the capitalist transition, then, one had to examine only the transforma-tion of the labor relation inside, say, England. Colonialism, mean-while, came to be associated more and more with commerce, and since we all know that in Marxist theory production takes precedence over circulation, it was said to be possible, by and large, to separate capitalism and colonialism as two different processes that had no necessary connection. This theoreticist separation between produc-tion (capitalism) and circulation (colonialism) was difficult enough to sustain even as a theoretical postulate, but the next step in this line of reasoning was indeed remarkable: Since there was discovered to be no theoretically necessary connection between capitalism and colonialism, one was now free to proceed as if there was no such necessary connection in historical fact either. A theoretically possible and potential history could thus be posited instead of the history that actually was.[7]

The effect, if not the purpose, of these lines of argument has been to revise Marxism once more in the direction of a Eurocentric world view. And once the originary formation of capitalism had been theoretically sundered from its colonialist links, once the contemporary metropolitan state had been conceptualized as an entity that had nothing basic to do with imperialism, and if quantitative analysis could show, in addition, that most values in contemporary capitalism were produced and exchanged within and among the metroplitan countries, then the penultimate question could in fact be asked: *Is imperialism necessary?* The Syzmanski-Magdoff exchange covers the terrain of that question fairly well,[8] and we need not dwell on it, except to say that even the posing of this question within a Marxist discourse is indicative of profound shifts in perspective. Instead of conceptualizing imperialism as capitalism itself, at the global/monopoly stage, this perspective takes imperialism to be perhaps a facet, possibly an adjunct, surely no more than an option that the metropolitan state may or may not wish to exercise.

There are, then, three questions: Does imperialism exist? Is it necessary? And is it bad? Warren begins where others have left off, and his answers have the virtue of clarity: Yes, imperialism exists; it exists because it is necessary; it is necessary because it is good, magnanimous, beneficent.

I have so far cited, in necessarily summary fashion and by way of example only, some of the highly influential debates among intellectuals who are, for the most part, free of party constraints. The case of the parties themselves is, if anything, worse. The crux of the matter here, bluntly put, is this: In the course of building what Togliatti used to call "national roads to socialism," the Western European parties have gradually come to identify themselves with nationalist agendas to such a degree that they have abandoned, for the greater part, the struggle against the imperialism of their own respective bourgeoisies. Thus, if the Spanish Party has failed to support POLISARIO because the Spanish bourgeoisie is itself an interested party in the struggle over the Sahara, the French Party (PCF) has been remarkably silent about military intervention by the French state in half a dozen African countries; instead, the PCF prefers to print in its own newspapers large pictures of the Mirage, the prized aircraft of the French military establishment, as a contribution by French workers to the export effort of the (beleaguered) French economy. The Italian Party (PCI), clearly the most influential of the Eurocommunist parties, follows much the same policies. It is well known that the term "dictatorship of the proletariat" disappeared from the lexicon of these parties after their Berlin Conference of 1976. At the same time, and as part of the same thinking, PCI also abandoned the term "proletarian internationalism," declaring it to be too sectarian, and substituted for it the term "internationalist solidarity," which has no class content. This classless "solidarity" makes it possible, in turn, for Mr. Berlinguer to establish party-to-state relations with such governments as those of Somalia and India; to endorse the economic integration of Western Europe under the rubric of the EEC, and to speak of a *strengthened* NATO as a bastion of Western European power against both the USSR and the United States; to conduct highly publicized meetings with Brandt, Mitterand, Gonzalez, and Soares—the leaders of social democracy in West Germany, France, Spain, and Portugal, respectively—in order to work out a historic compromise between social democracy and Eurocommunism; and to speak in his address to the European Parliament not of the imperialism of the European bourgeoisies but of a "framework of relations" between Europe and nations of the Third World based on "mutually advantageous cooperation," a term not much different in content from the "interdependence" so close to the heart of the American ruling class. And it has been a long time since programs of the PCI have spoken of Italy's own bourgeoisie as one of the imperialist bourgeoisies.

The case of France, and hence the outlook of the PCF, is possibly the most pertinent in this regard, since France is the most openly active of all the European imperialist powers. Some of the PCF's record goes back to the 1940s, when the party looked favorably at the reactivation of French colonialism in Indochina and Algeria. It is also indicative that in the current politics of France, the PCF has volubly joined the racist campaign against migrant workers, and that Georges Marchais himself has demanded for France draconian laws similar to the ones that exist in West Germany—some of them dating to the Nazi period.[9] These, again, are not fits of absentmindedness. These tactics are required by that variant of the "national road to socialism" which increasingly becomes a mere passageway of French nationalism. As a group of French communists, led by Étienne Balibar, noted in their criticism of the draft documents of the 23rd Congress of the PCF, held in May 1979:

> The Party's discourse has been based for too long on the non-recognition, indeed the systematic suppression, of two sizeable realities: French imperialism, and the existence and the nature of inter-imperialist conflicts. Thus, we could look in vain in the preliminary documents of the 23rd Congress for an analysis of *French* imperialism. Indeed, any reference to it has disappeared from the preamble to the new statutes. . . In its present argumentation the Party is trying to suggest that *France has in turn become victim of imperialism.* . . It is a matter of *denying that the structure of French society,* its productive apparatus and its work force, *is marked by our history as an imperialist power.* . . To put forward such an argument is in fact to give up on principle all criticism of *the structural distortion* which the development of imperialist capital has placed on the means of production and on mankind. It is like saying, for example, that socialism does not have to transform from top to bottom a specialization of the industrial branches which relies upon the use of raw materials taken by pillaging the Third World, and which aims at the conquest of foreign markets. . . At this stage, it seems to us, the class viewpoint so often claimed has completely disappeared [Balibar et al., 1980; italics in original].

This came from inside the PCF and seems accurate enough. Interestingly, criticisms such as these have led not to the rectification of party policies but to the expulsion, instead, of Balibar and others who were opposed to the party's racism and proimperialism.

Obviously, Warren's text is not an offspring of the Eurocommunist parties. Nor are his formulations derived directly from the politics and the debates I have cited above. It remains nonetheless true that the terms of those debates and the persistence of those practices have contributed immeasurably to a general climate of opinion in which Warren's thoughts become thinkable, even to a degree plausible, within a political framework that continues to define itself as Marxist. That is, extremist as Warren's text surely is, it is also symptomatic of something wider.

Notes

1. I use the term "Western Marxism" not to cover the entire body of Marxist writings published in the Western countries but in the narrower, though not quite specific, sense given to this term by Perry Anderson and others of New Left Books.

2. I am referring here—and in the slightly lengthier discussion toward the end of the chapter—not to the totality of the writings of these authors but to the principal texts of the debate, which are as follows: Poulantzas (1969), Miliband (1970, 1973), and Laclau (1977).

3. Some of the purely economic aspects of Warren's assertions regarding the latest phase of imperialism have been addressed, albeit briefly and rather charitably in Lipietz's useful review of the book in *New Left Review* (No. 132, March-April 1982). Lipietz correctly traces the genealogy of Warren's thought back to Rostow, not Marx.

4. Even within the spectrum of New Left Books, one might have gathered as much from, for example, the note on "The 'Asiatic Mode of Production' " in Anderson (1979). Warren does not even acknowledge that most historians who have written recently about precolonial India take a very different view of the matter.

5. Poulantzas is very much in the mainstream of Western Marxism when he characterizes parliamentary democracy as the "normal" form of regime in the capitalist state, while dismissing Bonapartism, fascism, and military dictatorship as "exceptional" forms which arise in particular and presumably transitional conjunctures (see Poulantzas, 1976; also his otherwise highly useful book, *Fascism and Dictatorship,* 1974). There is a remarkable disjuncture within this mode of thought. It sets out to theorize the state of the capitalist mode as such, in Europe or elsewhere; it would undoubtedly insist that capitalism is now the globally dominant mode; it takes parliamentary democracy to be the normal form of regime in the capitalist mode; and the data it cites always refer to the metropolitan state, never asking itself why the capitalist state of the periphery rarely adopts the parliamentary-democratic form. The capitalist state formations of the periphery are in fact never analyzed within this discourse.

6. Significantly, British revenues from these areas of genocidal famines continued to rise. After the famine of 1769-1770, Warren Hastings, Governor of Bengal, wrote to the directors of the East India Company on November 3, 1772:

> Notwithstanding the loss of at least one third of the inhabitants of the province, and consequent decrease of cultivation, the net collection for the year 1771 exceeded even those of 1768 . . . owing to its being very violently kept up to its former standards.

7. The basis for this separation (between production and circulation, capitalism and colonialism, internality and externality, Europe and non-Europe) was already there in the formulations of those, such as Rodney Hilton and Eric Hobsbaum, who focused attention on the question of the prime mover—that is, the single most important factor in the transition. Mercifully, they were historians, and though what they knew best was the history of the developments inside Europe, their work had the merit of never presupposing, as Foster-Carter and Brennan later did, that the theoretical question underlying the whole debate could be settled on the ahistorical basis of the formal construction of theoretical paradigms.

8. See Szymanski (1977). Magdoff's reply is reprinted in *Imperialism* (1978).

9. For a brief account, see Lloyd (1981).

References

Anderson, Perry
   1979   Lineages of the Absolutist State. London: New Left Books.

Avineri, Shlomo (ed.)

1968a Karl Marx on Colonialism and Modernization. New York: Doubleday.

1968b The Social and Political Thought of Karl Marx. London: Cambridge University Press.

Balibar, Etienne, et al.

1980 "Is the crisis 'above all national'? A view of the policy of the French Communist Party." Contemporary Marxism 2 (Winter).

Brenner, Robert

1977 "The origins of capitalist development: a critique of neo-Smithian Marxism." New Left Review 104 (July-August): 25-87.

Brown, L. and G. Finterbush

1972 Man and His Environment: Food. New York: Harper & Row.

Buchanan, D. H.

1966 The Development of Capitalist Enterprise in India. New York: Augustus Kelley.

Foster-Carter, Aidan

1978 "The mode of production debate." New Left Review 107 (January-February): 47-78.

Laclau, Ernesto

1977 "The specificity of the political," in Politics and Ideology in Marxist Theory. London: New Left Books.

Lloyd, Cathie

1981 "What is the French CP up to?" Race and Class 22. 4 (Spring).

Miliband, Ralph

1970 "The capitalist state—reply to Nicos Poulantzas." New Left Review 59 (January-February).

Nasrullah, Syed and J. P. Naik

1951 A History of Education in India. London: Macmillan.

Omvedt, Gail

1975 The Political Economy of Starvation: Imperialism and the World Food Crisis. Bombay: SSET.

Poulantzas, Nicos

1969 "The problem of the capitalist state." New Left Review 58 (November-December).

1974 Fascism and Dictatorship. London: New Left Books.

1976 The Crisis of the Dictatorships. London: New Left Books.

Szymanski, Albert

1977 "Capital accumulation on the world scale and the necessity of imperialism." Insurgent Sociologist 7 (Spring).

Warren, Bill

1973 "Imperialism and capitalist industrialisation." New Left Review 81.

1980 Imperialism: Pioneer of Capitalism. London. New Left Books.

Weeks, John and Elizabeth Dore

1977 "International exchange and the causes of backwardness." Latin American Perspectives 6 (Spring): 62-87.

Carlos Johnson: Ideologies in Theories

of Imperialism and Dependency

> We must flatly reject, as sophistry, all references to an inadequate discussion on the
> difference between national and international tactics. . . . This is sophistry, because a com-
> prehensive scientific analysis of imperialism is one thing—that analysis is only under way
> and, in essence, is as infinite as science itself. The principles of socialist tactics against
> imperialism, which have been set forth in millions of copies of Social-Democratic news-
> papers and in the discussion of the International, are a quite different thing. . . . Capitalism
> will *never* be completely and *exhaustively* studied in *all* the manifestations of its predatory
> nature, and in all the most minute ramifications of its historical development and national
> features. Scholars (and especially the pedants) will never stop arguing over details.
> —V. I. Lenin (1972: Vol. 1, 211-212)

Lenin's analysis of imperialism has been declared insufficient by dependency theorists such as Theotonio Dos Santos who hoped to articulate the perspective of the dependent countries. According to Dos Santos, for example, Lenin analyzed imperialism only from the perspective of monopoly capital: "Therefore, we should consider the approaches of the authors of the theory of imperialism to be limited. Lenin, Bukharin, Rosa Luxemburg, the main Marxist writers who concerned themselves with the theme, as well as Hobson, have not focused the subject of imperialism from the point of view of the dependent countries" (Dos Santos, 1970a; 23). Much time has been spent attempting to justify the space occupied by dependency theory.

Author's Note: I wish to thank Tania Calvimontes, Takis Economopoulos, Armando Sanchez, and Gema Solano for their critical comments on this chapter.

Some analysts have simply tried to unite the two different theories of imperialism and dependency by alluding to their complementarity (Ianni, n.d.: 41p.), while other analysts are in turn attempting to bury dependency theory (Fagen, 1977). I should state early on, however, that it is impossible to combine Lenin's materialist analysis of imperialism with the critical-idealist perspective of the dependentistas (see Johnson, 1977, for a more extensive critique of dependency theory).

One cannot, in fact, pose an abstract question of a theory of imperialism *versus* a theory of dependency, as some analysts claim (Santi et al., 1971). Rather, as Lenin once noted, it is a question of understanding imperialism (monopoly capitalism) and the national liberation movements in the colonies (Lenin, 1972: Vol. 39, 738). The accent is thereby placed on a question of *transformation* (Economopoulos, 1978) instead of the difference between abstract models of classical capitalism and a supposed deformed, dependent capitalism. This latter approach in fact constitutes a question of sophistry.

Hence, much of what has been held against Lenin's analysis and cited in favor of a "theory of dependency" generally results from two elements: a lack of historical perspective in knowing what *theses* have already been ideologically produced by other political economists and the absence of a method of theoretical reasoning capable of approaching reality in order to identify the dialectical (relational), historical (temporal) and material (spatial) reasons for the occurrence of specific socioeconomic and political events.

By showing the manner in which nonmaterialist analyses and sophistry are effected by dependency theorists themselves, I hope to set the groundwork for comprehending the manner in which dialectical-historical-materialist analyses of space, time, and motion events within social relations are to be approached. It is this method of reasoning that determines the theoretical production of ideological or scientific knowledge.

One specific need of theoretical analysis is that of taking the word concepts, such as "capital," "labor," "imperialism," and "dependency" and explaining their different meanings. Such a task is essential before proceeding into other realms of theoretical analysis (for example, that of identifying the needs of transformation at a given moment). It is necessary to distinguish the different theses involved, for dependency theory has dominated socioeconomic and political literature on the left in Latin America for some ten to fifteen years. For this reason alone, such ideas merit consideration and scrutiny.

"Imperialism" and "Dependency" as Concepts of Bourgeois Political Economists

Marx reminded his contempories that he did not discover the existence of classes or even that of class struggle. Consider Marx's letter to Weydemeyer, March 5, 1852: "And now as to myself, no credit is due to me for discovering the existence of classes in modern society or the struggle between them. Long before me bourgeois historians had described the historical development of this class struggle and bourgeois economists the economic autonomy of the classes." The very concept of "class" was itself a product of class struggle and class analyses of social relations. However, Marx did explain in *Capital* ("capital" being another bourgeois concept) the contradiction between social production and private appropriation which produced classes and the struggle for surplus values. The materialist objective is to precisely explain the class meanings of the concepts in terms of the social relations.

Similar to what Marx accomplished regarding class analysis, Lenin went on to explain what "imperialism" meant in terms of the social relations of capital production and appropriation, specifically in terms of monopoly capital and competitive capital and the struggle for the accumulation of surplus values (Lenin, 1972: Vol. 22, 116-117). In the works of Marx and Lenin one will not find the petty bourgeois characteristics of fetishizing a particular word concept. Marx and Lenin simply explain what the abstracted concepts mean in terms of historically existing relations.

Lenin constantly made the point that the petty bourgeois analysts were merely debating over concepts, "arguing over words" and definitions around a particular word (Lenin, 1972: Vol. 39, 267, 373). This same characteristic of the German petty bourgeois intelligentsia was pointed out by Marx and Engels in *The German Ideology* (Marx and Engels, 1976: 711). Lenin's emphasis, in contrast, was to identify the "component parts of the concept 'imperialism' ": "I Monopoly, as the result of concentration, II export of capital (as the chief thing), III + IV division of the world a) agreements of international capital, b) colonies, V bank capital and its 'threads', VI replacement of free trade and peaceful exchange by a policy of force (tariffs, seizures, etc., etc.)" (Lenin, 1972: Vol. 39, 202).

Lenin placed the word "imperialism" between quotes in order to convey the idea that it represented the other side's choice of words.

That which was identified by the bourgeois economists as imperialism was explained by Lenin as due to specific material reasons of capital production. Even the title of Lenin's book, *Imperialism: The Highest Stage of Capitalism* (Lenin, 1972: Vol. 22, 185-304) appears to follow the wording of Steffen, who pointed out that "Imperialism is a universal [sic!] political stage of development, through which every [!!] great people with large internal forces and a momentous mission must pass" (1972: Vol. 39, 260; italics in original). Consider also Lenin's "Approximate Title for Censorship: 'Principal Features of Modern (Recent, the Recent Stage of) Capitalism' " (Vol. 39, 230). Other expressions in Lenin's *Notebooks on Imperialism* concern "Imperialism, the highest (modern) stage of capitalism" (p. 202); "The *Special* stage of capitalism in our time" (p. 230). By using the idea of the highest stage of capitalism, Lenin was merely emphasizing the fact that call it as you will, capitalism was on its last leg, historically speaking. Thus, in order to emphasize the economic character of imperialism as a product of capitalist development itself and not merely the political significance of imperialism, Lenin turned the word concepts of the bourgeois political economists against themselves.

In their sociopolitical meaning (not to mention their everyday use before that), one must remember that both imperialism and dependency were concepts produced and emphasized by the bourgeois political economists of Lenin's time. Before Lenin wrote *Imperialism,* in 1916, already such titles had appeared as Fraisse's *International Situation of the Dependent Countries of the Congo Basin* (1904) and Redslob's *Dependent Countries* (1914), among others. To think, as some dependentistas do today, that dependency is a new phenomenon of contemporary imperialism is to ignore the relations that gave rise to relations of class dominance. Independent movements against imperialism and colonialism meant the existence of dependent countries during Lenin's time, simple mechanical dialectics would illustrate this point. But the ideological point is to understand that "dependent" already reflected the imperialist's class perspective: convincing the colonies that they *depended* on the imperial countries. Furthermore, Lenin did not make his analysis from the perspective of the dependent countries, just as he did not make it from the perspective of the imperialist countries. Lenin made an analysis of imperialism and dependency from the theoretical perspective of historical materialism.

Most of the word concepts used even today by bourgeois political economists and by many Marxists to identify dependency were thought up several years before Lenin completed his synthetical study of imperialism. For the sake of example only, consider the following popular phrases in vogue today. The expression "less developed countries" appeared in *The Annals of the American Academy of Political and Social Science* in 1915 (Lenin, 1972: Vol. 39, 49)— not to mention the literature before Marx. But with respect to the studies on imperialism, also common were the concepts "colonial dependence" (Lenin, 1972: Vol. 39, 68) and even "internal colonisation" (Vol. 39, 112). This latter concept calls to mind the concept of "internal colonialism," another supposed theoretical "advancement" disputed by authors such as Rodolfo Stavenhagen and Pablo González-Casanova (1974). As to who originated the idea, a case could be easily made that Wakefield (see Marx, Vol. 1) or Hildebrand (Lenin, 1972: Vol. 39, 112) beat both Stavenhagen and González-Casanova to it long ago—if, that is, one wishes to waste time considering the origin of word concepts. "Financially dependent countries" (Vol. 39, 195), "dependence of independent countries" (Vol. 39, 240), "periphery" (Vol. 39, 531), among many others are just some of the concepts that are held to represent the conceptual backbone of contemporary dependency theory. Such concepts, however, were the daily bread of the bourgeois political economists of the early twentieth century. Today, ideological debate remains at the level of the struggle over word concepts. The scientific discussion of social relations corresponds to the level of the materialist explanation of those relations and word concepts and remains ignored by the dependentistas.

The foregoing critique of dependency concepts is of relatively little significance, even though it directly contests the pretentious efforts of the dependentistas to create *a* theory of dependency, or to modify Lenin's theoretical understanding of imperialism. For even when the dependentistas invent "new" word concepts—some have done through "poetic license" with terms like "lumpenbourgeoisie" and "lumpendevelopment" (Frank, 1971)—the theoretical issues remain obscure and unanswered. The invention of a new word concept would appear to be the resolution of the theoretical analysis. The problem does not concern the coining of new word concepts which supposedly reveal the secrets of an entire historical period. The need is to offer materialist explanations of the sociohistorical relations that exist.

Dependentistas fail to achieve this, however, because of a disproportionate concern for the originality of concrete socioeconomic formations and the idealistic attempt to construct *a* theory of social relations around a particular word. This may be seen in the ahistorical nature of the definitions of dependency some authors have constructed:

> Dependency is a situation in which a certain group of countries have their economy conditioned by the development and expansion of another economy to which itself is subjected. The relation of interdependence between two or more economies, and between these and world trade, assumes the form of dependency when some countries (the dominant ones) can expand themselves and self-propel themselves which the other countries (the dependent ones) can only do so as a reflection of that expansion, that can act positively and/or negatively upon its immediate development. Anyway, the basic situation of dependency leads to an over-all situation of the dependent countries that places them behind and under the exploitation of the dominant countries (Dos Santos, 1970a: 45).

Such neutralized, ahistorical definitions may be used to apply to capitalist as well as socialist relations between countries. In fact, as stated here, even the developed countries would be subject to this definition, since they too are subjected to the expansion and production of surplus value by the dominated countries; if these do not produce, imperialism does not grow. I have critiqued such "definitions" elsewhere in greater detail (Johnson, 1979b).

A critique such as this of these idealist procedures is itself open to misinterpretation. This critique may give the initial impression of arguing against the word "dependency" as though it were inadequate, incorrect, or unnecessary. This is not the case, certainly, just as it is not the case to argue against Lenin's having analyzed the word concept and relations of "imperialism." The objection concerns the absence of materialist explanations of the social relations represented by the concept of dependency, as well as the absence of analyses of other aspects of those relations excluded by the concept.

The Socioeconomic and Political Theses of Imperialism and Dependency

Socioeconomic Theses

Lenin concerned himself with explaining the concepts and relations of imperialism, whose ideological counterpart was, and remains today, dependency. Neither did Lenin occupy himself with creating a theory of dependency, a concept with which, as we have seen, Lenin was more than familiar. To even suggest, as Dos Santos does, for example, that Lenin did not review this side of the imperialist coin is simply a distortion of Lenin's work. You cannot study one without studying the other.

Many of the *theses* Lenin postulated about the historical significance of imperialism came from the works of the bourgeois, liberal, and socialist political economists of the day: Agahd, Bauer, Baumgarten, Cromer, Dietzel, Hildebrand, Hilferding, Hobson, Steffen, Ulbricht, among many others (Lenin, 1971: Vol. 39, 792-827). Lenin argued mainly against the thesis that imperialism was a deformation of capitalism's expansion (Vol. 39, 264-268)—that is, an undesired political policy that could be avoided if capitalism were effectively reformed. Lenin also argued in favor of utilizing the imperialist war as a time for promoting socialist revolutions in different countries (Vol. 39, 316-317).

Some of the most significant socioeconomic theses forwarded by Lenin in his analysis of capitalism and imperialism, common to the work of other writers before him, though not expressed in these exact terms, regard the following (Vol. 39, 69-75):

(1) finance capital is imperialism (R. Hilferding);
(2) imperialism represents the beginning of the end of capitalism (Paul Louis);
(3) imperialism represents a specific moment of the dialectical process of capitalism to socialism (Paul Louis);
(4) capital/labor relations produce imperialism (R. Hilferding);
(5) the level of analysis is maintained at that of the relations of production (capital/labor) and not at that of international exchange relations (R. Hilferding);
(6) surplus value extraction from the colonies facilitates the bribing of the petty bourgeoisie and upper strata of the proletariat in the imperialist countries (J.A. Hobson);
(7) the question of who is more dependent on whom, the banks on industry, or vice versa (I. SchulzeGaevernitz);
(8) imperialism hampers development of industry (that is, represses levels of production/consumption) (Sigmund Schilder);
(9) capitalism/imperialism is parasitic (J.A. Hobson);
(10) technological progress is hindered rather than promoted by monopoly capital formations (Louis C. Fraina, F. Nahas); and
(11) socialism does not need colonies (Editors, Gazeta Rabotnica).

It should also be remembered that in order for Lenin to have demonstrated some of these points, he had to censure himself to keep his book from being censured.

The dependentistas of the 1960s and 1970s in Latin America apparently ignore the significance of Lenin's theses when they identify dependency as a deformity of classical capitalism and speak about the *sui generis* nature of dependent capitalism. Consider: "For that reason, more than a precapitalism, what one has is a *sui generis* capitalism, which only makes sense if we contemplate it in the perspective of the system as a whole, at a national level, and mainly, at an international level" (Marini, 1973a; 15)

Because of this, the dependentistas have difficulties in identifying materially when dependency actually comes into existence, and what represents its unique historical characteristics. Dos Santos, for example, cannot make up his mind whether Latin American countries were born into dependency or whether dependency is a more recent consequence of imperialism (1970b: 44-45). Many speculators of Latin American dependent capitalism claim that the concept of dependency reflects something new, something original that was nonexistent under classical capitalism (Bambirra, 1974). These new features refer to theses about the superexploitation of labor: "My central thesis, on which I insist in all of my texts, is another: dependent capitalism, based on the superexploitation of labor, divorces the productive apparatus of the needs of consumption of the masses, thus aggravating a general tendency of the capitalist mode of production" (Marini, 1978, 74); the marginalization of the labor force (Nun, n.d.); the existence of unequal exchange relations (Emmanuel, 1972); the problems of the realization of surplus value (Marini, 1973b: 86); and the impossibility of the domestic and international markets (Marini, 1973b: 53ff).

On such ideological constructions the dependentistas make the absolutist statement that capitalism is impossible in Latin America and only dependence is reproduced—that is, "more underdevelopment." They grapple similarly with concepts of "subimperialism" (Marini, 1973a), not recognizing that it is monopoly capital that creates itself again and again in the form of imperialism, out of the economic crises of capitalism and the concentration and centralization of capital.

The idealist task of attempting to develop a Marxist theory of dependency assumed today by many Latin American dependentistas immediately reveals their nonmaterialist conception of theory. The imperialist perspective produced both the thetically uncritical concept of imperialism and the antithetically critical concept of dependency, which harbored a hierarchically inferior value relative to the imperialist nations at that time. Imperialism and dependency were and still are word concepts of class combat, with specific ideological connotations and class meanings of struggle. They represent class ideologicl concepts.

Unlike Marx's and Lenin's disdain for an all-encompassing word that would supposedly explain reality to us, we see the dependentistas concerned with rescuing concepts, and creating various theses around the word "dependency." Such critical-idealist efforts represent exercises in sophistry, where one aspect of a process is brought out supposedly to explain the entire process. (Lenin, 1972: Vol. 39, 598).

At best, the concept of dependency reflects only one aspect of the process, on an ideological plane, by reflecting essentially an imperialist thesis. Dependency conveys the idea of inferiority vis-à-vis imperialist development by suggesting that Latin American countries depend technologically and financially on the United States, for example, for their existence. Historically the opposite obtains: Imperialism came first, then created that historical dependence. Consider, for example, "Just as it [the bourgeoisie] has made the country dependent on the towns, so it has made barbarian and semi-barbarian countries dependent on the civilized ones, nations of peasants on nations of bourgeois, the East on the West" (Marx, 1975: 38). It is the United States that depends on the surplus value production of Latin American labor forces in order to maintain its relatively high levels of production and consumption. Hence, Hobson and especially Lenin placed emphasis on the fact that finance, monopoly capital, was completely parasitic.

By emphasizing the word concept of dependency for identifying Latin America's socioeconomic formations vis-à-vis the United States, this particular dependentista thesis unknowingly (in the best of cases) posits an imperialist perspective. Despite this, the dependentistas in general articulate the needs of competitive capital (for example, local and national capital) in the face of monopoly capital. Dependentista theses in this contradictory vain reflected the critical tones of Latin American nationalism and anti-imperialism, though not always anti-capitalism. They coincided with the ideology of some sectors of the local dominant classes and their needs of capital accumulation. Nevertheless, at the same time, many dependentistas declared themselves to be politically against the national bourgeoisie and in favor of socialism, revolution, and international proletarianism (Frank, 1969).

In Latin America during the 1950s, one class ideological program of monopoly capital was represented in the theses of *developmentalism*. This school of thought postulated the need for foreign capital investment as a way to achieve development and eliminate underdevelopment. The imperialist class *need* was the exportation of capital; the class ideological *thesis* was that foreign capital investment would bring about "development"—obviously, capitalist development.

Against this program of monopoly capital, the dependentistas produced a counterclass ideological program (Dos Santos, 1970b: 109-110). The class need of competitive capital here was to remain with as much of the surplus value as possible that was being produced in Latin America. In the face of difficulties in remaining with a "fair" share of surplus value, the ideological class thesis concluded the impossibility of capitalist development in Latin America. The direct opposite was postulated, then, in the face of the imperialist thesis.

Neither of these two particular class ideological programs (theses) represents a scientific comprehension of how capital/labor relations become the dominant form of exploitation within a specific socio-economic formation—that is, how capitalist relations encourage (develop) some areas of an economy and repress (underdeveloped) others. In other words, how capitalist/imperialist "development/ underdevelopment" is created remains obscure. Dependency theses at this level concern themselves with how (surplus) values are transferred from one country to another—that is, how classes struggle over the accumulation of value.

The counterthesis concerning capital creating more dependence and underdevelopment was already put forward by authors Lenin identified as "arch-bourgeois and nationalist," such as E. Agahd, author of *Big Banks and the World Market* (1914), who committed precisely the same theoretical mistakes of interpretation as the modern-day dependentistas (Lenin 1972: Vol. 39, 120). Agahd maintained the level of analysis at the point of market relations and the unequal exchange of surplus values (for similar errors, consider Amin, 1978). In this light capitalism always appears impossible to attain, for one is seeing things through the perspective of the underdog capitalist who can never seem to make it imperialistically big. Furthermore, the thesis concerning the existence of a second-rate technology, also forwarded by contemporary dependentistas, was already expressed by Fraina during 1913-1914: "This technical progress, which alone can guarantee the continued ability to export, is, however, hindered rather than promoted by monopoly formations" (Lenin 1972: Vol. 39, 594-595).

Dependency theorists like Dos Santos, among others, perceived a crisis in the developmentalist program of interpretation (Dos Santos, 1970a: 173).

> This crisis of the model of development and of the project of development implicit in it, which is dominant in the social sciences in our countries, brought about a crisis in this same science. It brought about a crisis in the very notion of development and of underdevelopment and the explanatory role of said concepts. From such a crisis is born the concept of dependence as a possible explanatory factor of this paradoxical situation. It is a case of explaining why we have not developed in the same manner as the developed countries of today.

In less obstruse language, the question would read: Why are we not imperialist countries? The answer would read: Because we have been dominated by imperialism.

One must realize, however, that a class program, like the one articulated by the political economists of developmentalism, has little to do with the actual material production of surplus values, which was being carried out then (and is still being carried out) effectively in Latin America. Succinctly, capital production remains in and flows out of Latin America before, during, and after the supposed theoretical crisis of developmentalist thought. Actually, there is no crisis in the production of surplus values, only in the possibility of their total appropriation, hence the struggle of monopoly capitalists (imperialists) against other dominant, competitive classes in Latin America for surplus value appropriation. A result of that conflict is the need for constructing ideological class theses supporting foreign investment, and the counterclass theses of the dependentistas denouncing imperialism in nationalist tones. There is no crisis in the practical apparatus of imperialism, only in getting the different classes in Latin America to accept foreign investment and capital extraction smoothly. In the face of such difficulties regarding direct foreign investment, imperialism devises other methods of capital exportation and exploitation. One form is that of international loans.

The construction of class ideological programs and theses is nothing new in the struggle over surplus value exchange and accumulation. The counterideological theses of the dependentistas were maintained earlier by the Russian Narodniks, or the Russian populists, against whom Lenin incessantly fought (Vol. 3, 37-69). Such theses referred to the deformed nature of Russian capitalism, the problem of the realization of surplus value, the problems of the domestic and international markets, and also basically the idea that it was impossible to establish capitalism in Russia then. There is one obvious reason for the similarity of socioeconomic theses between the dependentistas and the Russian populists. If one maintains the theoretical level of analysis at that of relations of the circulation of commodities, markets, and unequal exchange, then the conclusions are going to be similar—irrespective of the concrete historical moment and socioeconomic formation one may be dealing with. To further maintain the analysis of circulation and market relations at the level of the *nation*, where the nation represents the basic spatial unit of analysis, only leads to further theoretical error. Analysis must be maintained at the level and moment of production/appropriation, as Lenin—and Marx before him—emphasized in his study, *The Development of Capitalism in Russia* (1899), for understanding the process and the needs of socialist transformation. Despite the lessons of history to this respect, such elementary Marxist-Leninist theses are combated consciously by such dependentistas as Marini (1973b) and Amin (1978).

The dependentistas thus replace the developmentalist binominal wording of development and underdevelopment with a supposedly more accurate word concept: dependency. An example of the theoretical sophistry carried out by the dependentistas can be brought out if we consider two analogous themes: the relationship of the dependency of *capital/labor,* and the relationship of the dependency of one nation on another. I will first refer to Marx's theoretical work regarding capital/labor relations. Then I will apply the logic of the dependentistas to Marx's analysis of capital/labor in order to exemplify their error in reasoning.

In *Capital,* Marx shows the various *moments* of the production process, where at one point

    (a) capital is *dependent* on labor for the production of surplus values (that is, for its very own reproduction as a class); at another moment,

    (b) labor is *dependent* on capital in order to sell its labor power, given the historical conditions of the forced separation of labor from the means of production; and at still another moment,

(c) capital and labor, as a system of social relations, are *(inter)dependent* on one another in order to reproduce that set of social relations.

Conversely, it is pointed out that

(d) capital is *independent* of labor, given its conditions of control over the means of production;

(e) labor is *independent* of capital, capable of producing its own historical process materially, without the assistance of the totally parasitic capitalist class; and

(f) capital/labor relations are *independent* of other systems of production as they exist in relation to one another.

To explain materially each of these specific moments of capital/labor relations, as Marx did, represents a dialectical-historical-materialist analysis of socioeconomic relations of capitalism. Each thesis represents a specific relation of capital/labor, social relations, and is exclusive of the other. All are correct apprehensions of capital/labor relations, and none denies the other. Each represents a specific moment of the entire process.

Each of these empirical theses reflects a particular aspect of the production and surplus value under capitalism. Each one of these empirical events have been and is used as an ideological thesis to promote specific class needs at a given moment in the history of class struggle. Each of these scientific theses, empirically identifiable in history, may have a significantly opposite ideological value, given the conditions of class struggle itself. For example, if one were to emphasize solely the particular thesis that "labor is dependent on capital," the historical process of socialism would be obscured and capitalists' needs would be openly supported. Something similar occurs ideologically with the thesis that "Latin American countries are dependent on the United States."

Within the realm of analyzing nation to nation relations one could cite the dependentistas' theses in a more complete manner, at the level of international relations of capital production:

First, the United States (monopoly capital) *depends* on Latin American countries (competitive capital) for the production and appropriation of surplus-value; second, Latin American countries *depend* on the United States for finance capital and technology, given the historical conditions of imperialism's control over the means of production and capital; and third, the United States and Latin American countries (inter)*depend* on one another, given the international division of labor and the system of capital production.

Conversely, one could construct other formulations of these same theses, in an opposing, antidependency sense:

First, the United States is *independent* of Latin American countries, given its control over the means of production, its own labor forces, and its control over capital accumulation; second, Latin American countries are *independent* of the United States, given their productive, creative potential to construct their own historical process; and third, the United States and Latin American countries are *independent* of one another based on each other's relative position of autonomy within the international division of labor, and so on.

Any one of these particular postulates can be, and has been, used by both imperialists and dependentistas alike to forward ideological theses about their specific class needs of capital accumulation and appropriation. What becomes clear, however, with these two examples of scientific theses are their ideological potential use is the fact that the concepts of dependence, independence, and interdependence correspond to the most superficial level of analysis, given that all matter/energy is in relation to (dependent/independent of) other matter/energy events. The materialist level of analysis identifies and explains the conditions of existence and relation of each specific *thesis/need* regarding those relationships.

The level of abstraction exercised by the dependency theorists begins erroneously by maintaining the unit of analysis at the level of interrelations between nations, regarding market and exchange relations of the circulation of commodities, capital, and labor. The dependentistas make the obvious point that the United States depends parasitically on Latin American countries for the extraction of surplus value, which explains in part the relatively high levels of production and consumption of the United States and the relatively high wages paid to its labor force. Such theses were already made by the bourgeois political economists before Lenin and were simply emphasized by Lenin in his work on imperialism. But from this important materialist thesis (which reaffirms the parasitic nature of capital on labor in general and not merely between national capital) the dependentistas turn the ideological table. They place all of the theoretical and critical emphasis of their approach on the idea of the dependency of Latin America vis-à-vis the United States. By concentrating on this moment of dependency, their work objectively supports an imperialist thesis, in spite of the dependentistas' attempt to illustrate exactly the opposite. By emphasizing that Latin America is the inferior element of the hierarchical scale, unable to survive and exist without U.S. capital and technology, the ideological coup serves imperialism well. For their work actually accepts the existing levels of U.S. production and consumption as being historically high, as actually representing "development." Never is it explained that those levels of U.S. production and consumption do not represent "development" *in abstractio,* but, on the contrary, those levels themselves are historically *low* levels. For they are repressed levels in relation to the material capacity and potential of socialized production and appropriation unfettered by capitalist relations. In fact, all levels of production (and therefore of consumption) in the "highly developed countries" are repressed. The simple fact that machine production runs constantly at a percentage level below its productivity capacity confirms this point, as does the fact that the capitalist system produces repressed levels of employment and wage-earners (that is, unemployment and the nonmaterialization of labor power).

Instead of emphasizing the U.S. dependence on Latin America for capital extraction, they choose to identify their entire theoretical effort of interpretation by citing the technological and financial dependence of Latin American countries on the United States. With that simple point, the mystification of the power of capital and technology is maintained as a remedy to "development," while the class contradiction of production and appropriation is all but ignored. They distract attention from the essential Marxian concept (and materialist point) that labor power alone is the creative force of social history (and of technology and capital), while capital is but a mere form of social relations, a product itself of that labor power. Hence, it is not a point of who depends on whom, but rather what are the social relationships and their contradictions. The fetishism with the ideology of growth in terms of capital and technological production *as* progress thereby remains dominant in their writings.

By limiting their analyses to emphasizing the word "dependency" the dependentistas then allow for imperialist ideologues to take that particular word and counterattack with other ideological theses. Such is the characteristic of class struggle over words as Marx and Engels pointed out in *The German Ideology.* The negative connotations of dependency pointed out by the dependentistas are thus established and applied to other social relations. At the level of abstracted theoretical analysis, the use of the concept "dependency" has played an important role for the imperialist ideological construction: "Cuba and Eastern European countries depend upon the Soviet Union in the same manner as Latin American countries depend upon the USA" (Eckstein, 1978), or, "We live in an interdependent world, and should live together peacefully, harmoniously" (Rock, 1964), or "the USA depends now on foreign oil and must eliminate such dependence" (Werner, 1978), ad infinitum. The ideological uses of dependency concepts are too numerous to list here. These are some of the outstanding examples of ideological class theses that support the capital needs of U.S. imperialism today. Since the dependentistas concentrate on a superficial aspect of international relations of surplus value exchange, they have been unable to combat the very relations they explicitly hope to eliminate: the imperialist relations of production and appropriation of capital.

Had Marx limited his theoretical efforts to constructing, for example, the "theory of dependence of labor on capital," or had Lenin merely spoken about the theory of the "dependence of Russia on France" (when, in fact, Lenin emphasized the opposite relationship of "the dependence of France on Russia" [Vol. 39, 91]), then we would simply have more examples of sophistry. The inability to identify theoretical sophistry, combined with the superficiality of the conceptual level of dependency theses, explains in part dependency theory's popularity. Dependency theses are easy to handle precisely because of the simplistic theoretical postulates and the lack of historical memory reflected in the petty bourgeois intelligentsia's work. This very lack of memory regarding similar theoretical positions that have been produced earlier in history is itself an imposed feature of capitalist/imperialist relations: the repression in education, a repression that has assisted in the diffusion of dependency theses, an example of spontaneous forms of resistance to imperialism.

All capitalist societies are hierarchically structured, where those perceived structures are assigned values determined by class needs. The hierarchies are visible ideologically in the theoretical interpretations and apprehensions. Practically, they are visible in reality where class values are assigned to the hierarchical arrangements of relations. From the perspective of capitalist-imperialist values, the kind of "development" in the so-called central economies is assigned a high value, that which is to be aspired, the ideal concept. Despite all the critiques by such authors as Frank (1969), dependency concepts correspond to and accept those hierarchical arrangements, for they do not reject the ideal type of the kind of "capitalist-imperialist development." They merely draw attention to the fact that Latin American countries are unable to achieve a similar kind of development. Ultimately, dependentistas simply identify and talk about certain arrangements of hierarchically structured class relations of domination. Thereby they state nothing new, but simply refer to the superficially obvious: that hierarchical class relations depend on other relations (that is, certain space-time and motion events). They identify relations of superiority (such as imperialism) and inferiority (such as dependence) of specific moments of relations. Then they go on to state that these relations (in fact, the products of these relations) determine the entire process of hierarchically structured relations, which is simply false.

The relations of dependency are a product of (and therefore reflect) the structured hierarchies, and are themselves in that manner determined. The need is to understand what determines their material existense: the struggle created by the contadictions of social production and private appropriation. Thinking that simply pointing to their existence tells us how the entire process and system exist constitutes an ideological postulate. It is this elevation of the specific, particularistic thesis to an absolutist, all-encompassing thesis for the entire process which represents the ideological construction. The specific thesis may even represent a scientific apprehension of that moment of the process to which it refers. But when that thesis is assigned to the other moments of the process as a material reason for explaining the overall process, then it loses all scientific meaning. Marx and Engels referred to this ideological procedure in *The German Ideology* as the inversion of moments within a process. It is at this point that one must be able to link up the ideological theses within the social sciences with specific class needs at particular moments in history.

Political Theses

The main dependentistas articulated socioeconomic theses regarding the needs of national, competitive capital in the face of monopoly capital (imperialism) in Latin America. Yet they proposed political actions to be carried out against the local dominant classes. Consider especially the thesis that identified the immediate enemy as the national bourgeoisie (Frank, 1969). This represents another outstanding contradiction of dependency theses. While the dependentistas' socioeconomic interpretation of Latin America's economy reflected class needs of the local dominant classes (competitive capital), the political interpretation of those same conclusions led to the idea of excluding the local dominant classes from national revolutionary praxis. Instead of basing themselves on a political praxis of the unity of class alliances in practice, they went against the class needs they articulated in their theoretical interpretation by ignoring and denying the potential role of the local dominant classes in national liberation movements. With that they thereby isolated the proletariat even further.

The thesis concerning the immediate enemy, however, did not go against the needs of imperialism during the 1960s. At that time the United States, licking its wounds from the Cuban Revolution, tried to break up the alliances in Latin America between the popular social movements and certain sectors of the local dominant classes. These broad front nationalist movements proved to be politically threatening during the 1950s in Latin America and were put down by coups d'état and extensive repression.

Immediately after World War II, when U.S. imperialism was once again turning its sights toward Latin America, an immediate imperialist need was to weaken the local dominant classes, which had become strengthened during the war years. In this sense, the radical political position of some of the dependentistas did not contradict the counterrevolutionary programs being drawn up then by the United States (ABT Associates, 1966; Condit, 1968). In fact, the dependency thesis of nonalliance with the national bourgeoisie objectively fit right into those programs (consider Menges, 1968). Recognition of this fact by the critics of dependency theory caused some of the dependentistas to be accused of being agents of imperialism—something they vehemently rejected and still reject (Frank, 1974). Furthermore, the antinational bourgeois thesis effectively countered the efforts of the work of the communist parties in Latin America during that time. It also offered an ideological support among sectors of the petty bourgeois intellectuals to carry out guerrilla actions in Latin America, especially during the late sixties and early seventies. Such actions further isolated the intellectuals from the workers, as well as from the local dominant classes, as well as further isolating the workers from socialist struggle. And given that such theses of struggle appeared to be the result of nationalist socioeconomic analyses of dependency and imperialism, it was all the more difficult to combat the political implications of such theses.

The political theses of the need for armed revolution and socialism formulated by some of the dependentistas (Marini, 1969; Frank, 1969)—again, similar to the political theses of the Russian Narodniks—cannot be concluded from an analysis of the circulation relations of capital. Only from the contradiction of production and appropriation and the recognized need of gaining control over the means of production can one understand Marx's political conclusions about the historical need for socialist revolution.

Dependentistas like Dos Santos, who propose reformist policies, would appear to be more consequential with their analyses of market relations—that is, the contradiction of *production and circulation*. They suggest the need to politically renegotiate dependency in the face of imperialism, by renegotiating the terms of trade and the exchange of surplus values: in short, get a larger share of the surplus value exchanged. Such theses openly articulate and represent a competitive capitalist perspective. Such nationalist, political theses of struggle over surplus values are more in line with the theories of unequal exchange, marginalization, underconsumption, and the needs of nationalist, competitive capitalists. Hilferding's conclusion of the need for socialism was quite similar to that of writers like Frank and Marini: "The reply of the proletariat to the economic policy of finance capital, to imperialism, can only be socialism, not free trade" (Lenin, 1972: Vol. 39, 337). This was the conclusion Marx arrived at after analyzing capital-labor relations and the contradiction of *social production and private appropriation.* It does not result from a characteristic of monopoly capital (imperialism) alone, which is merely a specific historical degree of capital accumulation. A critique of monopoly capital can only reinforce the original conclusion drawn up scientifically by Marx from relations of capital and labor. To attempt to draw the conclusion about the historical need for revolution and socialism from relations of the unequal exchange of surplus values ultimately avoids the contradiction of socialized production and private appropriation, for as Marx showed time and again, capitalist relations mean precisely the exchange of unequal (nonequivalent) exchange values. Marx and Lenin emphasized that it was this contradiction of *production and appropriation* that was present in all class societies, no matter what particular sociohistorical form they may take. Obviously, as the dependentistas' theses show, one may propose the idea of the need for socialism for the wrong reasons, and worse still propose actions that have no chance of achieving socialist transformation whatsoever.

Again, however, it is not a question now of concluding the historical need for socialism *in abstractio* based on an analysis of production and circulation relations for some twenty-odd Latin American countries. Nor is it a question of concluding the need for armed revolution *in abstractio,* and denouncing all forms of alliances with sectors of the local dominant classes (for example the national bourgeoisies). For *socialism* is the historical outcome of the presence of the contradiction between production and appropriation; and *revolution* is the outcome of the forms of control that the capitalist classes exercise over the means of production and the means of appropriation. The ideological socioeconomic theses of dependency, however, appeal to many analysts because they seem to offer a theoretical and practical substantiation for political praxis itself. As Lenin once showed, however, it is a question of comprehending the strategy for socialist revolution in a concrete situation of class struggle. In other words, it is not a question of repeating Marx's nineteenth-century conclusions about the historical need for socialist revolution, but a question of how to produce the knowledge that serves as a material base for the hows, whys, and wherefores of socialist revolution—that is, how to effect such transformations in concrete historical situations. According to Lenin (1972: Vol. 39, 271):

> The *struggle for socialism* lies in the *unity* of the struggle for the immediate interests of the workers (including reforms) and the *revolutionary struggle* for power, for expropriation of the bourgeoisie, for the overthrow of the bourgeois government and the bourgeoisie.
>
> What have to be combined are *not* the struggle for forms + phrases about socialism, the struggle 'for socialism,' but *two forms* of struggle.
>
> For example:
>
> 1. Voting for reforms + revolutionary action by the masses . . . ,
>
> 2. Parliamentarism + demonstration . . .
>
> 3. The demand for reforms + the (concrete) demand for revolution . . .
>
> Economic struggle *together* with the unorganized, with the masses, and not only *on behalf of* the organized workers . . .

4. Literature for the advanced + free, mass literature for the most backward, for the unorganized, for the 'lower masses' . . .

5. Legal literature + illegal.

The above socialist strategy of struggle runs contrary to the polemics of proposing either a proalliance policy with the bourgeoisie (characteristic of some communist parties in Latin America) or an antialliance policy with the bourgeoisie (characteristic of many dependentistas and new left groups in Latin America; see MIR, 1973). Lenin, to the contrary, emphasizes the materialist nature of political analysis: knowing *when* to employ whichever particular form of struggle at a given moment in history and in a concrete case of class conflict. It becomes idealistic to abstractly support a priori one specific form of struggle as being *the* form to win a revolution, while rejecting and excluding the other political forms of struggle. For all of the above-cited aspects in the brief strategy noted by Lenin are already an integral part and product of class contradictions—that is, they remain present in class struggle whether one agrees theoretically with them or not. Therefore, it becomes a materialist question of knowing when and how to promote and organize these different existing aspects *in correspondence* to the needs of transformation. Choosing abstractly one form or another as the omnideterminant form of struggle and transformation results in (and comes from) a conceptual fetishism of the form itself, as though a change in the form of struggle itself were not determined by struggle but capable of singularly determining the outcome. No revolution has occurred with only one form of political struggle. Such a historical fact alone should further reveal the theoretical sophistry of the dependentistas, who forward the end (for example socialist revolution) as the means for achieving that very end.

With the dependentistas' apparently radical propositions for political praxis one can now see the complete framework. In dependency theses there exists then a nationalist articulation of competitive capital's needs, which ultimately denies those same needs at both the level of socioeconomic relations of production and circulation and political policies for struggle. The socioeconomic theses do not effectively question the relations of production of monopoly capital, while the political propositions attack the local dominant classes, thereby isolating the workers in an abstracted international proletarianism, and encouraging the petty bourgeois intellectuals into isolated acts of guerrilla violence. With that monopoly capital (imperialism) remains untouched in the end. History would seem to repeat itself, in that the objective process of capital surplus value production and appropriation effectively continues, while the "prevailing 'subjective' ideology consists of 'national' phraseology which is being spread to fool the masses" (Vol. 39, 236-237). The ideological theses of dependency theory in this light can easily be understood to be the dominant ideas among the petty bourgeois left, a school of MarxismLeninism that even monopoly capital tolerates and diffuses, in spite of the stated opposing aims of the dependentistas themselves.

One specific historical case of this contradictory situation may be found in Mexico. During 1970-1976, the president of Mexico, Luis Echeverría Alvárez, spoke out strongly against U.S. imperialism in international forums with a nationalistic phraseology of dependency concepts. These actions were coupled at home by populist policies in education and an apparent "democratic *apertura*" in politics. Parallel to these populist policies, however, was the penetration of monopoly capital in the form of international banking loans, which ultimately reached almost $30 million by the end of Echeverría's regime. At this point in time, the dependency rhetoric appears to have been an ideological camouflage for the movement of monopoly capital. As always in capitalism, freedom of speech is highly compatible with the free movement of capital: surplus value can withstand—even needs at times—the rhetoric.

Hence dependency theory reflects, on one level, a spontaneous ideological reaction to imperialist theses of socioeconomic interpretation. On another level, it signifies a reflection of the local competitive capitalist classes' interests and needs of surplus value accumulation. And on still another level, it reflects a means of camouflaging imperialist capital penetration. Such theses, then, can be and are given different meanings at different moments of struggle. In that, dependency theory has no one specific meaning.

In light of such historical events, the theoretical discussions and polemics of dependency theory seem to dwell on false problems— problems which, however, have concrete solutions in reality: national liberation movements and socialist revolutions. The basic question remains, then, to be not the abstract debates of the theory of imperialism and/or that of dependency, or both, but rather, as Lenin pointed out: "imperialism is oppression of nations on a *new* historical basis . . . . the other half (of the problem) = emergence of national movements in Eastern Europe . . . , in Asia and Africa . . . . 'in the colonies'" (Vol. 39, 736).

Debating theoretical sophistications founded on ideological interpretations as to whether it is because of imperialism or because of dependency that something occurs only distracts analytical efforts from
the essential issue of imperialist relations as against the historical
need to transform those relations into socialist ones, through national
liberation movements, national revolutionary movements, through
the very social relations determined by imperialist monopoly capital.
The polemics of imperialism versus dependency reveals a scholastic
review of conceptual details and different wordings. This polemic
simply talks about the differences between capitalist and imperialist
relations and their specific sociohistorical products: relations of
forced domination and forced dependence, historically imposed on
entire nations, while the contradiction of imperialism against national
revolutionary movement requires questions and answers of an entirely
different historical nature: the whys, hows, and wherefores of achieving socialist transformation in the face of monopoly capital.

In order to advance to the analytical level of the socialist theses of
1915 about "socialism not needing colonies" (Vol. 39, 757), or that
socialism and not self-determination works for "joint determination"
(p. 757), is not possible as long as these other issues are still concep-
tually imprecise and the various meanings of dependency theses are
obscured under the abstract polemics of dependency theory and the
theory of imperialism. In other words, an analysis of socialist international relations, or communist relations at the level of what is
the contradiction of production and appropriation relations and those
relations between nations under capitalism/imperialism, is difficult
to assess as long as one does not recognize the false polemics established by the ideologues within capitalism-imperialism itself.

From Dependency Theory
to World-Systems Analysis

At this conjuncture, the political significance of dependency theory
itself has changed greatly from that of the 1960s and early 1970s.
Particular theses and word concepts about dependency have become
assimilated into the socialist language of struggle and reflect a certain
political consciousness. The imperialists now fight this tendency in
order to eliminate the ideological cut of certain dependency theses. In
effect, they are attempting to reestablish the imperialist thesis that
"development" is possible and present in Latin America: in other

words, they are now attempting to counter the dependentistas' counterthesis which stated that only more underdevelopment and dependence was created (Friedman, 1978). And even though dependency theses are erroneous in many ways, the critical edge and political consciousness that the words themselves now reflect are a product of acute class struggle—which occurs in spite of the existence of dependency theory itself. The existence of such consciousness occurs because of the contradictions in the social relations themselves, and would occur with or without the theoretical constructions of the socioeconomic theses. In fact, dependency theses themselves are the product of the battle between competitive capitalists and monopoly capitalists (Johnson, 1979b). Nevertheless, this kind of articulated ideological nationalism expressed in dependency theses provides a material basis for struggle, though not for its scientific analysis and interpretation. Such occurs with all of the spontaneous ideological reactions to the contradictions of capitalist class struggle.

While many analysts today are seeking to understand dependency theory, some of the dependentistas who initiated the theoretical pretensions are now trying to pronounce dependency theory dead (Cardoso, 1978b; Frank, 1974), an equally idealist task which confirms their previous idealist reasoning about trying to draw up a "theory." Some students in North America want to know, on the other hand, what dependency is and attempt to adopt it for their own analyses of Latin America (Cardoso, 1976). Again, this is a contradiction of the system that reflects its logic: Some of the forefathers of the so-called theory of dependency now visualize such a theory as a "no no," while their students see it as an enigma and frustration, unable to understand what it was, much less use it. Other dependentistas are seeking to press beyond dependency theory and theories of imperialism in order to explore newly perceived contradictions of capitalism and imperialism. "The present crisis in 'imperialism theory' is no exception—nor is it unusual, though perhaps tragic, that it occurs as a response to a profound structural crisis in the world-economy" (Friedman, 1978: 131). Such is the perception of analysts who are endeavoring to create a world-systems approach, or something similar, with the world-economy as the center of analysis. These analysts (some of whom are former dependentistas) see a need for "a more consistent theoretical model of the functioning of the world-economy" (Friedman, 1978: 141). On the other hand, some analysts, like Samir Amin are declaring "that there can be no economic theory of the world economy" (1978: 64) without an analysis of class struggle.

In order to carry out imperialist policies, one needs an imperialist ideology. Of this the imperialists and their ideologues are well aware (Hagan, 1964). A specific need of an imperialist ideological perspective is to reflect the idea of a unified, interdependent, integrated, harmonious—or at least working—world-system. The concept of world-economy or world-system, used by bourgeois political economists for ages, fits the bill quite nicely. In fact, definitions of the world-economy, offered by authors like Samir Amin, simply replace the concept of imperialism (with all of its negative connotations) where "capitalism" refers to the central economies, and "world capitalist system" refers to the central economies plus the peripheral ones. Such are the practices of ideological debate, not scientific materialist discussion.

Lenin identified imperialism as the beginning of the end for capitalism. History has since been that of national liberation movements and socialist revolutions, each one confirming that theoretical apprehension. Since its very birth, capitalism-imperialism has always been in constant *relative* growth, while in absolute terms of space alone on this planet it has been diminishing. In the face of a floundering, spatially receding economic system of social relations, an important ideological thesis of imperialism today—and of yesterday—is to state or convey exactly the opposite notion. Thereby one may deny historical processes of time by concentrating on facts and statistical figures of relative quantitative growth in order to portray an image of *absolute* imperialist growth. The world-systems analysts (some knowingly, some unknowingly) lend themselves to such a task through their theoretical pretensions.

The ideal concept used around World War I to convey a similar idea was that of a "United States of the (Civilized) World" (Lenin, 1972: Vol. 39, 684), based on analyses of the so-called world-economy then. Today similar theses of a more abstract nature appear in the suggested form of concepts of "world-systems analysis," "world-economy," "world capitalist system," and so on, over and above the conception of a capitalist/socialist process of development. With that the very *object of study* ("world," "world system," etc.) has been identified as determining the nature of the theory of theoretical approach, suggesting an undifferentiated world-economy where capitalism and socialism are but forms of that abstract system. The hierarchy of *center and periphery* defines, then, the system to which both capitalist and socialist economies can be subjected. The relations of the contradiction of socialized production and private appropriation are ignored once again, abolishing the concept of a capitalist/ socialist process. That is, the struggle and transformation throughout history of eliminating the contradiction of social production/private appropriation and the establishment of social production and appropriation.

By using the center and periphery hierarchy, on a nation-to-nation basis, relativized statements obtain that seem to deform all of the defined categories: "Europe is a strange sort of periphery" (Friedman, 1978: 140). This point appears to be contradictory because the analysis was made at a superficial level to begin with, where the concept of periphery is held to be a negative spatial position within the perceived hierarchy. When reality and relationships turn out to be more complex than the simple center/periphery definitions of space, then the poles are reversed, and the relationship (reality) would seem to be positivistically contradictory of the ideal concept. Europe, then, could never be conceived to be a periphery, and conceiving it as such would apparently contradict the center and periphery theory from the start. Obviously, to overcome such silly ideas, one would have to abandon these positivistic lines of reasoning in the dependentistas' and world-systems analysts' spatial categories of center and periphery and establish a dialectical-historical-materialist analysis of the relations themselves. This, however, has been accomplished on only few occasions throughout history.

Within the center and periphery hierarchy, the ideological thesis now surfaces in the word concept of "world-system" or "world-economy," while the object of study itself (that is, capitalist-imperialist economic relations) vanishes before the researcher's eyes. The new relations (socialism) that are being constructed are generally ignored, then, in an attempt to return to a period of time that time itself has assisted in destroying. The process toward socialism is the result of the conscious class effort of millions of workers who have fought and died in the imperialist wars in the national liberation movements and in the socialist revolutions of this century against the very system of capitalist relations itself. These sociohistorical events alone signify the socialist process of transformation and the process of the elimination of capitalist relations. This scientific thesis must be emphasized in the face of the suggested and explicitly stated imperialist ideological theses about constant capitalist world growth and domination, now surfacing once again in abstract concepts of world-systems and world empires (Wallerstein, 1979).

By ignoring many historically significant Marxist theses about the capitalist-socialist process, and the contradiction of socialized production and private appropriation, critical idealists will continue to produce abstract analyses that advance a specific object of study as defining its own theoretical outlook. In other words, the dependency theorists and the world-systems analysts conceive of the object of study (dependency, world-system) as that which supposedly defines and represents their theoretical approach, when actually, as we have attempted to demonstrate here, one should understand that the specific theses about the object of study are *already* a product of a theoretical conception—in this case, of positivistic misapprehension and misconception.

The very suggestion that specific theses represent the theoretical framework of analysis (the theory) already shows that a dialectical-historical-materialist conception is absent, that theory as such is denied. The specific theses about a concrete space-time/motion event are already the result of an idealistic/materialist theoretical apprehension. With that procedure, however, such analysts distract attention from analyzing what theory represents in the social sciences; again an ideological coup is achieved in favor of class values and perspectives of capitalism/imperialism. There is, then, one may say, a crisis in this particular concept of theory, ever present, however, in an infinite number of forms throughout history. But it is an ongoing crisis which signifies the existence of class struggle at the level of ideology; the crisis in no way represents its possible demise. Such misconceptions represent the empirical manner in which man has had to relearn history as well as relive it. Many analysts think that the particular theses proposed represent the theoretical approach, and that adhering to a specific thesis makes one a dependency theorist or a world-systems analyst. In fact, in both cases, each is simply an idealist who produces sophistries and perceives crises where no crises exist in reality. They limit themselves to constructing value systems about perceived hierarchies, not knowledge about reality.

One of the by-products of a world-systems analysis is the avoidance of identifying the historical process of capitalist and socialist production and the contradiction of social relations of production and appropriation. Polemical debates continue to revolve around the contradictions of production/circulation, which easily allow for capitalism and socialism to be conceived as specific forms of the world-system," a dependent function of this larger 'global' transformation" (Friedman, 1978: 145).

There is no resolution to the counterposing of different theses within sophistry. Ideological debate is waged every day at this level. Materialist explanations of space and time processes are not produced therein. Some world-systems analysts are attempting now to accommodate the opposing ideological theses of the developmentalists and the dependentistas (Friedman, 1978: 136-137). When two sets of ideological theses are counterposed regarding the possibility (developmentalism) or impossibility (dependentista) of development, it would seem that one or the other opponent sustains the correct thesis. Now it is being suggested that since the system changes, therefore the theses reflect the change in the system, which means that neither is wrong, but only wrong at a later date and correct for when the thesis was actually stated (Friedman, 1978: 83-104). Such are the mental gymnastics of an attempt by one world-systems analyst to propose apologias for the developmentalist and the dependency thesis of sophistry. Obviously two sophistries do not make a right.

Furthermore, all theoretical and practical knowledge is space-time determined inasmuch as it is produced at a specific level and moment of the process and apprehends specific events, but that does not necessarily mean that those theoretical apprehensions are exact representations of those events. One must discuss the apprehensions in terms of the levels and moments of the process that they reflect.

"The capitalist world regards imperialism, its last card, as the last refuge against the bankruptcy and spontaneous disintegration that threatens to engulf it with fatal certainty. But imperialism is also a remarkable, incomparable artisan of revolution" (Lenin, 1972: Vol. 39, 251). Contrary to much scholarly opinion, there are no crises in theories of dependency or of imperialism. There are only those crises created by imperialism itself in the social relations of production and appropriation, which are resolved by the hand of its own products: class-conscious processes of socialist transformation.

References

Abt Associates, Inc.
    1966   The Development of a Simulation of Internal National Conflict under Revolutionary Conflict Conditions, Vols. I and II. Washington, DC: Abt Associates.
Amin, Samir
    1978   The Law of Value and Historical Materialism. New York: Monthly Review Press.
Bambirra, Vania
    1974   El capitalismo dependiente liatinoamericano. Mexico City: Siglo XXI Editories.

Cardoso, Fernando Henrique
1976   "The consumption of dependency theory in the United States." Latin American Research Review 12, 3: 7-24.
Chilcote, Ronald H.
1974   "Dependency: a critical synthesis of the literature." Latin American Perspectives 1 (Spring): 4-29.
Condit, D. M. et al
1968   Challenge and Response in Internal Conflict: The Experience in Africa and Latin America. Washington, DC: American University.
Dos Santos, Theotonio
1970a   "La crisis de la teoría del desarrollo y las relaciones de dependencia en América Latina," pp. 147-188 in Helio Jaguarbie (ed.) La dependencia político-económica de América Latina. Mexico City: Siglo XXI Editores.
1970b   Dependencia y cambio social. Santiago, Chile: Centro de Estudios Socio-Económicos.
Eckstein, Susan
1978   Cuba and the World-Economy: The Limits of Socialism in One Country. World Congress of Sociology, Uppsala, Sweden. (unpublished)
Economopoulos, Takis
1978   "The political economy of the transformation process." Montreal: Department of Economics, McGill University.
Emmanuel, Arghiri
1972   Unequal Exchange. New York: Monthly Review Press.
Fagen, Richard
1977   "Studying Latin American politics: some implications of a *dependencia.*" Latin American Research Review 13, 2: 3-26.
Fraisse, M.
1904   "International situation of the dependent countries of the Congo Basin." Thesis, Carcassone.
Frank, André Gunder
1969   "Who is the immediate enemy?" in Latin America: Underdevelopment and Revolution. New York: Monthly Review Press.
1971   Lumpenburguesía; lumpendesarrollo. Mexico: Series Popular ERA.
1974   "Dependence is dead, long live dependence and the class struggle: a reply to critics." Latin American Perspectives 1 (Spring): 86-106.
Friedman, Jonathan
1978   "Crises in theory and transformation of the world economy." Review 2, 2.
González, Gilbert G.
1974   "The internal colony model." Latin American Perspectives 1 (Spring): 154-160.
González-Casanova, Pablo
1969   "Internal colonialism and national development," pp. 118-139 in Irving Louis Horowitz (ed.) Latin American Radicalism, A Documentary Report on Left and National Movements. New York: Vintage.
Hagan, Roger
1964   "Counter-insurgency and the new foreign relations." The Correspondent, pp. 79-87.

Ianni, Octavio
　n.d.　"La dependencia estructural." Asociación de Becarios del Instituto de Investigaciones Sociales, Universidad Nacional Autónoma de México.

Johnson, Carlos
　1977　"La teoría de la dependencia: ciencia e ideología." Instituto de Investigaciones Sociales, Universidad Nacional Autónoma de México.
　1979a　"Critical comments on marginality: relative surplus population and capital/labour relations." Labour, Capital and Society 12, 2: 77-111.
　1979b　"Dependency theory and the capitalist/socialist process." Centre for Developing Area Studies, McGill University.

Lenin, V. I.
　1972　Collected Works (45 vols.). Moscow: Progress Publishers.

Marini, Ruy Mauro
　1973a　"Brazilian subimperialism." Monthly Review 23 (February): 14-24.
　1973b　Dialéctica de la dependencia. Mexico: Serie Popular ERA.
　1978　"Las razones del neodesarrollismo (o por qué me ufano de mi burguesía)." Revista Mexicana de Sociología 40 (special number): 57-106.

Marx, Karl and Frederick Engels
　1975　Manifesto of the Communist Party. Peking: Foreign Languages Press.
　1976　The German Ideology. Moscow: Progress Publishers.

Menges, C.
　1968　Democratic Revolutionary Insurgency as an Alternative Strategy. Santa Monica, CA: Rand.

MIR (Movimiento de Izquierda Revolucionaria)
　1971-　El Rebelde, Nos. 1-99. Santiago, Chile.
　1973

Nun, José
　n.d.　"Superpoblación relativa, ejército industrial de reserva y masa marginal." Asociación de Becarios del Instituto de Investigaciones Sociales, Universidad Nacional Autónoma de México.

Redslob, Robert
　1914　Dependent Countries (An Analysis of the Concept of Original Ruling Power). Leipzig.

Rock, V. P.
　1964　A Strategy for Interdependence. New York: Scribner's.

Santi, Paolo et al.
　1971　Teoría marxista del imperialismo. Buenos Aires: Cuadernos Pasado y Presente.

Wallerstein, I.
　1979　"The Ottoman Empire and the capitalist world-economy: some questions for research." Review 2, 3: 389-400.

Warren, Bill
　1973　"Imperialism and capitalist industrialization." New Left Review 81: 3-44.

Werner, Roy A.
　1978　"The economic impact of American oil dependency." Current History 75, 438: 1-4.

Part Two: Case Studies in Dependency

and Mode of Production Analyses

Aníbal Quijano: Imperialism, Social Classes, and the State in Peru, 1890-1930

Translated by Susan Gregory

The organization of this work constitutes the crystallization and redefinition of the ideas that have been elaborated in the discussion of the "structural dependency" of Latin American social formations.

I believe that the principal insight of that discussion is the recognition that the specific, historically determined character of these social formations cannot be understood without placing the problem of imperialist domination at the center of analysis. This insight, however, has not always been handled in a manner congruous with the theory of reference, according to which imperialism is a particular stage in the process of production and reproduction of capital. Due to this fact, the problem of the articulation between international relations and relations among classes in the imperialist chain was seen as a problem of "external-internal dependency" and of "metropolis-satellite" or "center-periphery" relations, focuses which, not-

Editor's Note: *Edited selections from Aníbal Quijano,* Imperialismo, clases sociales y estado en Peru, 1890-1930 *(Lima: Mosia Azul, 1979).*

withstanding their partial contributions, were not fully effective in explaining the problem inasmuch as they were biased toward the national problem in examining the order of imperialist domination.

In one way or another, there has been confusion in the thought and research of the majority of us, a situation that has persisted because for a long time we have continued to study Latin America only in its entirety, neglecting the examination of well-defined, specific situations. This has given rise to formulations in which frequently no distinction is made between generality and theoretical abstractions.

I have chosen to limit this chapter to the study of the Peruvian case in particular, and I have taken the question of capital accumulation as the basis for the construction of a problematic of imperialist domination in this country. The most striking result of this manner of focusing the issue is that some of the principal received hypotheses regarding the relations between capitalism and precapitalism and among the respective social classes, as well as regarding the articulation of the interests of specific classes in a specific state and the resulting international relations, require thorough reworking. This requires an effort in which the theoretical explanation is necessarily influenced and formulated by specific historical factors.

Imperialism in Peru

Since Lenin, imperialism has been known as the stage of capitalism in which, as a consequence of the known processes of technological development, entrepreneurial reorganization, concentration of capital, and domination by finance capital—processes historically initiated in England and other European countries—the international circuit of accumulation is expanded by means of the export of capital. Capital export proceeds from countries where these processes take place toward other territories or countries where the capitalist mode of production has not yet reached that level of development, or where the economy is basically or totally precapitalist. In this way a new international structure of capitalist accumulation was created, characterized by the establishment of a few countries as the centers of and in control of that accumulation. As a consequence, the center bourgeoisies establish economic domination and in varying degrees political domination, according to the level of development of the national state in the countries to which they export capital.

The degree to which a country is incorporated into that imperialist structure and the consequences of this on the specific history of its national society depends not only on its condition as a recipient of capital, but also on the nature of the relations of production which predominate and/or exist within it, on the development of its social classes, and on the form and development of its political organization. The nature of imperialist domination assumes characteristics determined by the specific, concrete conditions.

The Export of Capital and
the Export of Relations of Production

In dealing with countries which at the time of their incorporation into the imperialist chain have a totally or predominantly precapitalist economy, the export of capital to them necessarily also constitutes capitalist relations of production. Of no less importance is the fact that these relations of production are precisely those of the imperialist state of capitalism—that is, they are dominated by international monopoly capital, whose centers of accumulation are located beyond their own borders.

While during the precapitalist period capitalism based on the export of commodities and the financing of this export encountered above all a problem of the realization of surplus value, in its imperialist stage capitalism based on the export of capital found another very different problem, that of the accumulation of capital.

With regard to the first problem, capitalism did not necessarily require the establishment of capitalist relations of production in the territories and countries with which it came into contact. The expansion of mercantilism—the expansion of the monetization of the relations of exchange—were sufficient. On the other hand, the difficulties of accumulation originating from the concentration of capital and the consolidation of monopoly capital in its first stage made it necessary to establish capitalist relations of production in colonized territories or territories economically subordinated to the capitalist market to allow for the expansion of the circuit of production and reproduction of capital. Thus, investment in these countries of capital from the principal centers of capitalist development fulfilled this need and gave rise to the nuclei of capitalist relations of production characteristic of the monopoly stage.

Since the generally precapitalist nature of the country dominated by or recipient of capital did not allow for the internal utilization of production resulting from that capital investment, the realization of the corresponding surplus value could not be carried out within the country's domestic market, but rather in monopoly's own market. Likewise, since in the dominated country an internal circuit of capital accumulation did not exist, the majority of surplus value realized there was also accumulated in the centers.

For international monopoly capital of that period, the recipient country was basically converted into a location for the production of surplus value, the majority of which was later realized in the international market and in the production of the imperial center. Thus, that which was an external market for the dominated country was an internal market for monopoly capital from the point of view of the realization of surplus value. What for the dominated country was an external accumulation of surplus value generated within its own border was for monopoly capital an internal accumulation.

The nonexistence of an internal circuit of accumulation in the recipient country inevitably impeded the internal integration of the various sectors of production. As a consequence, each of these sectors became separately integrated into the circuit of accumulation of the capital-exporting countries—that is, an external or foreign circuit.

Thus, external capital, markets, and accumulation constituted the central mechanisms of the structure of imperialist domination during that period. This continued until transformations within international monopoly capital and in the economic structure of the dominated country required a new structure.

It was less this capital's foreign origin than its monopoly status that gave it its imperialist character. In other words, it was not so much its national character as its class character and, within this, its specificity which imparted on this structure its imperialist nature.

In fact, before, during, and after this invasion by international monopoly capital, other foreign capital came to our countries but in the capacity of competitive capital. For these capitals the domestic market and internal accumulation were vital. This was not the case for international monopoly capital in that stage, for which the domestic market and internal accumulation were not essential.

For this reason, when Latin American political parlance incessantly refers to the problem of the foreign location of the "centers of decision-making" in regard to our economy, in practice it reflects a symptom or a result but does not reveal the real structure that sustains the problem. For this reason, this manner of focusing our problems obscures the roots of these problems. It removes from sight the monopoly capitalist nature of imperialism to project only the foreign character of domination.

The Historical Conditions of the
Invasions of Imperialist Capital in Peru

Peru's definitive entrance into the imperialist order did not come about until the end of the nineteenth century. This does not mean that before this time important relations did not exist between the Peruvian economy and the economies of those countries where capitalism was developing and entering into its monopoly stage.

The first direct investments of European capital were recorded around 1850, in the development of guano on the islands. However, imperialist capital's first presence in Peru was short-lived. Notwithstanding the importance of the economic and political consequences for Peruvian history, it was not able to consolidate imperialist investment or capitalist production in Peru under the control of monopoly capital.

The development of cotton cultivation in the valleys of the central coast and the north of the country, in association with the markets of London and New York, which were affected by the Civil War in the United States, was done under the immediate control of the Peruvian landowners even though they were subordinate principally to the financing and commercial hegemony of the English bourgeoisie.

The construction of a network of railroads was done at the expense of the Peruvian state, even though this served to enrich the foreign contractors and in particular the "Yanqui Pizarro," Henry Meiggs, and it consolidated the state's financial mortgage to the English capitalists.

The relations between the Peruvian economy and European capitalism before the end of the nineteenth century were characterized principally by being finance-mercantile relations; and if indeed they formed part of the first forms of imperialist penetration, they still did not constitute mechanisms of direct exportation of productive capital to Peru and consequently of capitalist relations of production under the control of monopoly capital. These finance-mercantile relations allowed for the revitalization and expansion of mercantilism in the Peruvian economy and stimulated the appearance of the first precarious bases of capitalist relations of production in the country in small, scattered nuclei, interwoven and framed in the matrix of a basically precapitalist structure but still under the direct control of strata of the landed bourgeoisie. Some of the fractions of this class were feebly beginning the transition to capitalism, and while still tied to the appendages of its seigniorial-mercantile origin, they projected their possible capitalist future. Nevertheless, it was on this basis that the Peruvian economy was integrated into the international division of labor of that period. This restricted the economy to the production of raw materials and importing manufactured goods, and subordinated it to the control of the imperialist bourgeoisie.

The Displacement of International Hegemony

The first stage of the invasion of monopoly or imperialist capital in the Peruvian economy coincided with two historical situations which determined the depth and specific conditions in which that domination was established. On one hand was the displacement of the imperialist hegemony of the British bourgeoisie by the bourgeoisie of the United States. This process involved significant consequences. British capitalism had concentrated on exportable industrial development, principally in the textile industry, which required cotton and wool as raw materials as well as foodstuffs such as wheat, meat, and sugar. For these needs the development of direct capital investment in our countries was not essential, nor were large-scale capitalist relations of production. This type of raw materials and foodstuffs could be advantageously produced under precapitalist relations of production. Commercial and financial control were sufficient to establish the respective international division of labor and the resulting "unequal exchange."

In contrast, the industrial development of U.S. capitalism came about in connection with metallurgical production. For this the principal needs were mineral and energy resources. The production of these resources in the necessary scale could not be done in Latin America—and Peru in particular—without using advanced technology and consequently the implantation of capitalist relations of production on the basis of direct capital investment. In this way, as the displacement of the axis of imperialist hegemony toward the United States reflected the greater development of the forces of production in that country with respect to England and consequently greater concentration of capital, these same factors pressed toward the modification of the type of economic relations with other countries that were incorporated into the sphere of capitalism through the direct exploitation of productive capital and at the same time the displacement of monopoly capital's interests toward new raw materials.

The Situation of the Peruvian State

On the other hand, the national state that was forming in Peru became weakened, as did the most important groups of the landowning-commercial sectors that had developed on the Peruvian coast since the middle of the nineteenth century. This weakening of the fractions of the ruling class, which were trying to consolidate their economic and political hegemony in the country and in their class, was the direct consequence of the economic disarticulation and the subsequent financial ruin of these groups caused by the effects of the crisis at the beginning of the decade of the '70s and later during the war with Chile. This was the basis for the debilitation of the state apparatus that constituted the foundation of the growing control of these groups since the middle of the nineteenth century.

The weakening of the national state in formation was accentuated later as a consequence of the political breach inside these groups resulting from the kinds of imperialist domination entering Peru under the control of U.S. capital and the U.S. bourgeoisie.

While under English control, Peruvian landowner-merchants, together with an incipient nuclei of a capitalist bourgeoisie, had the possibility of maintaining ownership and immediate control of their productive resources as the basis of a relative autonomy within their subordination to the financial and commercial control of the British bourgeoisie. This situation was radically altered with the invasion of U.S. capital. Indeed, because of its greater concentration, its greater need to expand its bases of accumulation, and its need for different raw materials—the exploitation of which required direct capital investment—this new capital advanced, taking away from these groups the ownership of their principal productive resources. In this way, it undermined the basis of relative autonomy which had been previously maintained.

For this reason several nuclei of landowner-merchants and of the capitalist bourgeoisie in formation did not easily resign themselves to the loss of their previous position, and they tried to resist by seeking to bargain with U.S. capital over the conditions of subordinated association, the limits of autonomy, and the distribution of benefits. These nuclei were basically tied to the ownership of the land and mineral resources. This was, for example, the case of the dispute for the control of the mines of Cerro de Pasco.

On the other hand, other groups which originated principally from more specifically commercial activity found that their interests were best served by subordinating themselves completely to U.S. capital. The presence of U.S. capital involved the expansion of international and domestic commerce and furthermore offered these groups greater possibilities of access to political power, since the maintenance of the other groups' bases of power also meant the continuity of their political hegemony. For this reason, the invasion of U.S. capital also involved the rupture of the political cohesion of the Peruvian ruling class. The groups which were able to gain control of the state, at the service of the new and more powerful imperialist order, had to attack and reduce the political power of the previous groups, making this struggle appear to be a process of the *desoligarquización* of the state (deposing of the oligarchy) and, as such, a progressive movement. This was basically the historical direction of the Leguia regime (1919-1930).

Under these conditions, the control of the new imperialist capital, mainly U.S., could establish itself in a profound way. The crippling of the historical possibilities of a national bourgeoisie, as proprietor of important productive resources and of the relatively autonomous management of the state within its general subordination to imperialist domination, was definitive.

Although the establishment of this new kind of imperialist control in Peru was in general a phenomenon inscribed in the conditions in which they economic relationship had been developing between this country and those countries in which capitalism was maturing, it was not equally necessary that this control be produced in such a massive and profound way. This was clearly the consequence of the previous economic and political debilitation of the most advanced fractions of the ruling class in Peru.

The First Structure of Imperialist Accumulation in Peru: Semicolonial Accumulation

Given the basically precapitalist character of the Peruvian economy, the introduction of capitalist relations of production under the control of monopoly capital into this matrix produced a characteristic combination of monopoly capitalism and precapitalism in a combined structure. That is, it produced a new economic structure in Peru. Even though from the point of view of the proportion of workers under its control and its geographical extension, precapitalism was overwhelmingly predominant and for this reason conserved ample autonomy within its own sphere, in its entirety and within the historical tendency to move forward, it became subordinated to the needs and the logic of monopoly capitalism. Precapitalism's place and its functions within the entirety of the new economic structure depended basically on this subordinated articulation to monopoly capitalism and secondarily to its own nature.

From this time on precapitalist relations of production in Peru could no longer be considered only in terms of their previous historical character, but also in terms of their articulation with capitalist relations of production, which were predominantly monopoly capitalist in nature. During the historical development of this new structure, this was the factor which determined the place and character of these relations of precapitalist origin in the Peruvian economy. This characteristic combination of monopoly capitalism and precapitalism and the history of this combination dominated and defined the character of and the changes in the Peruvian socioeconomic formation until not very long ago. This work is limited to the study of the mode of accumulation of monopoly capitalism grafted onto this matrix, and only in relation to this will the role of precapitalist origin in the new structure be dealt with.

Between 1890 and 1925, the investment of monopoly capital was established under the control of principally four large corporations: Cerro de Pasco Copper Corporation, Grace and Co., International Petroleum Corporation, and Peruvian Corporation, the first three being U.S. capital and the last, British capital. As an indication of the differences of power and interest between the two capitals, the former operated in the sectors of production (mining, export agriculture and textiles, petroleum, respectively) and the latter in railroad transportation. Along with these were several small firms, such as the British Duncan Fox in the textile industry. Parallel to this, a network of banks, of which the Bank of Peru and London was the most important, and international trading firms served this new monopoly formation in Peru.

The Bases and Mechanisms of Semicolonial Accumulation

There were two bases which defined the semicolonial character of the first structure of monopoly or imperialist accumulation in Peru: (1) the nonexistence of an internal circuit of accumulation, and (2) the enclave nature of the nuclei of capitalist relations of production controlled by monopoly capital. The former determined the type of relations between the Peruvian economy and the centers of monopoly capital accumulation as relations of structural dependency. The latter determined the type of relations between monopoly capital and the precapitalist matrix in which the enclave was established.

The Nonexistence of an Internal Circuit of Accumulation and Its Implications

During this period monopoly capital being exported to Peru was above all interested in broadening the bases of protection of surplus value, the majority of which was accumulated in the major centers and in the raw materials and energy sources to develop this central accumulation. On establishing itself in Peru, monopoly capital became concentrated in the primary sectors of the economy: mining, oil, agriculture, and only secondarily in the financial, commercial, and transportation services which permit productive activity. Only on a limited scale did monopoly capital become established in manufacturing.

The development of the forces of production capable of supplying an expanding manufacturing industry was incipient and weak, and for this reason this did not constitute an area of significant interest for imperialist capital. However, the bases for the development of industrial production were not negligible. An incipient textile industry was already established, as well as small factories for the production of beverages, food, shoes, and other nondurable consumer goods. Perhaps even more importantly for the future—in association with the needs of the export agriculture of cotton and sugar cane—important bases were established for metallurgical production, which began to develop and recruit a growing number of laborers.

As is well known, monopoly capital was interested in expanding the market for its own metropolitan industrial production, and consequently it was interested not only in not developing but in asphyxiating the possibilities of developing the bases of industrial production already established in the countries where it went. This is exactly what occurred in the Peruvian case. Monopoly capital took over the textile industry, the most developed industrial branch, but did not expand it and in a short period liquidated all the bases of the growing metallurgical industry.

The basis for an internal circuit of accumulation which was beginning to link agricultural production (cotton) and livestock production (wool) with industry as well as the possibility of linking industry with agriculture (the production of agricultural tools and machinery) and whose development would have necessarily permited the integration of mining and oil with industry, was soon reduced to an insignificant scale. Industrial development was incapable of generating a domestic market and a focal point of accumulation and integration of the diverse sectors of the economy. The consequences of this liquidation of the foundations for an internal circuit of accumulation and the concentration of monopoly investment in the primary sectors was decisive:

(1) The definitive consolidation of the international division of labor restricted Peru to the condition of being a primary producer with a limited market for industrial production.

(2) The nonexistence of a domestic market for the realization of a fundamental part of the surplus generated in primary production created a structure in which surplus value was entirely realized in a foreign market.

(3) Given the absence of an internal circuit of significant accumulation in Peru, the majority of this surplus value realized abroad was accumulated in the centers of monopoly capital. This constituted a mechanism of decapitalization of the Peruvian economy and of underdevelopment, hindering the expansion of capitalism, the economy, and the development of the forces of production.

(4) There was no internal focus of accumulation that could integrate the various sectors of the economy that were developing under the control of monopoly capital. Each of these sectors was separately articulated to what was an external focus of accumulation for Peru but an internal one for monopoly capital. This meant that the "centers of decision-making"—as referred to in the developmentalist-nationalist literature—regarding the "national" economy were foreign.

The structurally dependent nature of the capitalism established in Peru was due to the fact that monopoly capital controlled that capitalism, which for no accidental reasons had developed and had its centers of accumulation abroad. Its nature as monopoly capital more than its national origin constituted the imperialist character of its operation in Peru.

The Enclave Character of the Nuclei of Capitalist Relations of Production Established by Monopoly Capital and Its Implications

Since monopoly capital was concentrated in the primary sectors of production where the matrix of the relations of production was almost entirely precapitalist, the nuclei of capitalist relations of production it established in these sectors were grafted onto this precapitalist matrix, becoming an enclave. Such capitalist enclaves established within a precapitalist matrix were characterized by relations of exploitation between monopoly capital, an external center of accumulation, and wage labor. They were, therefore, capitalist relations of the imperialist stage of this mode of production. In this specific sense, then, they constituted *imperialist* enclaves.

From the point of view of the problem of accumulation, the relations between the precapitalist matrix and the imperialist enclaves were organized through two principal mechanisms:

(1) the combination of surplus value (generated within the enclave) and mercantile surplus (generated in the precapitalist matrix) in the establishment of global profits for monopoly capitalism; and

(2) the direct utilization by this capital of institutions and mechanisms which were part of the precapitalist relations of production for capitalism's own ends.

The first of these mechanisms is basically linked to the problem of the costs of production and reproduction of labor within the enclaves and the effect of these costs on capitalist profits. Everything produced in these enclaves was sold in the metropolitan market outside Peru. However, it was sold at the same prices as production originating within the metropolis. For example, Cerro de Pasco Copper Corporation sold copper in the United States from its Peruvian enclave at the same price as the copper produced in the United States. However, Cerro de Pasco paid its Peruvian workers much lower wages than those paid to U.S. workers in copper production. In this way, Cerro de Pasco obtained superprofits compared to copper-producing companies in the United States.

The central explanation resides in the differences between the capitalist cost of the reproduction of labor in Peru and in the metropolitan countries. The value of labor as a commodity is measured by the value of the products the workers uses to reproduce his labor power. In the countries which were the centers of monopoly accumulation, such products came from industry or capitalist agricultural and livestock production, and for this reason more value was incorporated into the commodity labor. In Peru, on the other hand, the limited significance of internal industrial production consumed by the workers in the enclaves and the high prices of imported goods which restricted their access to these products meant that the reproduction of labor was based on production originating in the pre-capitalist part of the economy. Therefore, less value was incorporated into labor power in relation to that of the central countries.

This meant that by means of low wages, monopoly capital was also extracting the surplus produced by peasants exploited by pre-capitalist landowners or the surplus produced by artisans under the domination of the mercantile bourgeoisie. Capital not only exploited the workers and thereby obtained surplus value, but it also indirectly exploited the peasants and artisans of the precapitalist part of the economy. The basis of greater profits was precisely the existence of precapitalist maturity which allowed capital to reproduce labor power in the enclaves at a lower cost. In this way, surplus value and mercantile surpluses were combined in the generation of global profits for imperialist capital, producing a structural articulation between monopoly capital and precaptialism in a global process of accumulation.

The imperialist enterprises which operated in agriculture or mining directly exploited peasant producers outside the enclave. Thus, given the difficulties of recruiting a sufficient and stable supply of labor to work all of their lands, Grace and later imperialist companies handed over part of these lands to various types of tenant farmers. They gave them some credit facilities for inputs and later collected the production from these lands at a very low cost and incorporated it with that produced by its workers in the process of realization and accumulation in the metropolitan market. In agriculture as in mining, these companies became the only purchasers of the production of the exportable agricultural products and livestock produced by independent peasants and landowners and of small-scale mining. The companies then sold these products at the same prices as those produced in their own enclaves.

The Resulting New Economic Structure

In connection with the central mechanisms which served the first structure of imperialist accumulation, a new economic structure in Peru was established. First, it was structurally linked to the international imperialist circuit of accumulation and was dependent on it for the mediation of the mechanisms of accumulation which operated inside it and not only as an imposition exercised from the outside, this being due to the foreign location of the "centers of decision-making." Second, it was a system of structural articulation between capitalism and precapitalism where the capitalist sector was characterized by being basically monopoly in nature and the precapitalist sector was characterized by basically servile and semiservile relations. However, relations of reciprocity (in the indigenous communities) and of simple commodity production of independent artisans and peasants were present. Thus the global economic structure of Peru during this period was composed of elements at the same time contradictory and complementary, articulated in connection with the domination of monopoly capital with external centers of accumulation, and in this sense it was imperialist.

Internally, then, what appeared in some ways to be a dual structure, in the sense of two structures—one capitalist and the other precapitalist—was in reality one combined structure. This resulted from the articulation of elements that were contradictory in their essential historical nature but complementary in relation to a specific moment in the needs of capital. From then until recently, the history of this contradictory and complementary relationship has internally determined the process of this structure. However, at the same time that this structure was created to serve the needs of the imperialist chain of capital accumulation, this internal history was also determined by the modifications of the imperialist chain and the mechanisms of articulation with it, and these at the same time were being modified in relation to the changes in the internal structure.

In this way the global economic structure of Peru was formed and consolidated, dependent on the laws of the international accumulation of capital. The relations of precapitalist production—independently of their specific character: servile, semiservile, reciprocity, or independent simple commodity production—not only remained organically articulated to the capitalist mode of production but also subordinated to its needs and its logic of future historical development.

Notwithstanding the ample initial predominance of precapitalist relations of production by virtue of the number of workers involved and the geographic area covered, within this new economic matrix the place and concrete behavior of precapitalist relations of production could no longer be defined solely or principally by their own nature, but above all by their subordinated articulation to the needs and laws of capital. In other words, they were no longer solely precapitalist relations of production. They were if taken separately; they were not completely so in relation to their link with capital. Perhaps from here on it is more appropriate to call them relations of precapitalist origin.

As international monopoly capital came to dominate the Peruvian economic structure, it was the central determining factor of the direction of the economy's historical development. The locomotive of this train was capital, and within capital, the monopoly sector. In other words, despite the predominance of the relations of precapitalist origin for a fairly long period in the specific sense already mentioned, the direction of the historical development of this economic structure was determined by the predominance of the capitalist sector and fundamentally by international monopoly capital.

This reveals well the complementary and contradictory nature of this articulation. On one hand, the presence and for a period even the expansion of the precapitalist sector was necessary for monopoly capital. Inasmuch as this was so, the presence of capital was also necessary for the precapitalist sector. On the other hand, capital cannot exist without constantly enlarging its bases of accumulation and expanding the monetization of the relations of exchange. In this sense, modifications in the internal structure of international monopoly pressured monopoly capital invested in the country to expand its bases of accumulation. However, the expansion of the monetization of the market, the dispersed and erratic appearance of competitive capital in the shadow of monopoly domination, also tended to deteriorate, crack, and finally disintegrate the relations of production of precapitalist origin.

Finally, since the domination of capitalism began and was consolidated in Peru on the basis of the domination of international monopoly capital and the bases of national internal capital were profoundly crippled, it was the evolution of international monopoly capital that came to define the later historical behavior of capitalism in Peru. Mariátegui referred to this process, maintaining that the more capitalism expanded, diversified, and modernized in Peru, the more the domination of imperialist capital would expand, diversify, and modernize in the country. He was not mistaken.

Imperalist Hegemony and Social Classes

The organization of this economic matrix was the fundamental factor governing the way in which basic social interests were organized, as social classes, and the way they were articulated politically in the state. The contradictory but complementary combination of imperialist capitalism and precapitalist relations in a common structure necessarily implied the formation of a coalition of interests between the dominating classes of both modes of production—the imperialist bourgeoisie and the native capitalist bourgeoisie on the one hand; on the other, the mercantile bourgeoisie and seigniorial landowners. This coalition of interests was also inevitably centered on the hegemony of imperialist capital—that is, the imperialist bourgeoisie. This defined the character of these classes, their behavior, the scope of their activities, their interests, and their struggles.

Meanwhile, the social interests of the exploited and dominated classes were shaped not only in relation to specific demands originating from their particular position in the productive structure, but also in relation to the global character of the coalition of dominant interests or dominant classes and of imperialist hegemony. The social interests of the dominated classes from that time on were defined not only in regard to the relations of each one with the ruling class under which it was directly situated, but also in connection with the relations with the whole coalition of dominant classes as such. This situation, which came to govern the relations between those who dominated and the dominated themselves, was marked by its combined contradictory and complementary character. It brought about a particular union of conflicts and convergences in class relations and class struggles.

Imperialist Hegemony and the National Bourgeoisie

The incipient nuclei of the Peruvian capitalist bourgeoisie that was beginning to appear arose from the transition from nuclei of the pre-capitalist mercantile bourgeoisie through the guano and saltpeter business and the production and commercialization of cotton after 1850. These nuclei of a Peruvian capitalist bourgeoisie still maintained the values and modes of behavior deriving from their origin as seigniorial landowners, who dominated a mass of indigenous peasants or African slaves. For this reason this domination was exercised in forms typical of internal colonialism after the separation from the Spanish colonial empire.

These first groups of the Peruvian capitalist bourgeoisie reached the end of the century with an extremely debilitated economic capacity and with its political articulation destroyed—that is, without the real class capacity to bargain the terms and conditions of association with the imperialist bourgeoisie at the precise moment in which imperialist capital was invading the Peruvian economy. Since it was precisely those nuclei of the bourgoisie (mercantile and incipient capitalist nuclei) which had, since the middle of the nineteenth century, been able to impose their hegemony over the control of the central apparatus of the nascent Peruvian state, the seigniorial landowners, who were not linked to the international market, were not in a condition to participate in the problem of the penetration of imperialist capital.

As a consequence, the imperialist bourgeoisie found a very easy and totally controllable economic terrain and nothing to stop it from taking control of all the principal productive resources in each of the branches of activity which were of interest to imperialist investment. The imperialist bourgeoisie took over the land suitable for export crops, mines, oil, trains, banking, international trade, and the incipient textile industry. At a certain moment it was also able to take over the direct administration of the principal port customhouse of the country, leaving the Peruvian state without revenues and forcing it, before 1930, to finance more than eighty percent of its budget with U.S. loans and credits.

Where, then, was the national bourgeoisie? Its incipient nuclei, which still had not entirely disposed of their seigniorial shell, were reduced to surviving on the crumbs left by imperialist capital from the productive resources of each branch of production and to using the state's resources to complement the meagerness of their own sources of economic power in the well-known combination of corruption and capitalist accumulation in our country. These reduced national bourgeois nuclei found themselves living not only off the crumbs of imperialism but entirely in vassalage to it. They were in a position analogous to that of serfs who lived on the lord's land, even though they appeared to live autonomously on that remnant of land. The national bourgeoisie thus appeared fixed in and surrounded by the financial, commercial, technological, and ultimately political mechanisms which imperialist capital had established—in the economic and political terrain of the imperialist bourgeoisie.

The character of the national bourgeoisie—that is, of the social interests of these groups—was above all shaped by their essential link with imperialist capital and constrained in its development by the limits set by imperialist capital. In the framework of a process in which imperialist domination was disputed between the English and the U.S. bourgeoisies, the former being the first to dominate the Peruvian economy, the nuclei of the capitalist bourgeoisie appeared divided by their association with each of the imperialist bourgeoisies. Finally, in a process which required that the relations of production become capitalist in the areas which were of interest to imperialist capital, the seigniorial traditions—either genuine or adopted—of the nuclei of the national bourgeoisie served as another factor of discontinuity and internal conflict within these groups.

For these reasons, but fundamentally because of the character of their relations with the imperialist bourgeoisie, the Peruvian nuclei of the bourgeoisie from the beginning were weak and fraught with internal conflicts; they were also economically and politically disarticulated as a consequence of the disarticulation of the branches of activity within the internal ambit of the Peruvian economy and as a consequence of the situation in which each of them was separately articulated to the demands and fluctuations of the economy of imperialism. In other words, these nuclei of the Peruvian bourgeoisie were structurally unable to develop as an effective national class in order to bargain with the imperialist bourgeoisie for their national interests of domination. They increasingly had to develop in relation to the expansion and consolidation of imperialist capital in the country.

Imperialist capital was able to impose the conditions of its hegemony in Peru without difficulty because the Peruvian bourgeoisie was too weak to establish itself as a national ruling class before the imperialist invasion. Once this imperialist hegemony was established, the Peruvian bourgeoisie was conditioned by the interests and forms of domination of the imperialist bourgeoisie, which also imposed on it the conditions and limits of its development. From that time on the concrete behavior and the concrete interests of the Peruvian bourgeoisie reinforced these conditions and reinforced the hegemony of the imperialist bourgeoisie. *It thus could never be a national class,* except in terms of its origin; *it could never be nationalist, much less anti-imperialist.*

Imperialist Hegemony and Precapitalist Classes

With the integration of the surplus value generated in the imperialist enclaves and of the marketable surplus produced in the precapitalist haciendas in the formation of the global profits of imperialist capital, the seigniorial landowners were increasingly pushed toward their conversion to landowner-merchants while the export-import merchants saw their scope of operation expanded. The result of this was the expansion of mercantilism and the progressive conversion of the landowner-merchants into a mercantile-seigniorial bourgeoisie.

The commericalization of surplus became a central interest of the most important nuclei of this class. The search for the expansion of the resources which would permit the production of such surplus was the inevitable consequence in the conduct of this class. As a result, the most important and extensive process of concentration of agricultural property in the hands of this type of landowner began through theft of the lands of the "indigenous communities" which had survived from the colonial period and through the first wave of the concentration of agricultural land with the beginning of the republic.

This process let loose a series of peasant uprisings throughout the first three decades of this century, above all affecting the regions in which the greatest number of "indigenous communities" were located. Thus, class struggle in the precapitalist countryside in that period correspond to the new position of the landowning class in the country's economy through its organic connection with the imperialist bourgeoisie and to the new positions which the serf and free peasants assumed under imperialist hegemony. Considered in an isolated context, this struggle between landowners and peasants in a way reproduced the characteristics of the social struggles within feudal society. However, the content of these struggles was not determined solely by the precapitalist character of these relations of production, but also by the articulation of these relations to the interests and means of exploitation of the imperialist order.

The concentration of agricultural property not only affected the property of the indigenous communities, even though this was its principal base. The process also involved theft of the lands of the small and medium landowners. The rural banditry, which reached its highest point during this period, was in great part fed by the rebellion of the dispossessed landowners. Luis Pardo and Benel were its typical representatives, and their names became part of popular legend.

Thus, the redefinition of the position and role of the landowners in the global structure of this economy under imperialist hegemony also redefined the class relations between peasants and landowners, forcing the great masses of peasants into servitude in order to produce the surplus which could be sold in the market generated by capitalist penetration. It also redefined the relations among the stata of the landowning class, pushing members of the lower strata toward commercial occupations and producing an exodus toward the cities and capitalist centers and, in part, the proletarianization of these strata.

On this base appeared a stratum of rural and semirural (or semiurban) commercial bourgeoisie—both small and medium—which was closely tied to the landowning class and dependent on it during a particular period. Later, however, it was destined to dispute the control of the land and the rural economy with the weakest sectors of the landowning class. This stratum of the small and medium rural commercial bourgeoisie—an intermediary in the relations of exchange between the landowners and the dominated native imperialist bourgeoisie—was also an efficient and ubiquitous intermediary in the relations of exploitation between the bourgeoisie and the free and servile peasants. This stratum of rural merchants, recruited mainly from the intermediary ethnic strata, which in the indigenous language of that period were included under the generic name of "mistis" (mestizos), intensified the exploitation of the indigenous peasants. In this way, the social relations typified by "internal colonialism" between Indians and non-Indians, founded on the expansion and strengthening of servile-merchantile relations of production, were expanded and strengthened. The precapitalist economic base was indispensable for the model of capitalist accumulation of that phase and for the social relations of internal colonialism, its social foundation, and its ideological justification in that sphere.

Imperialist Hegemony and the Proletariat

In the imperialist enclaves and in the smaller ones under the control of the Peruvian groups of the bourgeoisie, a population of workers was created which formed a new social class. In the nineteenth century, a disperse stratum of precapitalist and incipient capitalist wage laborers had been forming through a new dynamism of mercantilism in Peru, particularly since the period of the height of the guano industry. However, because of the precariousness of capitalist activities in guano and in the urban centers, and because of the massively predominant character of precapitalist relations of production in the country, nothing recognizable as free labor market was formed, nor did the first groups of workers stabilize this situation. The replacement of black slaves by the importation of Chinese laborers under labor contracts which tied them to the land in the mercantile haciendas of the central and northern coasts also impeded the formation of a rural proletariat there. However, these same practices of coercive recruitment of labor proclaimed the nonexistence of a process of the liberation of labor from servile agricultural activities. As a consequence, it was only after the introduction of imperialist capital in the different branches of production that the formation of the proletariat began in a stable and significant way.

Given the enclave nature of the principal forms of capitalist exploitation and the lack of internal articulation among the different branches of production under imperialist domination, this new class in formation also emerged disarticulated and scattered in nuclei which were not only economically but also geographically separated in enclaves without close communication among them. As a class in formation whose members were principally peasants from a servile or communal tradition, the process of social and psychosocial proletarianization developed very slowly. This situation was reinforced as much by the fluctuation of some of its members between working-class and peasant activities as by the character of the primary activities in which they were mostly concentrated—that is, by the continuity of their position in the rural world. In their new position, workers coming from the countryside gradually began to liberate themselves from the sociocultural relations of internal colonialism, and this differentiated them in the sphere of the peasant population.

The proletariat which was forming in the cities, actually almost exclusively in Lima, originated in great part from the urban-mercantile artisans and from the middle peasant sectors which were robbed of their resources. They constituted a special fraction within the new proletariat in formation, characterized by their mainly urban extraction, their relatively considerable level of education expressed in their ability to read, write, and publish numerous papers and pamphlets during the entire period prior to the 1930s. This allowed the urban-industrial fraction of the proletariat to exercise an active leadership role in the ideological-political and syndical formation of the new class, despite their small numbers and their secondary importance in the economic structure of the country. The great struggles for the eight-hour day, the organizing of trade unions, and the revolutionary politicialization in Lima prior to 1930 bears witness to this fact.

The internal characteristics of the remaining sections of the proletariat in formation were conditioned by the organization of imperialist capitalism at that time. The nascent proletariat was numerically small, disarticulated, fluctuating, basically non-urban-industrial, mainly of peasant origin, linked by its patterns of consumption to the cultural patterns of peasants, and coercively recruited and subject to the will of the patron. As such, this proletariat closely corresponded to the type of imperialist presence and its concrete model of capital accumulation. It must be added that with the little diversification of economic activities and the persistence of seigniorial patterns in the internal regime of imperialist as well as dominated native capitalist enterprises, the relations between the proletariat and the bourgeoisie took on a paternalist-authoritarian ("oligarchical") character for a long period.

Due to all these factors deriving from the particular combination of imperialist capitalism and precapitalism in the country, the relations of production between the bourgeoisie and the proletariat were subjected to a system of organization remote and different from that which corresponded to the same relations in the imperialist centers.

The prolonged duration of the work day, the obstacles to union organizing, the paternalist-authoritarian discipline, the adherence to internal colonialism, the lack of social rights, and coercive recruitment were the characteristics which defined the concrete relations of imperialist exploitation of the proletariat in formation during the major part of the first three decades of this century in which imperialist domination and its first model of accumulation were established and consolidated.

Imperialist Hegemony and the Middle Strata

The concentration of capitalist agricultural property in the valleys of the central and northern coasts, where the land was suitable for export crops in which imperialist capital was interested at the time, meant the displacement of the peasants of the zone toward proletarianization on the capitalist haciendas as well as the displacement of members of numerous seigniorial-mercantile landowning families outside that class. The members of those landowning families were thus pushed toward liberal professional or bureaucratic occupations, swelling the ranks of the new middle social strata, which had been slowly forming since the recuperation of the Peruvian economy's association with the capitalist international market.

The same process of forming a domestic market around the capitalist activities in the enclaves and the principal urban centers stimulated the gradual growth of a stratum of middle-level merchants in the countryside as well as in the cities, and of people to provide services for the needs of the new dynamism of the urban population, particularly in Lima. A petty bourgeosie was forming in the sphere of the development of semicolonial imperialist capitalism.

The required expansion of public services, as well as of financial institutions and international and domestic commerce, enlarged the bases of a bureaucracy that was recruited from the members of the declining landowning families and from the members of the small middle urban groups previously formed during the course of the revitalization of mercantilism during the second half of the previous century. Incipient professionalization of a classical liberal type, bureaucratization, the formation of a new petty bourgeoisie, and the expansion of the small and medium mercentilist bourgeoisie in the countryside, constituted the principal channels of the formation and expansion of these middle social strata. The socioeconomic destiny of these middle strata was conditioned by the characteristics and the fluctuations of imperialist capitalism, by the type of relations it had with precapitalism, and by its relations with the matrix economy of imperialism. The rhythm of growth of each of these fractions of the middle strata depended on the rhythm of expansion of imperialist capitalism in the country.

At the same time that capitalist accumulation was also founded on the maintenance and expansion of precapitalist relations in the countryside, the margins of growth of capitalist activities and of their spread in the Peruvian economy were limited in advance by the small domestic market's own needs, which were generated around the capitalist activities of the enclaves concentrated in certain areas. During this period the possibility of a rapid expansion of the economic activities of the middle strata was restricted to these limits. The problem, however, was that the concentration of property and of the control of productive resources, in the capitalist as well as the precapitalist sphere, increasingly pushed more human contingents toward a middle social position without expanding the economic activities in which they could engage themselves.

The austerity of the economic sphere suitable for sustaining the middle social positions obliged an important part of the contingents from the landowning ranks to look for refuge principally in the area of public bureaucracy. They pressed for the expansion of public positions even if they were not really necessary. The tendency toward the inflation of the bureaucratic sectors of the middle strata was one of the resulting characteristics of this type of imperialist hegemony in the Peruvian economy, more than a response to the real need for the growth of public services.

On the other hand, the maintenance of precapitalism, founded on relations typical of internal colonialism and for this reason impregnated with all the seigniorial values to the point of becoming encrusted in these conditions, meant that the social ideology of the whole society, and in particular of the middle groups formed by the explusion of a part of the landowning class during the course of the concentration of argricultural property, also tended to become stronger as the last barrier to defend their social position. People tried to stay in middle social positions while still maintaining a perception of themselves as members of the seigniorial class. They sought to imitate and maintain the conduct, norms, and social values of that class, despite the fact that the actual material conditions were not even sufficient to convert them in any stable way into middle strata. The formation of a socially and psychologically seigniorial middle stratum with very precarious, indeed impoverished, economic bases was one of the characteristics of this process. The ideological and political consequences of these phenomena later formed part of the base of many of these middle group's political conduct after the 1920s, as will be discussed later.

However, the austerity of the economic sphere of the middle sectors forced the poorer strata and the groups not originating from the landowning ranks toward proletarianization in the incipient industrial-urban formations, which the activity of immigrants with entrepreneurial aptitudes and imperialist capital established under the total hegemony of the latter. The majority of Lima's urban artisans and the middle groups originating from past mercantilism in activities of personal services constituted the major part of the first working-class contingent in the textile factories and foodstuffs industries which were established in Lima since the beginning of this century, as well as in the semifactory activities (particularly bakeries). This social origin marked the conduct and the social ideology characteristic of the first groups of the urban proletariat during the first thirty years of this century; they quickly accepted anarchosyndicalism.

As in any process of change from a mercantile to a capitalist economy, the middle strata corresponding to that economy were forced toward proletarianization—that is, petty commercial bourgeoisie was proletarianized. However, in its place in the specific conditions of the combination of imperialist capitalism and precapitalism, new middle social strata appeared whose channels of formation, social values, and political behavior were not only the result of capitalism as such, but also the result of the particular form of reproduction of capital which imperialism had established in the country.

The Political Organization of These Classes: The Dependent National Oligarchical State

The formation of a national state had not been completed during the nineteenth century, not even under the direction of the nuclei of the bourgeoisie which were distancing themselves from the seigniorial-mercantilist ruling class. With the repercussions of the national defeat in the war with Chile, the political and administrative apparatus precariously constructed after 1850 had practically disintegrated. As reconstruction was beginning, imperialist hegemony was in the full process of establishing itself. Later the political organization of social classes—that is, of Peruvian society—could no longer correspond solely to the previous national or class conditioning. The socio-economic articulation which imperialist hegemony shaped in the country implied the presence of capitalist and precapitalist classes, woven into one structure in which these classes contradicted and complemented each other in relation to the combination of capitalism and precapitalism in capital accumulation and in the production of mercantile surplus at the service of the former. This implied a coalition of class interests between those controlling both sectors of this structure of exploitation which is expressed as a coalition of power for political domination. The class character of the new state was necessarily impure, hybrid, at the same time bourgeois and seigniorial. The history of this state from that time on consisted not only of its confrontation with the dominated classes but also of its complex and contradictory dialectic of opposition and combination of class interests, in different degrees at different times.

The problem of class was not, however, the only one that affected the setting-up of this new state. In the coalition of power that was established as the social base of the state, the hegemonic fraction was the imperialist bourgeoisie. This was, of course, imperialist due to the characteristics of *capital* and to the capitalist relations of production which correspond to it. It was not by chance that the *bourgeoisie* controlling this capital and these relations of production was of foreign origin. As a consequence, the problems of the definition of the state's class character were joined by the problem of its national condition. For this reason part of the later history of the state was also conditioned by this national problem. The problem of the definition of its class character along with the definition of its national character has since dominated this history.

Ideological Conceptions of the National Problem

In this coalition of power the dominant capitalist and precapitalist classes were articulated:

(1) Bourgeoisie: imperialist bourgeoisie + dependent capitalist bourgeoisie
(2) Landowners: mercantile-landowners + seigniorial landowners

In this coalition of power, the imperialist bourgeoisie was clearly hegemonic, as a result of the type of organization of the economy. However, because of its foreign character, it could not directly and explicitly assume the control and management of the state, since the state was formally independent. Only the national fractions of this coalition of power were in a position to assume the immediate and explicit control of the state. Nevertheless, given that the central function of the state was determined by the needs of imperialist capital accumulation, it consisted of politically and administratively guaranteeing the conditions of his model of capitalist accumulation. The new state fulfilled a central function of the service of imperialist domination—a class function. However, since the bourgeoisie that controlled this domination was foreign, this function *appeared* to serve the domination by foreigners, as a national function. In other words, *the national problem concealed but also manifested the essential class character of the basic function of the state.*

The problem of imperialism—that is, the class character of this state—presented itself as a national problem. The *ideological* form characteristic of the social perception of the nuclei of the dependent bourgeoisie and of the middle strata retained only the national dimension of the problem of imperialism. This ideology also pervaded the perception of even the dominated classes, including the majority of the proletariat even until today.

The ideological posing of the problem of the national character of the state corresponded, for that same reason, not to a mere invention of reality. The new state that represented that coalition of interests and power was actually a dependent national state, in that it guaranteed the interests of a foreign bourgeoisie. However, as with all ideologies, it confused appearance with reality. As a consequence, it made that which was really essential disappear; the imperialist character did not reside above all in the foreign character of the imperialist bourgeoisie, but in the nature of the established ruling relations of production in the Peruvian economy—in other words, the capitalist relations of the imperialist stage. The class content of the problem was hidden and at the same time expressed by the foreign character of the bourgeoisie which controlled imperialist capital. This superimposition of the national problem over the class problem, which established the ideological perception of imperialism as an exclusively national issue, was determined by the fact that the essential class character of the state, consistent with its position as a guarantor of imperialist hegemony, was manifested during this period fundamentally in the fulfillment of this function but not in the concrete composition that directly and indirectly assumed the control and management of the state. Actually, keeping in mind the class composition of the national fractions of the coalition of power, which were the only ones in a position to assume direct control of the state, it is clear that the class character of the state on a concrete level was much more precapitalist than capitalist. In the association of the dependent capitalist bourgeoisie with the landowning class (mercantilist and seigniorial), both shared dominance from the point of view of an external description of the situation.

In the first place, because of the nature of its relations with the imperialist bourgeoisie, the dependent capitalist bourgeoisie was reduced in numbers and economically and socially weak because its productive resources consisted of the crumbs left by imperialism; it was internally disarticulated as a class in the productive structure because of the disarticulation among the branches of production in the internal national order; it retained all the seigniorial adherences derived from its historical origin; and the possibilities of expanding its domestic market more rapidly and massively were limited because of its vassalage to imperialist capital. This meant admitting the type of association of interests between imperialist capital and the pre-capitalist base of surplus production and maintaining this base as long as this association was necessary for imperialist capital. Above all, its own resources of power were congenitally limited, and it was not able to impose its style as a capitalist bourgeois class in the political domination of the society. In contrast, although now subjected to the hegemony of imperialist capital, the precapitalist classes—the mercantile landowners and the seigniorial landowners—found in this submission the material foundation of their concrete power in society, which was even strengthened by the concentration of mercantile agricultural property. By dominating the majority of workers in the country in the social sphere through relations of internal colonialism and in the economic sphere through servile and semiservile relations, these classes, among which there was no definitive break in practice, appeared as one class with functions in the process of becoming differentiated. The weakness of the central state apparatus over the economy and over a society with these characteristics permitted the establishment of immense autonomy on the part of the local power of the mercantile or purely seigniorial landowners which gave rise to the phenomenon known as "political caciquism," an analogy to the prehispanic chieftancies.

In this way a somewhat paradoxical situation presented itself. On one hand, in the coalition of political power the precapitalist classes were immediately predominant as the concrete social base of the state. This was a combination of bourgeois and seigniorial aspects in its concrete appearance, and in that appearance the seigniorial element was predominant. On the other hand, however, the very existence of this coalition of power, as well as the basic state function of guaranteeing the hegemony of imperialist capital, created a situation in which the state had a predominantly bourgeois character in its essential function despite its predominant seigniorial base.

The dependent national state, which criss-crossed the class problem with the national problem in relation to the hegemony of imperialist capital, also assumed its oligarchical continuity on new foundations. In other words, a national-dependent oligarchical state was emerging. It was oligarchical in the specific model of political domination with a social base that was bourgeois-seigniorial, hybrid, conflictive but combined; it was national in the formally independent condition of the nation-state; it was dependent (this word is not very appropriate) because the hegemony of imperialist capital in the functions of the state was dressed with the foreign origin of the imperialist bourgeoisie.

The State and Class—
A Theoretical Digression

Here a principal theoretical problem is posed. In Marxist theoretical discourse, the central thesis regarding the relations between social classes and the state is that the state is fundamentally an instrument of domination of a ruling class over the dominated class. In the *Communist Manifesto* Marx maintained that the administrative apparatus of the state is nothing more than committee which administrates the common affairs of the ruling class. In bourgeois society this refers to the bourgeoisie. Politically, the state is the organized power of the ruling class—in this case the bourgeoisie—to oppress the dominated class. Later, after studying the characteristics of the phenomenon of Bonapartism, Marx found that under certain historical conditions the state appears to rise above the social classes and establishes itself as the principal power of the society. Nevertheless, this political autonomy of the state with respect to classes can be neither total nor permanent. As long as the socioeconomic order consists of a system of class domination, even in a time when it emerges as politically autonomous over classes. It serves the interests of the ruling class even when it obliges this class to subordinate itself to state regulations.

This means that in the Marxist theory of the state, the relation between the state and social classes is more complex than it would appear to be if only the first of those theses were maintained, even though it continues to be the matrix of the theory. However, the study of Marx regarding Bonapartism clearly illustrates the necessity of permanently recovering the real potential of the theoretical-methodological focus of Marxism. The study of a specific state, in a specific historical situation, involves examination of the specific characteristics of classes and class struggle in every moment—of the greater or lesser capacity each class has in that moment to monopolize, share, influence, and dispute the power of the state.

The concrete study of the relations between the state and social classes implies focusing on the state as a center of power which is permanently disputed by the classes and where consequently the relative position of each of the classes to the state depends on its greater or lesser capacity to influence, participate in, control, or monopolize state power. The specific conduct of the state as an administrative apparatus and as a system of political articulation between classes depends on the historical variations that are produced in class struggles. As long as the basic structure of exploitation and domination are not radically altered, these variations in the *political* conduct of a specific state will continue within the framework of the system of domination of the time.

The Effects of Imperialist Hegemony

Unlike the situation resulting from the period of bourgeois revolutions in Europe, in which capital accumulation inevitably required the elimination of the seigniorial state as well as of precapitalist relations of production, the problems of accumulation during the new stage reached by capital in Peru required a combination of imperialist capitalist and precapitalist economic relations as well as the political combination among those in a position to dominate.

The rising bourgeoisie in Europe at the end of the eighteenth century and the beginning of the nineteenth needed to expand its *domestic* market and free labor to create a free labor market in order to expand and consolidate the bases for the internal accumulation of capital. The imperialist bourgeoisie in Peru needed to generate surplus value to be realized and accumulated in its own market, not in the Peruvian market. It was not interested in the complete expansion of the Peruvian market, or in completely freeing labor. To the contrary, it sought to maintain the bases of superprofits derived from the low cost of labor power and the appropriation of marketable precapitalist surpluses.

The ambivalence of the class character of the state was the principal basis for the ambivalence of the proletariat's political struggle. This was also the basis for the possibility, later materialized, of the hegemony of reformist-nationalist populism of the middle strata. The major part of the middle strata, which originated from the disintegration of many of the seigniorial-mercantilist landowning nuclei as a consequence of the war with Chile, imperialist invasion of the land, and the concentration of precapitalist agricultural property had similar difficulties. On one hand, the magnitude of the economic sphere of the middle strata was not ample enough, nor could it accommodate the ranks of those who were being pushed toward a middle social position or were struggling to maintain it. The reinforcement of seigniorial landowning domination and the enclave nature of capitalist operations hindered the rapid expansion of intermediate economic activities. On the other hand, the seigniorial presence in the state and the weak and dependent bourgeoisie with aristocratic pretensions which participated in political power with a primarily peasant base that was isolated, scattered, illiterate, and subjugated to the local power of the landowners, allowed for monopoly control of the state through this coalition of power—that is, the formation of an oligarchical state. The emerging middle strata were not acceptable in this combination of power, except as part of the subordinated bureaucracy or as professionals at the service of oligarchical-imperialist domination—that is, as bureaucratic professional clientele of the oligarchic system.

During this period the objective conditions were in no way present for the middle strata to exercise the political and social functions characteristic of these strata in pure capitalist societies, these being political and social mediation. The middle strata, for this reason, were forced to confront the oligarchical-imperialist coalition in the search for the expansion of their own social, economic, and political perspectives. Their social position and their social origin prevented them from grasping the complexities of the situation of this society, except in ideological terms, not in theoretical-scientific terms. The leadership of the middle strata understood the national dimension but not the class dimension of the problem of imperialist hegemony. From oligarchical domination and its functions relative to imperialist hegemony, they retained only the problem of democratic participation. The characteristic ideology thus constructed was thus marked by demands for the expansion of the channels of popular participation in the generation of power, without questioning the social bases of power, and by demands for the rescue and consolidation of the national independence of the state in the face of domination by the foreign bourgeoisie. Nationalist democratic reformism was the resulting political option.

The peasantry, due to its ethnic characteristics, its dispersal and lack of communication, and the continuous theft of its lands, was not in a situation to face the problem of the state. It perceived its principal problem directly in relation to the struggle for land. The peasantry did not have the basis that would permit it to distinguish the anti-imperialist component of this struggle for land.

All these conditions gave rise to a well-defined process.

1. The coalition of power had no fraction interested in or capable of even indirectly supporting or stimulating the struggle for political

democratization through the affirmation of the national independence of the state. The weak dependent bourgeois fractions were conditioned to move within the framework of imperialist hegemony and its commitments with the seigniorial landowners.

2. The middle strata had no ground for political mediation between the ruling class and the dominated class except in ideology, whose marterialization, however, brought them face to face with the coalition of power.

3. The proletariat found itself in an ambivalent situation between its antibourgeois direction and its antioligarchical direction, and through this its antiseigniorial direction.

4. The peasantry had no channel of participation in the national political confrontation except in an indirect way through its struggles for land.

The consequence of all these factors was the emergence of a coalition of the dominated and the middle strata in which the political participation of the peasantry was abstract or indirect. Thus, the dominant coalition was confronted by a coalition of the dominated and the middle strata. Historically, this meant the impossibility of a system of legitimate and stable political mediation that would permit the control and equilibrium of the order of political domination. Due to this situation, the dominant coalition soon was forced to maintain itself in power by means of the permanent presence of the armed forces in the direct management of the political apparatus—retaining, however, the direction of the administrative apparatus and the political direction of the armed forces' conduct in the state. The sphere of stable legality, a correlate of political legitimacy and the middle strata, from then on was out of reach of this oligarchical coalition, subordinated to the conditions of imperialist hegemony. The permanent illegal and repressive character of the oligarchical regime notably served to reinforce the leadership role of the middle strata over the proletariat and to consolidate the populist-nationalist ideology among the masses. The relevance of the struggle against the dictatorship and repression relegated the limitations and political-social incongruities of the middle strata's leadership in the popular movement to obscurity. This complicated history would be literally incomprehensible if it were thought of in terms of the hypotheses received from the European experience or from a reification of the central categories of Marxism. Any analysis can grasp reality only after an adequate understanding of the problem of the character of imperialist domination.

Norma Stoltz Chinchilla: Interpreting
Social Change in Guatemala:
Modernization, Dependency,
and Articulation of Modes
of Production

For most of the post-World War II period, neoevolutionary
and structural-functionalist paradigms dominated the study of change
in Third World societies and dictated research agendas under which
data are collected, theoretical categories through which information
is analyzed, and political strategies with which goverments and international agencies attempt to intervene in change. The situation began
to change only when Latin American scholars themselves (such as
Rául Prebisch and the economists with the Economic Commission on
Latin America; see Baer, 1969; Vitale, 1968; Cardoso, 1969; Cardoso and Falletto, 1969), and others who were influenced by them
(such as Frank, 1967, 1969, 1972; Dale Johnson, 1972, 1973; Cockcroft et al., 1972; Bodenheimer, 1970a, 1970b) directly challenged
the assumptions of the modernization view and offered the dependency perspective as an alternative. Discussion of the alternative, in
turn, generated interest in other alternative frameworks and methodologies, particularly mode of production, in both its "traditional"
evolutionary and modern articulationist versions (John Taylor, 1979;
Hoogvelt, 1980; Oxaal, 1975; O'Brien, 1975; Bradby, 1975; Chinchilla, 1980, 1981; Chinchilla and Dietz, 1981; Henfry, 1981; Car-
olos Johnson, 1981; Angiotti, 1981; Howe, 1981; Smith, 1978;

Dieterich, 1978; Harding, 1976; Laclau, 1971; O'Laughlin, 1975; Luporini and Sereni, 1976; Cueva, 1976, 1977; Foster-Carter, 1973, 1976; Assadourian, 1977; Godelier, 1974, 1977; Rey, 1976).

The paradigmatic debate which these discussions initiated called everything related to the interpretation of Latin American societies and social change into question: the formulation of the questions, the methods for gathering data, the interpretation of answers and the policy and political implications of evidence and analysis. Even the most narrow and empirical of scholars found it difficult to ignore the raging debates since the categories for which they were collecting data were being challenged as to meaning, validity, and usefulness.

The hemisphere-wide discussion of methods and models for studying society and social change had an important impact on a fledgling indigenous social science endeavor in a country like Guatemala that had long been dominated by the descriptions and interpretations of North Americans, in this case anthropologists such as Tax (1941, 1953), Redfield (1939), Gillin (1948), Tumin (1945, 1949, 1952), Adams (1956, 1957, 1967), Nash (1958) and their North American and Guatemalan students. North American social science models were in vogue throughout the hemisphere after World War II, partly because of their superior access to funds for research and training, but were particularly hegemonic in countries like Guatemala where, after the counterrevolutionary coup of 1954, academic and intellectual life, including research, was seriously repressed and many of those Guatemalans who might have contested the formulations of the North Americans chose exile over persecution.

The challenge to North American social science interpretations finally came in the 1960s, when, stimulated by the discussions elsewhere and by the emergence of an opposition movement at home (based on the Cuban guerrilla foco model—see Debray, 1975), Guatemalan scholars directed their attention to concrete questions about their society's history, sociology, and economic development. These included: What was the character of the Spanish conquest and why did it differ in Guatemala? To what extent did the liberal reforms of the late nineteenth century represent a break from, rather than continuity with, the social structure and economy of the colonial period? When and how did capitalism emerge in Guatemala and what have been its specific characteristics? In what ways and to what extent were the changes of the 1944-1954 period revolutionary ones? What has been the impact of the infusion of foreign capital and the expansion of export agriculture in the last two decades, and what are the political and strategic implications of these changes? Finally, the most controversial but perhaps most important question of all, of what significance is it that more than half of Guatemala's population is Indian? What, in particular, does this imply for the success of opposition and revolutionary movements? (Torres Rivas, 1971a, 1971b, 1980, 1981; Martínez Peláez, 1973, 1975; Figueroa Ibarra, 1974, 1976; Cambranes, 1975; Flores Alvarado, 1971, 1973; Ciro Cardoso, 1969; Mejía, 1970; Guzmán Bockler, 1975; Guzmán Bockler and Herbert, 1974; Guzmán Bockler et al., 1971).

All of these questions are of importance to the reconstruction of Guatemalan social history and to the understanding of possible emergent trends for the future. But they also are of theoretical and methodological importance, although they are not explicitly framed as such. Linked to their answers are key issues in the larger paradigmatic debate, and that debate will be advanced by a better understanding of social change and development in concrete empirical and historical settings. The purpose here is to explore the larger issues in the context of Guatemala, evaluate critically the contending theoretical frameworks—modernization, dependency, and mode of production, and contribute to and argue for the elaboration of one, articulation of modes of production.

The Modernization Paradigm

The modernization paradigm draws on various schools of thought: nineteenth-century evolutionists (such as Comte, Spencer, and Durkheim), twentieth-century neoevolutionists (such as Sahlins and Service, 1960), and modern structural-functionalists (such as Parsons, 1951, 1964, 1966, 1971; Smelser, 1964; Hoselitz, 1960; Rostow, 1960; and Moore, 1963), a subcategory of neoevolutionists.

Like the nineteenth-century evolutionists, the modernizationists conceive of change as a unilinear and continuous progression along continua with fixed endpoints: folk and secular, gemeinschaft and gesellschaft, traditional and modern. Unlike the nineteenth-century evolutionists, however, they acknowledge that social evolution (defined as greater specialization, differentiation, and adaptation—(Parsons, 1951, 1964, 1966, 1971; Semlser, 1964; Moore, 1963) can occur not only within societies but in the development of social systems overall. Thus, primitive or traditional societies can develop from contacts with modern, developed social systems as well as from their own internal evolutionary change. While some theorists allow only for contacts characterized as "diffusion" (Parsons, for example) and others include domination and conquest (Sahlins and Service, 1960), the direction of change is always hypothesized as the same: more developed, more modern, more adaptive. Resistance to change is assumed to be inevitable, especially on the part of nonelites, because of lack of information, traditional values, and psychological fear of anything new, but resistance always eventually gives way to acceptance, since only acceptance ensures survival.

The modernization model includes both evolutionary notions of change from one endpoint to another and the structural-functionalist notion that societies tend toward states of equilibrium to which interdependent and interrelated parts contribute after changing from one "ideal type" to another. Within each type (i.e., traditional, modern), cohesion among individuals and institutions is guaranteed by consensus on basic core values, which not only give the system its "glue" but define its basic character. Feudalism, capitalism, and socialism, in this view, are distinguished not by their structures of production and reproduction but by their dominant economic values. The Panajacheleños studied by Tax (1953) are considered "penny capitalists" because of their commercially oriented attitudes and behavior. Social classes, such as Indian peasants and ladino intermediaries (i.e., non-Indian) are likewise defined attitudinally and interactionally (how an individual thinks of himself or herself and how he or she is treated) rather than structurally (Tumin, 1945, 1949, 1952).

Within this framework, the problem of modernization is the problem of smooth and orderly change from one set of core values to another. Public policy must see that change proceeds rapidly enough for adaptation to new environments but not so rapidly as to seriously dislocate the interdependent parts from each other. It must promote changes that will favor adaptation to new realities and social order: physical integration of regions through transportation and markets and social integration through a common language and value system.

Modernism, then, is rational and functional for survival, and social integration of regions and groups is necessary for the modernization of nations. As Adams argues,

The process of nation-making requires the substitution of the direct exercise of power over all individuals for the indirect exercise of power through corporate segments of individuals. The national power center must be able to communicate directly with, and exercise control direct-ly over, the population. To do this, it is necessary to contain local and provincial power nuclei that can compete for control [1967: 469].

Toward this end, the haciendas and Indian towns *(reducciones)* in Central America created under Spanish colonialism were the first step. For several centuries, however, physical isolation of regions and towns from the centers of power and dominant culture made their control precarious and their existence a potential threat to national cohesion. Only with improved transportation and communication as a result of the liberal reforms of the late nineteenth century and the growing use of Indian labor directly on the plantations was national culture possible (Adams, 1967).

Parallel to the process of administrative and political units is the need to integrate individuals and social groups, since heterogeneity of cultures and languages, like regional isolation, is seen as an obstacle to national survival and a threat to social cohesion. But such integra-tion has been problematic in countries like Guatemala, where, as many anthropologists have observed, cultural differences between Indian and non-Indian are long-standing, in spite of numerous arenas of interaction. While the traditional modernizationist view might argue that contact between the cultural groups is simply not consis-tent or even enough, others have argued that heterogeneity might actually be functional and a guarantor of stability.

Application to Guatemala

The assumption that modern societies inevitably strive for and need social integration and cultural homogenity to survive presents certain problems in the study of a multiethnic, multicultural society of long duration such as Guatemala. Why, if Indians (of various ethnic nationalities) and non-Indians interact in certain spheres, such as towns and markets, do they maintain separate languages, behaviors, and world views? The Panajacheleños studied by Tax, for example, buy and sell goods in impersonal markets and calculate their worth without reference to sentiment or kinship ties. In a tradition dating to before the conquest, they are "practical, matter of fact, mundane and secular-mined" traders who "move around, go places on business and come back, or move to another town for a few years, or sometimes for the rest of their lives."

Yet, in noneconomic matters, the Indians from Panajachel retain a classic primitive folk world view.

> clouded with animism [in which] sun and earth, river and hill, are anthropomorphized; animals talk; plants have emotions; [and] it is possible for a hoe to work alone; such things as fire and maize are capable of direct, punitive action. . . . Animals, plants, humans alike change their natures with the phases of the moon [1941: 38].

Tax and Redfield suggest an amendment to the structural-functionalist assumption of universal adoption of modern values on contact with modern societies: that as long as certain types of values (i.e., economic value) are compatible with modern market behavior, others, such as primitive world views, can and may coexist simultaneously unless direct attack is made on them (Tax, 1941).

Other anthropologists who have studied Guatemalan village life argue that sharp distinctions between indigenous and nonindigenous behavior and attitudes may actually be necessary for the maintenance of social order. Indians are said to accept dominant values even though they do not benefit from them or are victims of a double standard in their application. Gillin (1948) argues that the Indian "chooses to accept his condition as a result of a reciprocal, symmetrical exchange for rewards of status or psychological security." As a result, Indians attribute misfortune to an angry god rather than to ladinos. Tumin argues that

> the forces of custom and traditionalism ('that's the custom;' 'that's the way things are;') tend to promote a general unawareness of and indifference, on the part of the exploited and deprecated groups, to these invidious aspects of the total situation. And, where awareness is present, these forces tend to reduce the quotient of sensitivity present in the awareness and thereby recommend to the Indian the passive acceptance of the status quo [1949:24].

and that

> in the situation described, there are no discernible stresses and strains pushing toward rapid or basic social change. Additionally, in those areas where cooperation or co-participation is indispensable to the

continuity of the social order, the caste arrangement is sufficiently flex-ible to permit clearly defined, hierarchically structured cooperation which for a variety of reasons, is mutually acceptable to both groups [1949: 25].

But the degree of stress and strain—or, more straightforwardly, underlying conflict—is a matter of dispute. Siegal, writing roughly in the same period (1941), locates Indian-ladino relations historically (something the structural-functionalists rarely ever do), and argues that apparent acceptance of an "invidious" system actually incor-porates realistic resistance to it:

Outward manifestations of hostility are relatively scarce partly because of the quick and harsh penalties imposed . . . on rebellious native groups. Instead, Indian hostility takes the form of a widespread, if passive, re-sistance to 'white ways' and a stubborn retention of native beliefs and practices. This resistance discloses itself variously: natives try to avoid public service; they apply public pressure against members who work for whites, associate with whites, or have sexual relations with whites; they perform religious rites and ceremonies as a closed group, completely excluding white participation (assuming that the latter desired to participate, which is hardly likely); they seek ways to keep their children from 'white schools'; they reject the national language, Spanish, as the chief medium of communication, always using the native dialect themselves; they wear native costumes clearly different from the dress worn by whites [Siegal, 1941:429].

Neopluralists such as Colby and van den Berghe, on the other hand, argue that functionalists are wrong, from the beginning, to assume that multiethnic, multicultural societies constitute single integrated systems that strive toward equilibrium. Rather, they posit, both inte-gration and separate parallel culture. Institutions may coexist with certain political or economic ties but retain autonomy to the extent that they are divided into socially and, in most cases, culturally distinct groups with a compartmentalized institutional structure of duplicatory (as distinguished from functionally differentiated) sec-tors (van den Berghe and Primov, 1977; Colby and van den Berghe, 1969; Boeke, 1953).

In other words, a plural society is composed of

a set of interacting groups which remain distinct by virture of not shar-ing all their institutions, and which constitute a single society by virture of sharing some crucial ones [Colby and van den Berghe, 1969:20].

Each cultural or ethnic group may have its own set of kinship institutions, religious and cosmological systems, voluntary association, child-rearing practices, and status-ranking criteria but interact together in key areas of the polity and economy, and only at these linkage points are they subject to common social and economic forces. Otherwise, they lack a common history and culture.

The coexistence of plural systems cannot be assumed, they argue, to be based on a lack of conflict or competition for hegemony:

> Colonial or plural societies were held together, not by consensus on basic values, as Parsonian functionalists had been claiming; or by the will of the people, as the amiable optimists of the Enlightenment had preached; or through the countervailing checks and balances of competing interest groups, as the liberal political scientists in the Tocquevillian tradition had advanced; but through the political and economic domination of one ethnic group over the others, a domination usually originating in conquest. Subject groups could continue to live semi-autonomously side by side and preserve separate sets of religious, family and other institutions, but under the overarching political and economic control of the conquerors [van de Berghe and Primov, 1977:6].

Since the divisions in plural societies are almost always religious and/or ethnic-racial, and since disparities in wealth and power usually coincide with ethnic-racial groupings, conflict generated by an attempt by dominant groups to impose their values on weaker ones is almost inherent. Certain institutions, such as godparenthood, and certain conditions, such as material interdependence, may mitigate the tendency toward conflict, but intergroup conflict will grow with the degree of ethnic difference and the degree to which rankings within the groups are loose.

Neopluralists challenge both the assumptions of diffusion and inherent acceptance of hierarchy. At the same time, however, they share with the structural-functionalists a major preoccupation with forms of culture, collective thinking, and daily interaction rather than the origins and development of the economic, political, and social structures that frame them.

Critique

The modernization model has a number of significant weaknesses—methodological, empirical, and political—not all of which need to be repeated here (Bodenheimer, 1970a; Frank, 1967; Cockcroft et al.,

1972; Bonilla and Girling, 1973; Foster-Carter, 1973, 1976; Hoogvelt, 1980; D. Johnson, 1973; J. Taylor, 1979). Its most fundamental problems relate to an overly linear, teleological, and ahistorical conception of change. The endpoints of the continuum of societal change are posited as fixed, a priori, and the characteristics ascribed to each are static and often idealized. Traditional societies, for example, are denied any significant history of change or evolution prior to their contact with modern ones. Modernism aspires to be a description of functional prerequisites for development that is independent of a particular economic system (capitalism or socialism) but in fact is a specific description of developed capitalism in Western cultures in this particular historical period. Even more, however, it is a description that is part empirical fact and part idealization in accord with the dominant ideology. Ascriptive status and personal relationships actually play an important role in individual opportunity, especially at the highest levels which might be assumed to be the most modern, and formal differentiation of functions (between private business, the executive branch and the military) is often more illusion than reality (see Frank, 1972).

Furthemore, the methodology of equating the *process* of change with movement between these two fixed points is highly problematic. Now developed societies did not necessarily pass along the continuum projected (the United States, for example was never a "traditional" society) and even if they had, the possibilities for repeating the transition cannot help but be influenced by a different international context (Frank, 1967, 1969, 1972; Bodeheimer, 1970a, 1970b). Nations like individuals, are not necessarily discrete autonomous units; they are members of social groups which interact in systems where some units have more power than others. Contact between dominant and subordinate nations in the modern period may actually result in the retardation of some aspects of change in the latter and the continued development of the former may actually depend on the retardation of progress of the less developed (the "development of underdevelopment," to use Frank's now-famous term—Frank, 1967; J. Taylor, 1979).

A model of development must take into account the possibility that contact between more and less developed societies does not necessarily lead toward linear change along the modernization continuum. In the absence of a more dialectical conception, the model inevitably favors the status quo distribution of power and wealth and dismisses as negative, disruptive and irrational, a priori, any challenges to developed country interests, even though such challenges may be necessary for the development of less developed societies.

Dependency and the Internal Racial Colony Thesis

The most controversial and polemical application of the dependency perspective to the interpretation of Guatemalan society was developed in the late 1960s by French anthropologist Jean-Loup Herbert and Guatemalan sociologist Carlos Guzmán Bockler (1970). Taking their cues from anticolonialist writers such as Franz Fanon (1963) and Albert Memmi (1967), Guzmán Bockler and Herbert argued that the fundamental contradiction in Guatemalan society was racism and the fundamental problem in all previous historical studies, be they dualist, pluralist, or evolutionary Marxist, was racial bias in favor of non-Indians.

Preconquest culture is pictured in previous studies as passive, stagnant, or degenerating and devoid of history, while postconquest society is characterized as dynamic, developmental, and civilized. Preconquest culture is variously characterized by scholars and chroniclers as "savage," "uncivilized," "pagan," "politheist," or "infidel," while postconquest society is characterized as having brought peace and forged a nation (Guzmán Bockler and Herbert, 1970:131-132).

Such characterizations only serve to reinforce racist justifications of the conquest and its brutal subordination of indigenous people and are, furthermore, historically incorrect. Rather than being passive and stagnant, or declining and degenerating, preconquest society was actually in transition from one stage to another (from partriarchal clans to city-state) when the conquest intervened to freeze its development for over 400 years (1970:5-32).

Other reconstructions (Carmak, 1973; Martínez Peláez, 1973) support the view of preconquest society in transition. Private property, in cacao and fruit farming, for example, and slavery, for use in transportation, agriculture, domestic production and ritual sacrifices, were already in existence. Because of the wars of conquest, in which larger nations consolidated their control over smaller ones, the role of calpulis, or collective kinship and production units, was being transformed. Their power was being challenged by a new class of landowners, the warrior nobility, and their duties had already shifted from primary emphasis on traditional clan activities to supervision of war-related production on state lands and the distribution and supervision of production on individual plots (Guzmán Bockler and Herbert, 1970:11-17). The beginnings of class differentiation and the dominance of warriors over others also may have been accompanied by changes in kinship and family ties toward greater patrilineality and patrilocality, although, according to the Spanish priest Las Casas, polygamy, promiscuity, and adultery were common at the time of the conquest and were not severely punished.

Preconquest technology was most developed, not surprisingly, in areas related to warfare (Guzmán Bockler and Herbert, 1970:11-12), and metal smelting was widely used in weapon-making and artisan activities but minimally in the production of agricultural tools. The sophisticated irrigation system in use was based on a profound knowledge of meterology and astronomy, but overall technological development in preconquest society was uneven. In commerce, agriculture, and construction, the Mayans never used their domesticated animals, nor did they apply the principle of the wheel (with which they were acquainted) to replace or extend human energy.

Pre- and Postconquest Modes of Production

Guzmán Bockler and Herbert argue that the characterization of preconquest society as degenerating derives from an overemphasis on intellectual, academic, and artistic criteria at the expense of material and technological ones. This "idealism and utopianism" results from a comparison of the architectural and artistic grandeur of Mayan culture at its height (during the Tikal period) with a more modest state of the arts at the time of the conquest. Although the authors do not build on this criticism by offering an explicit alternative, they clearly favor greater emphasis on material (i.e., technological and social) developments in the definition of the character of preconquest society.

When it comes to the definition of postconquest society, however, Guzmán Bockler and Herbert single out two dimensions over all others: its incorporation into world trade (changes in the sphere of circulation) and racism (changes in the dominant ideology and discriminatory practices). These changes produced, in their view, a new mode of production, a colonial capitalist mode, in which two poles, inherently linked to each other—metropolis/colonizer and peripheral/colonized—appeared. Racial ideology (supporting the dominance of non-Indians) and subordination to the world market, institutionalized as minifundia-latifundia, have sustained the poles, according to the authors, from the conquest to the present.

In Guzmán Bockler and Herbert's conception of the colonial mode of production, surplus extraction and periodic crises are externally determined, but these alone are not sufficient to generate united internal opposition. Rather, such opposition is mediated by the ideology of racism. Nonelite ladinos suffer from improverishment, as do Indians, but they respond, according to Guzmán Bockler and Herbert (1971), by waiting to recover their losses at the expense of Indians when an upswing occurs. Non-Indians (ladinos) have little capacity to organize because they lack a "positive collective identify" and a material base to support cooperation among themselves. Their existence is defined by isolation, atomization, alienation, and an individualistic, egoistic, "get it while you can" spirit. Ladinos have no other identity, in Guzmán Bockler and Herbert's view, than imitation of that which is foreign and the rejection of that which is "truly national"—that is, Indian (Guzmán Bockler et al., 1971; Guzmán Bockler and Herbert, 1974; Guzmán Bockler, 1975).

Indians, on the other hand, have "zones of refuge" (Aguirre Beltrán's term [Guzmán Bockler et al., 1971] as a material base from which to reinforce group identity (which persists even then they migrate as individuals) and the experience of discrimination to bind them together. Indians will lead the struggle for national liberation, the authors argue, because only Indians have the capacity to reclaim a national identity. Furthermore, this national identity can only be Indian, since only Indian culture recovers values that are "authentically Guatemalan." Mestizo culture can never be a superior synthesis of Spanish and indigenous culture, as many Mexican intellectuals argue, because forced confrontation between a superior (Indian) culture and an inferior (Spanish) one can never yield a more desirable result (Guzmán Bockler and Herbert, 1974:140-142).

Guzmán Bockler and Herbert do not clarify what the role of sympathetic ladinos might be in this recovery of national identity. They seem to imply that ladinos can unite with Indians if they agree to "renounce their privileges" and embrace Indian culture. The authors provide little reason for ladinos to do so, however (since they dismiss common material conditions as unifying factors), other than a desire to escape the alienation associated with having no identity. The role of the ladino as well as the end result of national liberation is therefore unclear. Herbert comments enigmatically:

Guatemala will be mestizo, ladino, integrated, Latin or Indian, we have no way of knowing. The sociologist cannot move ahead of the social dialectic; rather, he must express it, always with some lag. . . . The only belief he should have is that the dialectic is open; a society has not one possible path but many none pre-determined [Guzmán Bockler and Herbert, 1974:164].

Classes and the Racial Internal Colony

Guzmán Bockler and Herbert argue that the classes created by the conquest, Indian/colonized and non-Indian/ colonizer, are the same ones that define Guatemalan society today. The underlying criterion for their delineation is the relationship to colonialism—that is, whether they share in the privileges and spoils of the colonizers or whether they are denied the privileges of the colonizers and forced to supply the spoils. Admittedly, non-criollo, non-Indian ladinos are in a somewhat contradictory class position according to this schema because they are both exploited (subject to surplus extraction) by higher status ladinos and exploit (extract surplus from) the Indians. But racism, according to the authors, prevents this exploitation from defining their class position.

The bottom line of Guzmán Bockler and Herbert's definition is not relations of production (ownership-nonownership, command and control of labor), since if it were the majority of ladinos who are landless would occupy the same position as the majority of Indians and landed ladinos and landed Indians would both be exploiters. Rather, it is membership in the sociohistorical categories "Indian" and "ladino."

Guzmán Bockler and Herbert assert that their definition is not racial (i.e., genetic) but relational (created by history). Were Indians to recover their land and cultural identify and ladinos to give up their position as colonizers (the latter is a precondition for the former), there would be no more Indians and ladinos (Guzmán Bockler and Herbert, 1974).

Until that happens, however, no amount of change in outward appearance, geographical mobility, laws, educational achievement, accumulation of wealth, or intermarriage can erase or minimize racial discrimination. At every level of the social hierarchy, marginalization takes place. As much as Indians might want to lose their identity, they cannot choose to do so. They continue to be identified as and treated like colonialized peoples. Because of this experience, Guzmán Bockler and Herbert expect that the newly emergent bourgeoisie that has accumulated wealth in commerce and land since the 1930s will take a leading role in any Indian revolution, identifying with the cultural values of the Indian masses rather than those of the ladino elite (Guzmán Bockler et al., 1971).

Critique

The most serious methodological problem in Guzmán Bockler and Herbert's approach is its assertion that one part of a dynamic whole (the internal colony) can remain frozen and unchanged in essence for over 400 years and that, at the same time, it can be unfrozen and put into motion along the same path once national liberation is achieved.

The model gives little explanation of why Indians would suddenly mobilize to recover their identity at a particular point in history, unless it is the result of awareness of decolonization trends elsewhere in the world. The real cause of change in the model is the nonmaterial desire to resist alienation by recovering or strengthening collective identity. Psychology also explains the excessive violence of the Spanish conquest: the Spanish had been humiliated by over 700 years of Moorish occupation and had acquired a racial hatred which they took out on Latin America's indigenous population (Guzmán Bockler and Herbert, 1970). Material factors (such as loss of land or economic insecurity) may support and encourage national liberation movements, but they are not fundamentally determinant, for if they were, poor ladinos and poor Indians would join in common cause.

Ironically, the criticism of utopianism and idealism applies not only to previous scholars of pre- and postconquest Guatemalan society but to Guzmán Bockler and Herbert themselves. They attempt to be dynamic in their treatment of preconquest society, relational in their definition of Indian and ladino (arguing that it is impossible to imagine the dominance of one without the subordination of the other), and dialectical in their conception of the internal colony (as part of the same system as the colony, not parallel to it).

But their efforts to provide an alternative to structural-functionalist modernization theory flounders on some of the same shoals. The racial internal colony is in many ways the flip side of modernization theory. Preconquest indigenous societies are dynamic, but postconquest internal colonies—and therefore Indian-ladino relations—are not. Indians have the capacity to recover a positive national identify, but ladinos have no identity at all to recover, let alone a positive one. Ladinos can identify with the recovery of Indian values if they give up being ladinos, but Indians can never become ladinos (even when they intermarry or abandon their culture by choice or by force) because racist ideology and institutions will continue to treat them as Indians. And land and racial categories tend to be correlated—but when they are not, ideological and culture factors predominate over material ones.

Dependency and the Nonracial Interpretation of Internal Colonialism

It is possible to remedy the static character of the Guzmán Bockler and Herbert version of the dependency thesis without abandoning the framework altogether, but to do so requires a new conception of mode of production, social classes, and Indian-ladino relations since the late nineteenth century.

The colonial and neocolonial (or "dependent capitalist") periods of Guatemalan development can be conceived as two distinct modes of production with their own characteristic social classes as well as the forms of integration into the world market which are their determinants. Within the latter mode, stages of development can be delineated ("competitive-industrial," "monopolistic-technical-financial," etc.) that correspond to stages in the development of the external system on which the society is dependent. Classes and Indian-ladino relations vary not only according to the two modes of production but somewhat according to the stages of development of the dependent capitalist mode.

Guatemalan sociologist Torres Rivas, for example, argues in a 1971 essay that Guzmán Bockler and Herbert are correct to argue that colonialism instituted social classes based on racial and ethnic origin in Guatemala (i.e., Indian/colonized and criollo/colonizer), but they are incorrect to insist that such classes persist even after independence is granted and the mode of production changes to dependent capitalist with the expansion of coffee production for export.

Once the mode of production became dependent capitalist, Torres Rivas asserts, the basis for the determination of classes was no longer race or national origin but the relationship to the extraction of the surplus.

For the first time, in this period, a single nation was forged and classes were differentiated to a greater degree than any time after the conquest. Indians divided into rich, middle, and poor peasants. Some of them became seasonal or permanent wage laborers, and ladinos separated into those who owned property or possessed a skill, a subsistence plot, or only their unskilled labor power: some of them resided in rural and others in urban areas (Torres Rivas, 1971).

Cutting across social classes, a colonial element of discrimination and segregation, based on race or ethnicity, throughout the liberal period (and continues to exist to the present day), but the dividing line, Torres Rivas and others have argued, is not color, since physical appearance between Indians and the majority of ladinos differs little. Rather, discriminatory and segregationist practices are based on visible signs of cultural origin, behavior, kinship, or self-identification, even though such practices may be rationalized on the basis of racially argued explanations and Indians may think of themselves as racially distinct from ladinos and other indigenous ethnic groups.

Under colonialism, clear distinctions between native inhabitants and conquerors made a racially and nationally determined class structure possible, but the mixture of races, ethnicities, and national origins through intermarriage, legally sanctioned or not, made impossible the maintenance of a rigidly defined class structure based on color. The qualitative transformation in the basis of the class structure reflects the qualitative transformation in, not the continuation of, the colonial mode of production.

Likewise, an internal colonial condition of indigenous peoples cannot be conceived of, according to this view, until a single nation is formed, and this did not occur with the conquest but with the integration of the territory into a common unit through the extension of a national market into remote rural areas (beginning with the liberal reforms—Torres Rivas, 1971a).

Internal colonies should not be racially or ethnically but spatially or geographically defined units or groups from which surplus is extracted for the metropolis—that is, units which suffer the "development of underdevelopment" when they interact with more developed units. Such units may coincide with racial or ethnic differences, such as in the case of the Western highlands of Guatemala, where the majority of the Indian population is concentrated, but the basis of the determination of units is a common relation to a center which extracts surplus, not to an ethnic group, and the disadvantageous relationship that this surplus extraction represents to the statellite or peripheral unit can be overcome only by common cause with others who suffer a similar fate (poor ladinos in the Eastern region, for example) in the pursuit of socialism, not just national or national minority liberation (Torres Rivas, 1971a).

Dependent Capitalism and
Indian-Ladino Relations

From Guzmán Bockler and Herbert's colonial mode of production point of view, legal changes in the status of Indians and Indian communities after independence from Spain are largely symbolic—that is, changes in form rather than substance. For Torres Rivas and other Marxists, on the other hand, these changes are crucial, in that they change the context for discrimination and exploitation and create new possibilities for overcoming them by creating common conditions for the majority of Indians and poor ladinos. Changes in the legal structure, to the extent that they reflect and facilitate changes already occurring in economic and political structures, create new social and institutional arrangements that not only make possible the development of capitalism but pressure for a socialist alternative.

Even though liberal reforms in Guatemala included the reintroduction of various forms of "unfree" labor, and even though these unfree forms were almost exclusively applied to the recruitment of Indian labor, the abolition of differnt legal statuses for Indian and ladino meant that racial and ethnic criteria had to be couched in theoretically more general social and economic terms (indebtedness, vagrancy, etc.). Once Indian community lands were subject to individual title and sale on the market like any other and even disguised forms of labor were outlawed by the 1944 revolution, Indian and ladino workers occupied the same status with respect to the law and could, if they so desired, band together in common complaints.

While Indian and ladino labor continued to be separated on capitalist plantations by deliberate policies of landowners who benefited from such separations, and while linguistic and cultural differences often made communication and perception of common interests difficult, the recuitment of labor on the basis of individual rather than village contracts, mediated by a noble hierarchy, was an important step in the breakdown of colonial society and the development of capitalism.

The more rationalized and capitalist the work setting, the greater the possibility for common cause between Indians and non-Indians. On foreign enclave plantations, for example, banana companies such as United Fruit prohibited the maintenance of subsistence plots by recently proletarianized peasants, making their separation from the latifundia-minifundia complex of social relations more complete. Plantation bosses, like traditional landowners, attempted to maintain an ideology of racism by laying down special rules of behavior for Indian and black workers (such as removing hats when speaking to "white" people and entering through back doors of residences), but workers on these plantations (some of them recently immigrated Indians) challenged such rules (and included them in their strike demands) as early as 1921 (Immerman, 1982:74-75).

The changes that Indian villages underwent at the same time were anything but symbolic. Once landownership was individualized, titles could be lost through indebtedness or outright robbery to local ladinos and wealthy Indians. A small Indian bourgeoisie with private wealth in land emerged for the first time, and local governmental positions that had been almost exclusively in the hands of Indians passed to resident ladino middlemen (Colby and van den Berghe, 1969; Guzmán Bockler et al., 1971).

Furthermore, despite the fact that the 1944-1954 revolution was predominantly led and supported by urban ladinos, at least in the beginning, it initiated a program of land distribution to small capitalist farmers that, had it been allowed to prevail, would have transformed the conditions of Indian and ladino peasants into that of small capitalist farmers, breaking down the Indian communal village-ladino tenant farmer distinction.

In the most recent period of capitalist expansion, the changes are even more dramatic. Whole villages are forced to migrate every year where only certain categories of individuals (young men, widows, etc.) or the whole village in certain types of years (drought, depression, etc.) migrated before (Torres Rivas, 1980, 1981; Chinchilla, 1980). The penetration of foreign missionaries into Indian villages since the 1954 coup has challenged the autonomy of traditional Catholic Indian practices on the one hand, and brought a new social concern to religion on the other (Chinchilla and Jamail, 1982). The cooperatives and modest development programs advocated by the religious workers have drawn violent reactions from large landowners whose docile, cheap, and abundant labor supply is thus interfered with. The combination of attacks on the improvement efforts of Indian communities and the indiscriminate repression of Indian and non-Indian labor on the plantations has created, (as a consequence of capitalism,) non-symbolic changes in Indian-ladino relations even deeper than those that would have prevailed had the 1944-1954 revolution prevailed.

Critique

The dependent capitalist reformulation of the internal colonialism thesis is an advance, in that it makes the convergence of ethnic/racial groupings and units of surplus extraction an empirical question rather than an a priori assumption (and thus introduces the possibility that the relation between the two can change over time). Nevertheless, it is weak theoretically because it never clarifies the formal relationship between the two as sources of conflict: class exploitation and other forms of oppression (such as ethnic and racial). Stavenhagen recognizes this problem in commenting that some of the concepts he uses are ambiguous and are defined more in commonsense than formal theoretical terms (1970), but this does little to advance a theory of social change. Torres Rivas, likewise, does little to clarify the issue despite this comment:

> It is useful to use both concepts to analyze the social structure: colonial or internal colonial structure and class structure: this allows for the study and analysis of relations between sectors, regions, or ethnic-cultural groups in the economic order and for learning about the variety of diverse relations the population has with the means of production and distribution in the productive process overall. The concept of structure of internal colonialism allows for the enrichment and completion of the class analysis [1971a:53].

Granted that class analysis is incomplete and inadequate without an analysis of ethnic and other similar divisions, the central question is still in what kinds of categories should other relationships be analyzed and to what extent are these categories equivalent to, overlapping with, or different from the Marxist conception of social class?

If both exploitation and oppression are equated, on the basis that both constitute forms of surplus extraction, and no distinction is made as to the quality (or form) in which the surplus is extracted and re-production of the group is achieved, (i.e., if slavery is seen just as a disguised form of wage labor—Bodenheimer, 1974), both become social classes and the emphasis, theoretically and strategically, is placed on the amount rather than the kind of surplus extracted. This leads to formulations such as those put forth by advocates of the guerrilla foco strategy of the 1960s (Debray, 1975) and some feminists in the developed capitalist countries (Bennholdt-Thomsen, 1977; von Werhoff, 1981) that the more absolutely oppressed and materially impoverished any social group, the more revolutionary it is likely to be.

While this in itself may be true for given revolutionary situations, the formulation of classical Marxism was much more specific—in other words, that in a revolutionary struggle that is not only anti-capitalist but pro-socialist, only the sectors in which surplus is extract-ed in the form of surplus value is the conflict an inherent contradiction objectively resolvable only by socialism. This theoretical distinction between surplus in general and surplus value in particular is the basis for the central political role assigned to the urban and rural pro-letariats (i.e., those who have only their labor power to sell and whose reproduction depends on the circulation of their wages on the capitalist market). At any one point in time groups other than the proletariat may be more active, more mobilized, and more openly revolutionary in their demands, given the more absolute level of their poverty or the immediateness of repression directed against them. But this empiri-cal observation in no way contradicts the classical formulation that the linchpin of capital accumulation and reproduction occurs in the most proletarianized sector, no matter how small in absolute size; and thus, given adequate leadership and organization, it is potentially the most consistently anticapitalist and pro-socialist.[1]

Of course, the most fundamental characteristic of Third World social formations is the heterogeneity of their relations of production. But precisely because of this heterogeneity, the theoretical categories must be clear and capable of describing and explaining the origins and historical development (not just the correlates) of changes. As John Taylor comments in an evaluation of the work of Frank:

> The concept of economic surplus . . . precludes any rigorous analysis
> of the structure, reproduction and development of modes of produc-
> tion; hence it cannot provide an adequate basis for analyzing either the

development of capitalist penetration of non-capitalist modes or the existence of different forms of this penetration [1979:85].

Finally, even if the theoretical-methodological problems were somehow overcome, the empirical question remains: To what degree does surplus transfer actually occur from regions and zones (including those with high concentrations of indigenous population), and to what extent is this transfer associated with "underdevelopment"? While more scholars have repeated Frank's formulation than studied it, one researcher who did test it with regard to the Indian highland region of Guatemala concludes that

> While Guatemala developed very little during the successive stages of its export crop 'dependency,' it underdeveloped only when capitalistic agriculture came to dominate its economy and made the mass of its population dependent on wage labor. . . And before capitalism could develop, the old-metropole-satellite urban structure had to be destroyed in the western region and be replaced by a competitive form of commerce that would create the wage-dependent proletariat. Hence, I argue further, contrary to various dependency arguments that by preventing the creation of a proletariat, the earlier administrative commercial system—that is the metropole-satellite structure—hindered rather than caused dependency [Smith, 1978:602].

Articulation of Modes of Production

The missing elements in the evolutionary stagist conception of modes of production—a dialectical conception of interactions between modes, forces, and relations of production in the economic base, levels of the mode of production (economic, political, ideological), and between cycles of production and reproduction—are in fact necessary elements for the description and explanation of change in Third World social formations.

The evolutionary Marxists are correct to posit an overall evolutionary direction to the development of societies from simple and undifferentiated to more complex and differentiated. But the pattern of development is not without temporary regressions and qualitative breaks, and the direction is generally linear but not unlinear. Not every society passes through feudalism, nor does it experience capitalism in the same way, given its variety of origins (external as well as internal), stages, and interactions with preexisting forms.

It is true that there is a limited number of known societal types with more or less identifiable sets of fixed basic laws. Capitalism, for example, requires a free market in land, labor, and capital and the reproduction of its means of production and labor force primarily through the circulation of wages for goods and services on the market.

But the pace and evenness of change and development where capitalism is dominant will vary greatly according to the character of other modes with which it interacts, and the nature of the contradictions engendered and the changes to which they give birth will differ as well.

Third World societies, though different from each other in many respects, share certain general patterns of articulation occasioned by their contact with imperialism and certain unresolved contradictions or dislocations. Taylor observes that

> the existence of these dislocations and the effects that imperialist penetration has upon them in trying, as it were to adapt them to the political and ideological reproductive requirement of a capitalist mode of production, can produce—in specific conjunctures in the transition—the possibility for the emergence of the preconditions of a different mode of production. Thus, there can be no such thing as a 'linear succession' from dominance by a non-capitalist to dominance by a capitalist mode of production. Imperialist penetration, having as its object to create the preconditions for a transition to a specific form of capitalist production, can produce . . . the preconditions for the possibility of a socialist mode of production [1979:103].

As a result of imperialism, it became more and more common for externally imposed capitalism (in its various stages of development—merchant, industrial, and monopoly) to appropriate other modes of production and/or divisions of labor, dominant classes, or religious beliefs to facilitate or guarantee its dominance and reproduction. The first form of capital usually to penetrate Third World social formations, merchant capital, often remains dominant for long periods of time, drawing on precapitalist forms whose existence limits its further penetration into the agricultural sector.

Because the nature of the relationship between the old and new dominant modes depends on the character of both, and on relationships to other modes that may be present, there is no automatic or guaranteed period of irresolvable contradiction initiated on their contact (as the evolutionary Marxist view would sustain). Rather, there may be long transitional periods in which old modes or parts of them are actually reinforced or recreated. The long-term tendency is still hypothesized as dissolution or diminuition of an old dominant mode in favor of the new one, but in Third World social formations, transition periods are long and the norm rather than the exception.

Thus, while the overall direction of change is toward higher levels of development, defined by greater productive capacity and more complex, interdependent divisions of labor, the actual path of change is not linear but dialectical and interactive. Conflict is an ever-present part of the cycle of reproduction of the existing system as well as the reason for the emergence of its replacement. Mediating structures (education, religion, mass communication, and institutions such as godparenthood) can channel, displace, or mask conflicts, but they do not annul them. Part of the reproduction of the existing sytem, in fact, may be the reproduction of conflicts in ever more antagonistic forms. From the perspective of the historical materialist model,

> the basic movement of human history is . . . the dialectical development of the forces and relations of production. Marx did not see this movement as an even, progressive, and harmonious development of the division of labor, but as uneven, periodized, qualitative change, marked by revolutionary transition from one epoch of production to another. The new system of production emerges historically from the old, but not as the synthetic resolution of its contradictions. The dialectic between forces and relations of production in the new mode of production differs in its terms from that of the preceding epoch of production. To understand history is therefore to be able to define these historically specific terms [O'Laughlin, 1975:350].

Change originates not only in the conflict among modes of production and between production and reproduction of the dominant mode but in dislocations among different levels (economic, political, and ideological) of a single mode.

The overall determinant of the parameters of change is economic, but within the degrees of freedom allowed, especially at particular transitional conjunctures, political and ideological structures may be independent sources of conflict and make independent contributions to change. And within the economic base itself, the relationship between the two components should be conceived as dialectical, neither substituting the class and class struggle component for the technological (as the evolutionary Marxist have traditionally done), nor attributing unlimited powers of change and transformation (as the Maoists and some structuralist Marxists have idealistically done).

O'Laughlin seems to capture Marx's original conception when she says,

> The dialectical relationship between forces and relations of production is the key to the uneven, periodized and non-teleological process of human evolution. No understanding of social change can be analytically separated from technological change, for in acting on the external world and changing it, people at the same time change their own nature [1975:354-355].

She continues:

> The base . . . is not self-reproducing; it only can be realized within a social totality. In that sense every mode of production describes not only a base but corresponding forms of superstructure [1975:358].

Where more than one mode of production is present in a concrete society or social formation, the discrepancies among forms of labor recruitment and economic organization, institutions of power, and forms of ideology and culture can be great. Precapitalist, prefeudal world views may govern the thought processes of seasonal indigenous workers who are working on modernized cotton plantations whose production is supported by the state and internal financial institutions. Although the workers are recruited individually, the process of individualization of human labor on the capitalist market may be retarded by the extremely uneven development of the relations of production, level of technology, and the market. Collective and communal social institutions and cultural practices may persist, even among plantation workers (especially seasonal ones) and may even be essential to their survival and reproduction. At the same time that these institutions and beliefs may facilitate their use to the capitalist for certain periods of time (more individualized and less cooperative workers might die in greater numbers, for example from the harshness of the conditions), they can also generate a capacity to organize resistance (especially clandestinely) that is difficult to stamp out, once other methods or ideologies are fused. The results of the articulation of socialist and precapitalist communal ideologies, tactics, and methods of organization are nothing but explosive in a country like Guatemala.

Thus, what makes the development of capitalism in Third World social formations particular is not only that it is articulated with other modes of production but that these articulations make the rate of change within other modes and within capitalism, as well as among the different levels of the capitalist mode, highly uneven and potentially explosive. John Taylor posits, in a more general formulation:

> As a result of its being determined in the last instance by an articulation of modes of production, the Third World formation is characterized by a whole series of *dislocations* between the various levels of the social formation. As opposed to the previous period of determinancy in the last instance by a particular non-capitalist mode, in which the different levels were *adapted to one another,* the latter are now *dislocated* with respect to each other, and with respect to the existing economic structure itself. Imperialist penetration intervenes economically, politically, and ideologically within these dislocated levels in order to ensure the increasing dominance of the capitalist mode of production, and to create that restricted and uneven form of economic development (together with its political and ideological guarantees) [Taylor, 1979:103].

Since the sources of conflict and contradiction and, thus, change are multiple and more complex in this model than in the evolutionary Marxist view (which expects to find a one-to-one relationship between economic base and superstructure), the methodology for studying change must also be more complex. And since it, unlike the dependency perspective, holds that there is a distinction between the general abstract societal-type model—that is, mode of production—and historically concrete societies—that is, social formations—the methodology for elaborating a theory of social change must be both historical-empirical and abstract. It must move back and forth between the two levels, not because one is a higher form of thought, as the Althusserian school would claim, but because both types of analysis are necessary for each other. The elaboration of the abstract model depends on an understanding of the actual historical process. All systems of production may have invariant elements but, to agree with O'Laughlin,

> these provide only a tautological framework of analysis which says nothing of historically specific social forms of production [1975:351].

Further,

> Since the purpose of theory is to develop those abstractions through which the concrete (always historically specific) can be understood, a set of universal concepts cannot define any particular mode of produc-

tion. Analysis of a mode of production must be movement from abstract general determinations to observation and conception at the level of the concrete and then back to the theoretical articulation of general and specific categories [1975:351].

Application to Guatemala and Central America

Rescued from the mechanical and dogmatic formulations of the evolutionary Marxists, as well as from the overly abstract and structuralist expositions of the early articulationists, the mode of production-social formation approach can capture both the general patterns of development of common societal types—capitalism, for example—and the particularities that influence the rate, evenness, and type of change. As such it strengthens the potential links between concrete studies of concrete societies and the elaboration of more general and formal theoretical explanations of social change. The importance of the mode of production approach, with its emphasis on the ways in which internal social structures (particularly classes and class conflicts) influence external ties (of dependence, for example), can be seen in a quick review of the Central American case. There all countries were conquerored by Spain and have played a more or less similar role in the international capitalist market since the beginning of the twentieth century (exporters of a limited number of agricultural products, particularly coffee).

These countries have developed different class structures and forms of class conflict that shape the crisis of the state and influence the revolutionary and other opposition movements that function in the region today (Torres Rivas, 1980, 1982; Chinchilla, 1980; Chinchilla and Hamilton, 1982; Chinchilla and Jamail, 1982).

Articulations of Modes of Production and the Conquest

To paraphrase Marx, Spain conquered Latin America, but it did not conquer it exactly as anticipated. The degree to which feudal institutions, culture, and forms of labor appropriation were implemented and endured was dependent on the proximity to centers of Spanish rule, the effectivenesss of native resistance, and the "fit" or "incompatibility" of native institutions and social structures with those that were externally imposed. These factors, together with natural resources, geography, and population settlement patterns, explain many of the differences in development patterns in Central American countries still visible today.

Where native populations were scattered and/or nomadic, as in the United States, Chile, Nicaragua, and Honduras, organization and control of native labor for surplus production was virtually impossible. Populations were largely decimated, restricted to reservations or regionally isolated (Service, 1955; Wheelock, 1979; Woodward, 1976). Rather than extensive articulation between new and old modes of production, the latter were dissolved in favor of the former or their influence limited and isolated. Small or nonexistent native populations after conquest, as in Costa Rica and Argentina, meant that new forms of land tenure and agricultural production could be established without interference from preexisting structures (Cueva, 1977; Woodward, 1976).

Where highly developed tribal or Asiatic-type modes of production (or a combination of the two) existed, on the other hand, the conquest produced a combination or linkage of modes of production that guaranteed the reproduction of the dominant mode (Dieterich, 1978; Godelier, 1974, 1977; Wolf, 1955, 1959). In Mexico, for example, a tendency toward concentration of private estates in the hands of Indian nobles had already begun. The conquest accelerated the tendency through release of lands formerly in the hands of Montezuma and the temples (Chevalier, 1963:207-226). The Indian nobles soon lost their lands because of indebtedness or were forced to sell them to the Spaniards at minimal prices. A new class of landlords began to appear whose wealth was based on land, mining, and commerce. The rapid concentration of landownership in the hands of non-Indians and the high degree of racial mixing encouraged by the settlement of Indians and non-Indians in the same towns distinguished Mexico's social structure and economy from the colonial period on.

In Guatemala, on the other hand, the creation of exclusively Indian settlements, in which non-Indians were legally forbidden to reside, resulted in a whole different economic, political, and social dynamic. Indians living in settlements, rather than on vast estates, provided for their own reproduction as well as that of the Spanish settlers. The towns and land under indigenous community control provided the material base for a civil-religious hierarchy and preconquest religious customs, the latter combined with Catholicism, with which it was similar in many ways. Catholic priests who functioned in Indian areas were (and are still) forced to adapt to native rituals and beliefs as much as they were able to change them (Colby and van den Berghe, 1969). Native labor frequently resisted paying the amount and kind of tribute demanded of them, and their resistance forced revisions in Spanish colonial institutions and policies (such as in the New Laws of 1542). Resistance was not sufficiently organized or coordinated to make the conquest impossible, but it did make it incomplete, especially culturally and ideologically, and helped to shape the form by which the external mode of production was imposed. It also negatively influenced the extent to which wealth could be internally concentrated and accumulated.

Articulation and the Rise of Capitalism

The origins of capitalism in Central America are internal as well as external. Internally, the rapid expansion of coffee production by native producers and immigrants came in response to international demand (generated by internal changes within European countries). Externally, capitalism developed as a result of the penetration of foreign monopoly capital into banking, bananas, mining, railroads, and electric power. New mercantile and agricultural interests increasingly dominated over old colonial groups and demanded political changes that would make capitalist production in agriculture possible: centralization of a modern state apparatus, creation of a government bureaucracy, and the establishment of a national bank and educational system (Jones, 1966; Woodward, 1976).

In all countries, economic and political reforms under the banner of liberalism came to the fore during this period. But the extent to which the reforms were carried out and the degree of domination of the new class alliances over the old varied from country to country.

Costa Rica, for example, experienced the real differentiation of its society into classes for the first time. Prior to the conquest, it had had no native population of indigenous modes of production to speak of. During the colonial period, few towns arose and no haciendas were established. The economy was based on subsistence-level family farms with no real export market, making it the poorest country in the region. The desire to overcome this poverty stimulated interest in coffee production among government officials even before independence was achieved.

In the beginning, government incentives for coffee production (in the form of gifts of free land and plants from nurseries) accelerated the tendency toward minifundia family production that was dominant in the previous period. Increasingly, however, the inability to repay loans from intermediaries of London merchants or to borrow for capital improvements resulted in differentiation into landed and landless classes, the latter recruited to work on the lands of the former. Yet even with this proletarianization, labor was scarce relative to demand, and wages, even for imported Black and Chinese workers, were relatively high ($1 to $5 for a 10-hour day, the same amount earned by rural workers in El Salvador and Guatemala today—(Sáenz, 1972; Calvo, 1980).

Coffee production was relatively efficient and earnings from coffee exports relatively high. As much as four million kilos were exported by 1850, before the completion of the Panama Railway to the Atlantic coast, and total exports reached 20 million kilos by 1900 (Estadistica y Censos, Anuario de Comercio Exterior, cited by Edward Taylor, 1980). More than in any other Central American country, coffee earnings were invested in education, health, and sanitation (Woodward, 1976). Even when coffee earnings dipped, taxes remained relatively high and were used, along with earnings from the national lottery, to maintain a level of social welfare spending. Costa Rica developed a degree of social equality and political stability unknown in other Central American countries. The racial ideology that justified the conquest of native peoples elsewhere were relatively absent in Costa Rica, since native labor was also virtually nonexistent and the need for an army to intervene in politics was minimized. Liberal versus conservative rivalries, based elsewhere on material conflicts between emergent capitalist and colonial-based interests, often violent in form, were muted in Costa Rica, resulting in relative social peace accompaning the rise to dominance of the capitalist mode of production.

Coffee production in El Salvador, however, brought a different kind of political peace from 1870 to 1930. A tiny, highly homogenous coffee oligarchy (with origins in the merchants, moneylenders, indigo producer, and cattle ranchers of the colonial period) was consolidated rapidly at this time. It managed to gain control of the vast estates and undertake rapid and relatively complete expropriation of indigenous communal land. In part, this was due to the relative economic weakness of the Catholic Church (in contrast to Guatemala) and the progressive (i.e., economically liberal) character of the colonial merchant class opposed to the Crown (in contrast to the monopoly trading interests of its Guatemalan representatives). These factors, together with the smaller size and less concentrated character of the indigenous tribes, initially encountered by Spanish conquerors, and their relatively greater distance from colonial control, resulted in a different class structure and dominant ideology (more purely class than racial/ethnic and class) than in neighboring Guatemala.

Liberal reforms in Guatemala had stimulated the formation of a distinctly colonial class. There, as elsewhere in the region, with the exception of Nicaragua, a new merchant class successfully challenged the interests of colonially-tied conservative oligarchies. But challenging forces took a long time to consolidate politically and required heavy dependence on the army and foreign monopoly capital. This dependence, in turn, reinforced politically conservative tendencies, even among liberals, and a morbid fear of Indian uprisings as long as indigenous peoples remained distinct ethnic communities. Elaborate strategies had to be continually readjusted and reinforced, not only to diffuse working-class and peasant unrest in general but to ensure that ethnic identities and loyalties remained primarily local. While even progressive young intellectuals of the 1920s, such as Miguel Angel Asturias, argued for the disappearance of the Indian through intermarriage with Europeans, differential forms of appropriation of Indian and ladino labor actually prolonged the distinctions and reinforced different social and economic structures.

Labor recruitment in the early period of liberal reforms in Guatemala reverted back to the legalized forced labor of the conquest due to the need to lure indigenous workers out of their ample subsistence settlements onto estates and plantations. As long as large amounts of good land remained outside the control of large landowners and there was little internal market and very little money circulating to speak of, Indians, who constituted the majority of potential rural workers outside the estates, had little reason to want to migrate. Furthermore, coffee producers had little previous capital accumulation with which to lure them, either through wages or a combination of wages and payment in kind. Legally sanctioned forced labor under the guise of vagrancy laws and taxes made the transition to capitalist production in agriculture in a society with a strong colonial legacy possible.

Today in Guatemala, class differentiation as a result of capitalist expansion is once again proceeding dramatically, extending the economic changes begun in the liberal period (see Torres Rivas, 1980, 1981; Chinchilla, 1980; Chinchilla and Hamilton, 1982; Chinchilla

and Dietz, 1982). Small producers are made more and more dependent on the capitalist market and state or private loans for their own reproduction, and the artisan supplement to marketed surpluses and
cash wages is less and less available due to declining demand for
handcrafted as opposed to (cheaper) manufactured goods. As agriculture for export expands but not enough (or consistently enough) to
provide the basis for mechanization and rationalization, large amounts
of labor are needed, at least seasonally, to make production possible.
Once again, the highland Indian communities are undergoing a process of rapid transformation as whole villages migrate in search of cash
income from wage labor. Once again, in Guatemala this transformation in the mode of production and class structure has a particular
colonial or ethnic component.

As expressed by the Guerrilla Army of the Poor, one of the revolutionary organizations that has been working for over a decade in the
areas of greatest Indian concentration, class and ethnic consciousness interact differently for subsistence and semiproletarian indigenous
producers:

> Subsistence Indian farmers and semiproletarian Indians . . . produce
> and think differently; they share a sense of ethnocultural identity, but
> differ ideologically as a result of their different social and economic
> status.

Among semiproletarian Indians, now the majority,

> ethnic-national consciousness is permeated with political and ideo-
> logical elements which belong to the encompassing modern relations of
> production. These include an incipient awareness of exploitation, a
> beginning differentiation along class lines to visualize the existence of
> rich Indians, class consciousness in relation to exploitative and exploited
> ladinos, etc. For the subsistence Indian farmer, the relation with ladinos
> is one of ethnic-cultural oppression and discrimination. For the semi-
> proletarian, the ladino is also oppressor and discriminator but he
> begins to understand that the exploiter is the rich. Thus, two systems of
> parallel and apparently incoherent contradictions are introduced into
> his awareness, since the logical conclusion of this second aspect is that
> there are also exploited ladinos even if they are not culturally oppressed
> [1982:3].

In order for capitalism to develop in Guatemala, land for sale on the
free market had to be freed from the inherited monopoly control of the

Catholic Church and Indian communities. Little wonder, therefore, that the two allied strongly against the liberal economic, political, and social initiatives (Rodríguez, 1955). Resistance to the erosion of their economic base, the land, was unsuccessful but the success of other forms of ideological and cultural resistance may be evident in what is known as indigenous culture today. While the customs and rituals may have distant roots in the colonial and precolonial period, the context for and implications of their practice were radically transformed during the period of liberal reforms. The shortage of priests created by restrictions of religious orders simply made the practice of sacraments and rituals the responsibility of the autonomous community. The closed corporate community described by Wolf (1955, 1957, 1959) probably consolidated at this time in reaction to increased exploitation and attempted penetration by external forces. Rus and Wasserstrom, in a comment on a similar phenomenon in Chiapas, Mexico, argue that

> faced with a dominant ideology which in the 19th century demanded that Indians accept their position as landless (or near landless) laborers, indigenous people—at least those who did not become *mestizos*—chose to put up the strongest ideological resistance of which they were capable. . . . Exploited as occasional or transient laborers, they responded as Indians, as members of native communities which were themselves being pulled apart into different social classes. It is this paradox, then, fed by the emergence of new social relations within such communities, that cargo systems sought to mitigate and that—ironically, but inevitably—they only exacerbated [1980:475].

The extension of capitalism through primitive accumulation in the countryside and appropriation of surplus value in the modern rationalized factories in the cities has created conditions for a revolutionary movement that can no longer be based only in the cities or include only ladinos. Nor will it take the form of a race war, since the same process, differentiating ladinos along class lines, has differentiated some Indians from other Indians to an unprecedented degree. While the economic and political crisis is generalized throughout Central America because of the conflict between new forms of production and old forms of political domination, the crisis has a particular expression in Guatemala because of the dependence of capitalism on several articulated modes of production for its reproduction. This will influence not only the strategy of the revolutionary movement but the character of the new mode that takes its place.

Implications for
a Theory of Social Change

Capitalist development in two periods in Central American countries, the period of liberal reforms and the past two decades of the Common Market, has led not to increasing underdevelopment or stagnation, as the original advocates of dependency perspective would have predicted, and not toward cumulative, integrative modernization, as the structural-functionalists would have imagined, but to uneven internal accumulation of capital and explosive political crises. The rate of external surplus transfer has been high and external dependency has increased. Internal development of the productive forces and significant qualitative transformations of the internal class structures have also taken place. The absolute well-being of many direct producers and newly incorporated proletarians may actually have declined, but the qualitative transformation in their relationships to production and the market have transformed the character of their political struggle, not only making it highly anticapitalist in content but tending toward socialist transformation as well.

Proletarianized workers, even those in multinational firms with somewhat better wages and working conditions, are not the coopted "tail end" of the movement for change but its spearhead. At the same time, the highly interrelated and articulated nature of the contradictions bring other social forces into play: semiproletarianized rural workers, small and medium peasants, and the urban unemployed and underemployed as well as students, teachers, and housewives are drawn into a common strategy of revolutionary popular war (see Debray, 1975; Chinchilla, 1980; Nuñez, 1980).

A theory of social change in Third World social formations must account for both the generalities of capitalist development and the particularities of its expression in particular social formations. Neither oppressed Indians nor exploited ladinos alone can make a revolution in this modern context of articulation of modes of production that give a country like Guatemala its specificity. It is the intersection of contradictions, of classes, ideologies, and political structures, that makes the existing situation so explosive; it is the understanding of these intersections that makes it possible to put forth a strategy to overcome them.

Like the revolutionary strategy, a theory of social change must integrate the generalities captured in the concept of changes in the mode of production—changes that have affected all Central American countries in the past two decades—as well as their particular expression in countries that have developed differently despite geographical proximity and similarities in their participation in the international division of labor. Only a theory that moves back and forth between historical realities and generalized laws, between mode of production and social formation, has the possibility of capturing the essence of societal change and development.

Note

1. Meillasoux (1975), Wallerstein (1974), and others (Bennholdt-Thomsen, 1977; von Werhoff, 1981) have recently challenged this formulation, arguing that the reproduction not only of Third World formations but developed capitalist ones depends on non-capitalist forms of subsistence and surplus extraction, driving capitalist to move constantly throughout the world seeking the lowest absolute cost of labor. A number of critiques of this formulation have been developed elsewhere and an alternative formulation, which takes into account the contribution to reproduction of non-capitalist as well as capitalist

References

Adams, Richard
   1956   "Cultural components of Central America." American Anthropologist 58, (5): 881-907.
   1957   "Political changes in Guatemalan Indian communities," pp. 1-54 in Margaret A. L. Harrison and Robert Wouchope (eds.) Community Culture and National Change. New Orleans: Middle American Research Institute, Tulane University.
   1967   "Nationalization," pp. 469-489 in Robert Wauchope (ed.) Handbook of Middle American Indians. Austin: University of Texas Press.
Angiotti, Thomas
   1981   "The political implications of dependency theory." Latin American Perspectives 8 (Summer-Fall): 124-137.
Assadourian, Charlos Sempat
   1977   Modos de producción en América Latina. Mexico: Siglo XXI.
Baer, Werner
   1969   "The economics of Prebisch and ECLA," pp. 203-218 in Charles T. Nisbet (ed.) Latin America: Problems in Economic Development. New York: Free Press.
Baran, Paul A.
   1967   The Political Economy of Growth. New York: Monthly Review Press.
Barrera, Mario
   1979   Race and Class in the Southwest: A Theory of Racial Inequality. Notre Dame, IN: University of Notre Dame Press.
Beltrán Aguirre, Gonzalo
   1967   Regiones de refugio. Mexico: Instituto Indigenista Interamericano.

Bennholdt Thomson, Veronica
1977   "Subsistence reproduction and extended reproduction." Unpublished paper.
        Bielefeld, Germany.
Biderman, Jaime
1980   "The development of capitalism in Nicaragua: economic growth, class rela-
        tions and uneven development." Unpublished paper. Berkeley, California.
Boderheimer (Jonas), Susanne
1970a   "Dependency and Imperialism: the roots of Latin American underdevelop-
        ment." NACLA Newsletter 4 (May-June): 18-27.
1970b   "The ideology of developmentalism: American political science's para-
        digm surrogate for Latin American studies." Berkeley Journal of Sociology
        15: 95-137.
1974   "Guatemala: land of eternal struggle." pp. 89-219 in Ronald H. Chilcote
        and Joel C. Edelstein (eds.) Latin America: The Struggle With Dependency
        and Beyond. New York: Schenkman.
Blauner, Robert
1972   Racial Oppression in America. New York: Harper & Row.
Boeke, J. H.
1953   Economics and Economic Policy of Dual Societies. New York: Institute of
        Pacific Relations.
Bonilla, Frank and Robert Girling (eds.)
1973   Structures of Dependency. Stanford, California: Stanford Institute of
        Politics.
Bradby, Barbara
1975   "The destruction of natural economy." Economy and Society (May): 127-
        161.
Calvo, J. B.
1980   The Republic of Costa Rica. New York: Rand McNally.
Cambranes, Julio C.
1975   Desarrollo económico y social de Guatemala: 1868-85. Guatemala: Instituto
        de Investigaciones Económicas y Sociales, Universidad de San Carlos.
Cardoso, Ciro F. S.
1969   "Los modos de producción coloniales: estado de la cuestión y perspectiva
        teórica." Estudios Sociales Centroamericanos 4 (January-February): 87-
        106.
Cardoso, Fernando Henrique
1971   Ideologías de la burguesía industrial en sociedades dependientes. Mexico:
        Siglo XII.
1972   "Dependent capitalist development in Latin America." New Left Review
        74 (July-August): 83-95.
Cardoso, Fernando Henrique and Enzo Faletto
1969   Dependencia y desarrollo en América Latina. Mexico: Siglo XII.
Carmak, Robert
1973   Quichean Civilization. Berkeley: University of California Press.
Chevalier, Francois
1963   Land and Society in Colonial Mexico. Berkeley: University of California
        Press.
Chinchilla, Norma Stoltz
1980   "Class conflict in Central America: background and overview." Latin Amer-
        ican Perspectives 7 (Spring-Summer): 2-23.

1981   "Articulation of modes of production and the Latin American debate."
        Unpublished paper. Irvine. California.

Chinchilla. Norma Stoltz and James Lowell Dietz
1981   "Toward a new understanding of development and underdevelopment."
        Latin American Prespectives. 8 (Summer and Fall): 137-147.

Chinchilla. Norma Stoltz and Milton Jamail
1982   "The Origins of the revolutionary and popular movement in Guatemala."
        Unpublished paper.

Cockcroft. James D., André Gunder Frank, and Dale Johnson
1972   Dependence and Underdevelopment. Garden City. Doubleday.

Colby, Benjamin N. and Pierre L. van den Berghe
1969   Ixil Country: A Plural Society in Highland Guatemala. Berkeley: Univer-
        sity of California Press.

Cueva, Agustín
1976   "A summary of 'Problems and prospects of dependency theory.' " Latin
        American Perspectives 3 (Fall): 12-16.
1977   El desarrollo del capitalismo en América Latina. Mexico: Siglo XXI.

Debray. Régis
1975   Critique of Arms. Harmondsworth, England: Penguin.

Dieterich. Heinz
1978   Relaciones de producción en América Latina. Mexico: Ediciones de Cultura
        Popular.

Falla. Ricardo
1978   "El movimiento indígena." Estudios Centroamericanos. pp. 356-357. 437-
        461.

Fanon, Franz
1963   The Wretched of the Earth. New York: Grove Press.

Figueroa Ibarra, Carlos
1974   "Acerca de 'El Adamcismo y la sociedad Guatemalteca.' " Economía 12
        (April-June): 1-16.
1975   El proletariado rural en el agro Guatemalteco. Guatemala: Instituto de
        Investigaciones Económicas y Sociales, Universidad de San Carlos de
        Guatemala.

Flores Alvarado, Humberto
1971   "El proceso de proletarización." Alero (Suplemento) 3 (March): 24-46.
1973   El Adamcismo en la sociedad Guatemalteca. Guatemala: Editorial Piedra
        Santa.

Foster-Carter, Aiden
1973   "The modes of production controversy." New Left Review 107 (January-
        February): 47-74. (Preprinted in John Clammer (ed.), The New Economic
        Anthropology. London: Macmillian, pp. 210-249.)
1976   "From Rostow to Gunder Frank: conflicting paradigms in the analysis of
        underdevelopment." World Development 4 (March): 167-180.

Frank, André Gunder
1967   Capitalism and Underdevelopment in Latin America. New York: Monthly
        Review Press.
1969   Latin America: Underdevelopment and Revolution. New York: Monthly
        Review Press.

1972   "Sociology of development and underdevelopment of sociology," pp. 321-
        397 in James D. Cockcroft, André Gunder Frank, and Dale L. Johnson
        (eds.) Dependence and Underdevelopment. Garden City, NY: Doubleday.
Gillin, John
    1948   "Race relations without conflict: a Guatemalan town." American Journal
            of Sociology 53 (March): 337-343.
Godelier, Maurice
    1974   "On the definition of social formation." Critique of Anthropology 1: 63-
            73.
    1977   Perspectives in Marxist Anthropology. London: Cambridge University
            Press.
González Casanova, Pablo
    1969   "Internal colonialism and national development," pp. 118-139 in Irving
            Louis Horowitz et al. (eds.) Latin American Radicalism. New York:
            Vintage.
Guerrilla Army of the Poor
    1982   "The Indian peoples and the Guatemalan revolution. Compañero 5: 1-5.
Guzmán Bockler, Carlos
    1975   Colonialismo y revolución. Mexico: Siglo XXI.
Guzmán Bockler, Carlos and Jean-Loup Herbert
    1974   Guatemala: una interpretación histórica-social. Mexico: Siglo XXI.
Guzmán Bockler, Carlos, Julio Quan, and Jean-Loup Herbert
    1971   "Las clases sociales y la lucha de clases en Guatemala." Alero (Suplemento)
            3 (March): 5-23.
Harding, Timothy F.
    1976   "Dependency, nationalism, and the state in Latin America." Latin Amer-
            ican Perspectives 3 (Fall): 3-11.
Henfry, Colin
    1981   "Dependency, modes of production and the class analysis of Latin Amer-
            ica." Latin American Perspectives 8 (Summer-Fall): 17-54.
Hinshaw, Robert E.
    1975   Panajachel: A Guatemalan Town in Thirty Year Perspective. Pittsburgh:
            Univeristy of Pittsburgh Press.
Hoogvelt, Ankie M.
    1980   The Sociology of Developing Societies. London: Macmillian.
Hoselitz, Bert
    1960   Sociological Aspects of Economic Growth. New York: Free Press.
Howe, Gary Nigel
    1981   "Dependency theory, imperialism, and the production of surplus value on a
            world scale." Latin American Perspectives 8 (Summer-Fall): 82-102.
Immerman, Richard H.
    1982   The CIA in Guatemala. Austin: University of Texas Press.
Johnson, Carlos
    1981   "Dependency theory and the processes of capitalism and socialism." Latin
            American Perspectives 8 (Summer-Fall): 55-81.
Johnson, Dale L.
    1972   "On oppressed classes," pp. 269-301 in James D. Cockcroft, André Gun-
            der Frank, and Dale L. Johnson (eds.) Dependence and Underdevelopment.
            Garden City, NY: Doubleday.

1973   The Sociology of Change and Reaction in Latin America. Indianapolis, IN: Bobbs-Merrill.

Jones, Chester Lloyd
1966   Guatemala: Past and Present. New York: Russell and Russell.

Laclau, Ernesto
1971   "Feudalism and capitalism in Latin America." New Left Review 67 (May-June): 19-38.

Luporini, Cesare, and Emilio Serini
1976   "El concepto de 'Formación económico-social.'" Mexico: Siglo XXI.

Martinex Peláez, Severo
1973   La Patria del Criollo. San José, Costa Rica: Editorial Universitaria Centro-americana.
1975   "Racismo y análisis histórico en la definición del indio Guatemalteco." Economía 45 (July-September): 83-110.
1982   "Los pueblos inígenas y el proceso revolucionario." Polémica 3 (January-February): 47-56.

Meillasoux, Claude
1975   Femmes, greniers et capitaux. Paris: Maspero.

Mejia, José
1970   "Guatemala: país desconocido." Alero 1 (August): 9-17.

Memmi, Albert
1967   The Colonizer and the Colonized. Boston: Beacon.

Moore, Wilbert E.
1963   Social Change. Englewood Cliffs, NJ: Prentice-Hall.

Nash, Manning
1958   Machine Age Maya. New York: Free Press.

Nuñez Soto, Orlando
1981   "The third social force in national liberation movements." Latin American Perspectives 8 (Spring): 5-21.

O'Brien, Phillip
1975   "A critique of Latin American theories of dependency," pp. 7-27 in Ian Oxaal et al., Beyond the Sociology of Development. London: Routledge & Kegan Paul.

O'Laughlin, Bridget
1975   "Marxist approaches in anthropology." Annual Review of Anthropology, pp. 341-371.

Oxaal, Ian
1975   Beyond the Sociology of Development. London: Routledge & Kegan Paul.

Parsons, Talcott
1951   The Social System. London: Routledge & Kegan Paul.
1964   "Evolutionary universals." American Sociological Review 29 (June): 339-357.
1966   Societies. Englewood Cliffs, NJ: Prentice-Hall.
1971   The System of Modern Societies. Englewood Cliffs, NJ: Prentice-Hall.

Redfield, Robert
1939   "Primitive merchants of Guatemala." Quarterly Journal of Inter-American Relations 1, 4: 48-49.

Rey, Pierre Phillipe
  1976   Las alianzas de clases. Mexico: Siglo XXI.
Rodríguez, Mario
  1955   "The Livingston codes in the Guatemalan crisis of 1837-1838," pp. 1-32 in
          Applied Enlightenment: 19th Century Liberalism. New Orleans: Middle
          American Research Institute, Tulane University.
Rostow, W. W.
  1960   The Stages of Economic Growth. Cambridge, MA: Cambridge University
          Press.
Rus, Jan and Robert W. Wasserstrom
  1980   "Civil religious hierarchy in Central Chiapos." American Anthropologist
          7, 3: 466-478.
Sáenz, Carlos Joaquin
  1972   "Population growth, economic progress and opportunities on the land: the
          case of Costa Rica." Madison: University of Wisconsin Land Tenure Cen-
          ter Research Publication No. 47.
Sahlins, Marshall
  1960   Evolution and Culture. Ann Arbor: University of Michigan Press.
Service, Elman R.
  1955   "Indian-European relations in Colonial Latin America." American Anthro-
          pologist 57 (June): 411-425.
Siegel, Morris
  1941   "Resistances to culture change in Western Guatemala." Sociology and
          Social Research 25, 5: 414-430.
Smelser, N. J.
  1964   "Toward a theory of modernization," pp. 258-274 in A. Etzioni and E.
          Etzioni (eds.) Social Change. New York: Basic Books.
Smith, Carol A.
  1978   "Beyond dependency theory: national and regional patterns of under-
          development in Guatemala." American Ethnologist 5 (August): 574-617.
Stavenhagen, Rodolfo
  1970   "Classes, colonialism and acculturation," pp. 235-288 in Irving Louis
          Horowitz (ed.) Masses in Latin America. New York: Oxford University
          Press.
  1975   Social Classes in Agrarian Societies. Garden City, NY: Doubleday.
Stein, Stanley J.
  1970   The Colonial Heritage: Essays on Economic Dependency in Perspective.
          New York: Oxford University Press.
Sunkel, Osvaldo
  1967   "Política nacional de desarrollo y dependencia externa." Revista de Estudios
          Internacionales 1 (May).
Tax, Sol
  1941   "World view and social relations in Guatemala." American Anthropologist
          43 (January-March): 27-42.
  1953   Penny Capitalism: A Guatemalan Indian Economy. Washington, DC: Smith-
          sonian Institute of Social Anthropology No. 16.

Taylor, Edward
  1980   "Peripheral capitalism and rural-urban migration: a study of population
         movements in Costa Rica." Latin American Perspectives (Spring-Summer):
         75-90.
Taylor, John G.
  1979   From Modernization to Modes of Production: A Critique of the Sociologies
         of Development and Underdevelopment. Atlantic Highlands, NJ: Humanities
         Press.
Torres Rivas, Edelberto
  1971a "Reflexiones en torno a una interpretación histórico-social de Guatemala."
         Alero (Suplemento) 3 (February): 48-58.
  1971b Interpretación del desarrollo social Centroamericano, San José, Costa
         Rica: Editorial Universitaria Centroamericana.
  1980   "The Central American model of growth: crisis for whom?" Latin American
         Perspectives 7 (Spring-Summer): 24-44.
  1981   "Seven keys to understanding the Central American crisis." Contemporary
         Marxism (Spring): 49-61.
Tumin, Melvin
  1945   "Culture, genuine and spurious: a re-evaluation." American Sociological
         Review 10 (April): 199-201.
  1949   "Reprocity and stability of caste in Guatemala." American Sociological
         Review 14 (February): 17-25.
  1952   Caste in a Peasant Society. Princeton: Princeton University Press.
van den Berghe, Pierre and George Primov
  1977   Inequality in the Peruvian Andes: Class and Ethnicity in Cuzco. Columbia:
         University of Missouri Press.
Vitale, Luis
  1968   "Latin America: feudal or capitalist," pp. 32-43 in James Petras and Maurice
         Zeitlin (eds.) Latin America: Reform or Revolution. Greenwich, CT:
         Fawcet.
Wallerstein, Immanuel
  1974   The Modern World System. New York: Academic Press.
von Werhoff, Claudia
  1982   "Las mujeres y la periferia: Los puntos ciegos en la crítica de la economía
         política." Unpublished paper, Bielefeld, Germany.
Wolf, Eric R.
  1955   "Types of Latin American peasantry: a preliminary discussion." American
         Anthropologist 57, 3: 452-471.
  1957   "Closed corporate communities in Mesoamerican and Central Java." South
         Western Journal of Anthropology 13, 1: 1-18.
  1959   Sons of the Shaking Earth. Chicago: University of Chicago Press.
Woodward, Ralph Lee
  1976   Central America: A Nation Divided. New York: Oxford University Press.

Part Three: World-System and Class Analyses

André Gunder Frank: Crisis and Transformation of Dependency in the World-System

For half a millenium, a large and increasing part of humanity has lived in a single world economic system. Its fundamentally unvarying unequal structure and uneven development has, as its mode of production, been based on and reproduced the polarization of owned wealth and disowned poverty, of development and underdevelopment, and of periods of cyclical expansion and stagnation. Many transformations in the world-system have been more of hopes than of reality. I trace this capitalist structure and development through much of the crisis-ridden history of capitalism to the present world economic crisis. The recent experience and foreseeable future prospects of delinking from dependent capitalist development and opting for self-reliant socialist development are then examined, as are recent tendencies of the socialist economies to relink into the capitalist world economy again. This inquiry will qualify, for the foreseeable future, the realism of opting out of dependence and transforming the world-system.

Author's Note: This chapter is based largely on two lectures delivered at the Tokyo University of Foreign Studies and one at the Center for Mediterranean Studies Conference on Transition to Socialism in Athens, Greece in 1980. I am indebted to Dale Johnson for extraordinary substantive editorial help to fuse my three lectures into one paper.

The single world economic system is composed of many parts which are very unequal: a developed North and an underdeveloped South; a capitalist West (including, of course, Japan) and the socialist East. We distinguish the individual features of the various parts of the world, including the Third World, which is becoming more and more differentiated. Within the world-system there are different modes (I prefer to speak in terms of relations) of production. Today precapitalist relations of production are still very prevalent in many parts of the world, combined with capitalist wage-labor relations of production and perhaps also with postcapitalist (meaning socialist) relations of production. What is important, however, is that these diverse relations of production combine to contribute to the world process of capital accumulation in a single world capitalist system, whose common features and operation I have sought to examine previously and elsewhere (see notes 1, 2, and 3).

The world-system has experienced periodic crises throughout its history. A crisis is a period in which the previous expansion could not continue on the same basis. In order to survive at all during a crisis, it is necessary for the system to undergo vast economic, social, political, and cultural transformations, including technological change. During these periods of crisis there is a need to reduce the costs of production: lowering wages, moving production to places where production is cheaper, and (very important in the long run) technological change. In periods of crisis, there are new inventions which require vast investments in order to transform them into a new basis for production during the subsequent expansion.

The world-system is once again in such a crisis today. The question is whether the world capitalist system will be able to make the necessary readjustment. If it cannot, then of course the system will destroy itself. But if it can make these readjustments, then there is reason to believe that it may experience another period of expansion similar to that of the postwar years which would begin after these readjustments have been made. This may occur in ten or fifteen years or perhaps longer. During this period of readjustment, there will again be vast economic, social, political, and cultural convulsions in the world.

In periods of crisis, there is also a tendency for the leading economic power, now the United States, to lose its hegemony and to be challenged by new rising economic powers, now Western Europe and Japan. Productivity in Europe increased twice as fast and in Japan increased almost four times as fast as in the United States during the 1960s. In the 1970s productivity increased slowly in these economies, and in the United States it had declined since 1979. This is the real economic basis of the relative decline of the United States. The U.S. center of hegemony has not so far been able to make the necessary economic, social, and political readjustments quickly enough to be able to compete with the newer economies that are more easily able to do so.

The world-system is very unequal; the process of capital accumulation, although it is a single process, is very unequal from one place to another and from one sector to another and takes place through many different relations of production. The process is also very uneven; periods of relative stagnation follow periods of rapid expansion. There is a connection between these features: The nature of the inequality changes most rapidly during the periods of stagnation or crisis; further, the incorporation or exit, the linking and delinking from the world-system, also occur as a result of or in response to these crises of accumulation.

World Capitalist Crisis Development History in Brief [1]

Having started our historical review at the end with the present crisis, we go backwards to review the previous ones. The present crisis began in the 1960s after a period of expansion since World War II. That period of expansion was based very significantly on the changes that occurred during the long crisis from 1914 to the war, a crisis which included two world wars, the Great Depression of the 1930s, the rise of fascism, socialist revolutions in the Soviet Union and China, and the growth of state monopoly capitalism. In other words, that crisis generated vast economic, social, and political transformations that laid the basis for the new expansion. Another basis for the postwar expansion was the very seriously reduced wage rate of labor during that crisis. This was based in part on a process of primitive accumulation—that is, capitalist accumulation on the basis of noncapitalist relations of production. I point, for instance, to the concentration camp labor in Eastern Europe that Germany relied on substantially, and in general the mistreatment of labor in Eastern Europe as a whole. Perhaps there were also similar forms of accumulation in Japanese imperialism's Greater East Asian Co-Prosperity Sphere. That crisis was also the period of the absolute decline of Great Britain, prior to the dominance of the United States. It was a period in which there was no one completely hegemonic imperial power. This is one of the important factors that explains the violence of the two world wars, which were essentially fought to determine who would inherit the dominance of Great Britain in the world.

That particular deep and long crisis from which capitalism obviously emerged strengthened had followed a period of expansion from 1896 to 1913; this had followed another major economic crisis in the world from 1873 to 1895, which in turn had followed another expansion from 1850 to 1873. In summary, 1967 to the 1980s has been a period of stagnation; 1940-1945 to 1967 one of expansion; 1913 to 1940 one of stagnation; 1896-1913 one of expansion; and 1873-1895 one of stagnation and crisis.

The period 1849-1873 was one of expansion analogous to that of the postwar years in the twentieth century, when Great Britain was the economically and politically dominant force in the world, called Pax Britannica, like Pax Americana after World War II. This expansion led to a renewed period of crisis, analogous to the one today, a period of crisis in capital accumulation. The major manifestations of its resolution were the relative decline of Great Britain as the United States and Germany and, behind them, Russia and Japan began to rise and challenge Britain; the development of monopoly capitalism in the industrial countries; and, most important, the development of classical imperialism and recolonization, in this case particularly of Africa. These were the economic and political bases for the regeneration of the system, putting it on a new footing which permitted the expansion from 1896 to 1913.

Also, in each of these major crises there was a period of rapid technological invention representing an effort to reduce costs and expand production in new sectors. These inventions, in the view of Schumpeter, then resulted in innovations. Great investments in new technological processes occurred, and innovations in the creation of new leading industries became the basis of the next major expansion in world capitalism. We return to technological innovation after another brief historical excursion into crisis periods.

There was another period of semistagnation and crisis from 1816 to 1848, which led to the famous revolutions in Western Europe of 1848, and had followed on the first major period of expansion generally recognized as the beginning of industrial capitalism, from approximately 1790 to the end of the Napoleonic Wars in 1815. Now I depart increasingly from orthodoxy with regard to the interpretation of economic history, because Marxists, followers of Kondratiev, and many others would regard this period not only as a sharp historical break but in fact as the beginnings of the capitalist system. This was the time of the Industrial Revolution in Great Britain. Many would argue that prior to that there was no capitalism, because there was no dominance of industrial wage relations; since there was no industry, there could have been no industrial capitalism, or capitalism of any kind. My interpretation is very substantially different from this, and this has a considerable relevance for a theme of this book, mode of production.

Consider the period 1762-1790. That was a period of crisis in capital accumulation which led to cost-reducing inventions, particularly in the textile industry and Watt's steam engine, that were the technological basis for the Industrial Revolution. However, the real innovations in these areas did not occur until the expansion of 1790-1815 associated with the first Industrial Revolution. This led to another period of relative stagnation and crisis from 1815 to 1848, in which there occurred the invention of machines to produce machines, which led to another major investment drive around midcentury. In other words, the first Industrial Revolution was in the production of consumer goods, particularly textiles. What is sometimes called the second Industrial Revolution, or at least the second stage of the Industrial Revolution, was in the production of textile machinery, which previously had been produced by hand. Now machines began to be produced also by machines: textile machinery, steam engines, including mobile steam engines powering locomotives and then the steam ship. During the next crisis, from 1873 to 1895, came the technical inventions which provided the basis for what might be called the third stage of the technological and industrial revolution based on electricity and petroleum, and then the internal combustion engine leading to the automobile, which has completely transformed society in most parts of the world. Then came the 1920s-1940s extension of new technique into the petrochemical, electronic, and nuclear fields, which were the technological bases of the post-World War II expansion. At the present time, obviously, we are again at the beginning of another series of cost-reducing technical inventions based on the microchip, on biotechnology (that is, new techniques in genetics and in cloning of genes to produce new life forms). Technological leaps may extend into the field of energy, which could provide the basis for another technological revolution at the turn of the century.

So far I have confined myself largely to the center of the world-economic system and, to some extent and as part and parcel of this series of expansions and contractions, the shift of the metropolitan center from Great Britain to the United States in the course of this economic development. The rise of imperialism as a consequence of the crisis of one century ago, 1873-1896, has hardly been mentioned.

Until 1816, India exported more manufactures than it imported; and all through the eighteenth century until the beginning of the nineteenth century, India was a large exporter to the rest of the world. A major basis of the Industrial Revolution was the destruction of the Indian textile industry and the so-called deindustrialization of India. Marx talked about primitive accumulation and the separation of the producer from his means of production—that is, that landowners lose their land and that owners of tools lose them and become converted into proletarian wage workers. This is, of course, what happened in Great Britain, which served as the main example for this study. In a famous article written in 1852 in *New York Tribune,* Marx said that Britain shows India the mirror of its future. If that is true, it has not happened yet, because obviously India has not yet become developed like Great Britain. On the contrary, in this world capitalist process of development, the separation of producers from their means of production in the West and in the North was followed by their reabsorption into the productive process as proletarian wage workers. This caused a great deal of suffering, which was recognized by Marx and was very well described by Engels in his book on the working class in Britain. In the South, in what is today called the Third World, this process did not happen at all. There was also a separation of producers from their means of production in agriculture, manufacturing and handicrafts, but what never happened was the real reintegration or reabsorption of these people into the productive process in the same way as in the North. In this regard, then, Marx turned out to be very seriously mistaken. Up to 1816, India was still exporting far more manufactures than it imported. In many other parts of what is today the Third World, there was local manufacturing for local consumption. The Industrial Revolution transferred the locus of manufacturing from the world as a whole into what are today called "traditional" industrialized countries, and it substantially deindustrialized the rest of the world. Around 1800, there was no great technological gap between the West and the East and the South (except in certain sectors, such as weaponry). This technological gap first developed through the development of industry in the West and the deindustrialization of parts of what today is the South. During the second Industrial Revolution, still worse happened. Around the middle of the nineteenth century the West went on to the production of machines by machines, and the real technological gap developed; because the South did not participate in this process either, it fell two stages behind. Not only was it not able to produce manufactures through industrial methods as the West did, but it was still less able to produce machines for the industrial process; the Third World became dependent on importing both from the West.

In the crisis of the 1930s import substitution brought some industry to some nations. In the present crisis, through export substitution of export promotion, there has been to some extent a process of apparent reindustrialization of the Third World, as some so-called traditional industry is transferred from the North or the West to the South. However, for the most part, the industry that is transferred is that which has now become relatively old and obsolete in the West, as the West goes on to a new technological revolution based essentially on the production of technology by technology. First it was the production of consumer goods, then of producer goods, and now it is the production of productive techniques, of technology itself, in the West (now, of course, including Japan), which makes it again possible to produce in the South a number of consumer and even producer goods. Meanwhile, the West maintains a monopoly on these new processes of technological production, so that the technological gap continues to widen.

I have provided only the briefest historical sketch of crisis and expansion. The roots of the capitalist world-system go back much further than the Industrial Revolution, where conventional and Marxist historiography usually set them. There is no space to explore this here, but I would say this. If we try to understand capitalism and the history of capitalism as being based simply on Europe or Britain, and if we try to find a transition from feudalism into industrial capitalism at the end of the eighteenth century and then analyze its spread from one place to another, we are missing the very essentials of historical and contemporary capitalist development. If the essentials of past capitalist development are missed, we cannot possibly understand the essence of contemporary and future historical development. For these reasons I submit that it is absolutely essential to understand the present through the past, and to understand both the present and the past in terms of worldwide relations within the development of a single world economic system that has roots many centuries deep. This system, despite many transformations and the incorporation of one part of the world after another, of one culture, one nationality after another, has apparently maintained certain significant structural features all the way through. At least some of these essential structural features, I suggest, are that it is a single system that is very unequal from one part to another and that it goes through this continuously uneven process of development in which the crises are as much a part—and perhaps an even more fundamental aspect—of the process of development than the periods of expansion. And what is significant about that for us is the world is passing through another one of these periodic crises. The latest crisis will be essentially politically resolved in one way or another depending on how the class struggle comes out, as it depended in the past on how the class struggle came out at those times.

Dimensions of the Present World Crisis[2]

The present world economic crisis is another general crisis of capital accumulation in the world capitalist system analogous to those of a half-century (1914-1940/1945) and a century (1873-1896) ago. After the last major crisis during the interwar years, there was a renewed expansion during the postwar period. This expansion apparently lasted until 1973, but in fact it had already begun to slow down in 1967 and to turn into a renewed period of relative stagnation and crisis. Initially, this crisis took the form of reduced rates of profit and a renewed recessionary cycle. There was a recession in 1967, which excluded the United States and Japan, the former (and in part the latter) because of the American expenditures to finance its war against Vietnam. In this recession, official unemployment in the industrial capitalist countries (of North America, Western Europe, Japan, Australia, and New Zealand) rose to five million. Unemployment then declined again in the 1968-1969 recovery. Then came the 1969-1970 recession, in which the United States and Japan also participated. Unemployment in the industrialized countries then grew to ten million.

This recession already had very serious consquences. Before the recession, the world had been flooded with dollars issued by the United States to finance the Vietnam War. There had been important changes in relative productivity among industrial producers during the 1960s. Productivity in Europe had grown twice as fast as in the United States and in Japan twice as fast again as in Western Europe.

This change in the relative competitive abilities on the world market and the flood of dollars were exacerbated when growth rates declined during the 1969-1970 recession and led, on August 15, 1971, to what President Nixon called a "new economic policy" and what the Japanese called "Nixon Shokku": Nixon imposed wage and price controls in the United States, took the dollar off its fixed relation to gold, permitting it to be devalued, and imposed a special discriminatory surtax of ten percent on imports from Japan. Thereby he effectively destroyed the basis of the international monetary system that had been established at Bretton Woods after World War II with fixed exchange rates and opened the way to widespread currency fluctuations and further devaluations of the dollar. This decision was an attempt to increase American competitiveness in world markets and led to the rapid increase of American exports, especially of armaments and agricultural products. Then followed the recovery from 1971 to 1973, which was, however, short-lived and led to the major 1973-1975 worldwide recession, in which official unemployment grew to 15 million persons, with nearly nine million in the United States.

The world recession of 1973-1975 also led to the end of rapid Japanese growth rates and to a decline in output in 1974 in Japan as well as in the other industrial countries. Since that time there was another recovery—from 1975 to 1979—in which unemployment decreased again in the United States but continued to increase in Canada, Western Europe, Japan, Australia, and New Zealand. Total unemployment in the industrialized world during the so-called recovery rose from fifteen to seventeen million. In 1979-1980 renewed recession struck and unemployment increased to about twenty-three million in 1980; the OECD predicted an increase to thirty-one million by 1982. This is equivalent to nearly the entire labor force of a major industrial country. Moreover, these unemployment figures are the officially recorded ones. Real unemployment is much higher than what governments say. This seems to be particularly the case for Japan. In 1974, for instance, registered unemployment in Japan was 730,000; but according to an Employment Status Survey, real unemployment was 3,276,000, and male unemployment was twice as high and female unemployment was *ten times* as high as officially registered unemployment. These figures for Japan still do not include the four million other people who either worked part-time but wanted to work more or those who were discouraged from looking for work. This problem is now exacerbated by the enforced earlier retirement age.

Investment has also declined. The rate of profit began to decline in 1967. The major consequence for economic policy everywhere has been that expansionist demand maintaining Keynesian policy has been abandoned on the argument that it would be inflationary. Everywhere Keynesian expansionism has been replaced by deflationary policies in an attempt to reduce costs of production. In the industrialized countries this new strategy takes the form of the imposition of austerity policies, the decline of the welfare state, and the attempt to reduce real wages, which has been more successful in some countries than others. Real wages have certainly declined in the United States and Great Britain, and during part of the 1970s they also declined in Japan, as inflation grew more than money wages. The drive to reduce costs of production has also led to changes in the nature of investment in order to reduce labor and its costs in the industrial process.

In an attempt to justify and legitimate these measures, it has become common to appeal to the return to traditional values, to national unity, and to economic and political nationalism. In a word, there has been a very marked political shift to the right in the industrialized world. This shift is visible in the election and policies of Ronald Reagan in the United States and Margaret Thatcher in Britain. But it also extends to the Frazer and Muldoon governments in Australia and New Zealand and to the pronounced rightward shift in the municipal and parlimentary elections and the government of Japan. Even the labor and social democratic parties have experienced significant shifts to the right and are pursuing more conservative economic policies in Germany, Scandinavia, and elsewhere. Indeed, it was the Labour government of James Callaghan in Britain and Democratic President Jimmy Carter in the United States that first abandoned Keynesian economic measures and imposed the new austerity policies in their country. That is the reason why they lost their electoral support, which went to the Conservative and Republican parties, who, however, only continued and further extended these same monetarist austerity policies. Among the industrial countries only France has moved somewhat to the left, but with severe limitations to the economic policy of the Mitterand government.

Another significant way to reduce costs of production has been to move parts of the productive process from areas where labor costs are high to areas where labor costs are lower. The policy is to move those industrial processes that use much labor, such as in the textile, clothing, shoe, toy, and electronic components industries. More recently, capital-intensive crisis-ridden industries (and those that are polluting or incur high antipollution costs), such as automobiles, shipbuilding, steel, and petrochemicals, are also being moved increasingly to Third World and socialist countries. The northern border of Mexico south of the Rio Grande River began to see the establishment of factories for production for export to the American market in the 1960s. Then South Korea, Hong Kong, Taiwan, and Singapore began their so-called export-led growth in the late 1960s based on the production of labor-intensive commodities for export to the world market. Particularly in South Korea and in Southeast Asia (except Hong Kong), much of this investment was by foreign capital, especially Japanese.

Under the impact of the growing economic crisis of the 1970s, this process of industrial relocation has spread to Malaysia and the Philippines (it is no accident that President Marcos imposed martial law in 1972 when this policy began) and to Thailand, Sri Lanka, India, Pakistan, Egypt, Tunisia, Morocco, various countries in sub-Saharan Africa, everywhere in the Caribbean (except Cuba), and through most of Latin America. In this rapid change in the international division of labor under the impact of this world economic crisis, the Third World is also becoming a place for increased production of agricultural commodities for export by agribusiness. New mining methods on land and the sea bottom are also being introduced. What the Third World countries have to offer in this new international division of labor is first and foremost cheap labor. Additionally, their governments offer all kinds of concessions to international capital, including tax-free holidays to the corporation for several years. Third World states provide the infrastructure of ports, airports, railways, cheap electricity, cheap water, and free land, among other things, and often they even build the factory buildings and lend international capital the money or guarantee private loans to them in order to set up production in their countries to export to the world market—in competition with other countries that bid to do the same.

The worldwide political economic mechanism to promote a new international division of labor by relocating these manufacturing, agricultural, and mining—and even some financial—processes in the Third World and the socialist countries is fueled and oiled by the international financial system. The recessions and inflation (so-called stagflation) in the industrial capitalist countries, combined with increases in the price of oil, have sharply aggravated the balance of payments deficits of the non-oil-exporting countries in the Third World (and some socialist countries such as Poland). To cover these growing deficits, these countries have increasingly turned to the private international capital markets, which have recycled some of the OPEC surplus funds to them and have additionally lent them other funds at high rates of interest that found no borrowers in the industrial countries where investment has been low. The extension of these loans, and particularly their rescheduling to finance the growing debt service when the borrowers are unable to pay, have become the basis of stringent economic and political conditions imposed by the private banks and/or the International Monetary Fund (IMF), acting as their intermediary, on Third World (and some socialist and developed) countries. The standard "conditionality" to the IMF package governments are obliged to accept in their "letter of intent" before being certified to receive further loans always includes devaluation of the currency, reduction of government expenditures (especially on consumer subsidies and polpular welfare), the reduction of the wage rate through various devices, and more favorable treatment for private and especially foreign capital. These conditions have sometimes led to "IMF riots" as the people sought to resist the enforced curtailment of their standards of living. (It has been said that the IMF has overthrown more governments than Marx and Lenin put together.) An important political economic consequence, if not rationale, of these IMF-promoted government policies in the Third World is to promote "export-led growth" by cheapening Third World labor for international capital and foreign importers (by lowering the price of Third World wages and currencies) and to lend support to the domestic forces in these Third World countries that have an economic interest in export promotion. Thus, the international financial system and the financing of the Third World debt serves to fuel and oil the mechanism of the emerging international division of labor based on Third World export promotion.

The political consequences of all these economic policies are that it is necessary to repress the labor force in order to keep wages low or to reduce wages. In the case of Brazil, which, after Mexico, has been the principal example of this process in Latin America since the military coup in 1964, wages were reduced by over 40 percent. In Argentina since the military coup in 1976, wages were reduced by over 50 percent. (Even before the coup real wages began to decline as a result of the economic policy of the Right Wing of the Peronist government in

1974-1975.) In Chile, real wages since the coup have been reduced by two-thirds, from an index of 100 to an index of close to 30; unemployment increased from 4 to 20, then declined to 15 and rose to 30 percent. To be able to do this, it was necessary first to destroy or to control the unions, to eliminate—often physically—the leadership, to repress all political opposition and to throw people in jail, to torture, murder, and exile them. Second, it was necessary to reorganize the economy from producing for the internal market through so-called import substitution to producing for exports.

During the last major crisis of the 1930s and early 1940s, when the Third World was experiencing a balance of payments crisis and was unable to earn foreign exchange to buy imports, countries such as Mexico, Brazil, Argentina, India, and South Africa started to produce manufactures internally for the internal market, substituting these for imports. To be able to do that, however, they had to import capital goods—machinery and later technology with which to produce these goods—and they had to pay for these capital imports through exports. In order to earn these exports they invited in the multinational corporation, which they thought would bring capital and equipment into the country, to do this they had to borrow and increase their debt. Then, in the 1950s and 1960s, this movement spread through other parts of the Third World, most particularly through many countries of Latin America. This process of import substitution for the internal market required people with incomes with which to purchase these commodities. Therefore, there were political alliances between the labor movement and the sector of the bourgeoisies that worked for the internal market to support populist, more or less democratic nationalist governments. When these economies switched from this import substitution model of economic growth to that of export-led growth by promoting exports for the world market, they no longer required effective demand on the internal market to purchase the industrial or agricultural commodities they produced. Manufactured and agricultural commodity exports require the lowest cost of production possible. Military regimes reduce the wage cost of production.

However, this requires a significant reorganization of the ecoonomic and political structure of Brazil, Argentina, Chile, and elsewhere in the Third World as well. The sector of industry and its labor force that had been producing for the internal market, also has to be repressed politically. And this leads to the repressive political measures of these authoritarian and military regimes that have been observed nearly everywhere in the Third World in the 1970s. The repression is used first and foremost against labor and, second, against a sector of the bourgeoisie itself in order to restructure the economy and reorient it toward export production. This political economic process is behind the political repression of Kim in South Korea and Aquino in the Philippines, both of whom are bourgeois leaders who do not propose a revolutionary alternative but simply a more democratic alternative. They are the political representatives of bourgeois capitalist interests in these countries that are dependent on the development of the internal market. These economic interests and their political representatives have to be at least politically eliminated. Repressive regimes are based on an alliance between the sector of the bourgeoisie in these countries that is allied to international capital and particularly to the multinationals of the United States, West Germany, and Japan. Internally this alliance rests politically on the military as the force that cements these relationships. This is the political economic basis of the events we have observed in South Korea, the Philippines, Chile, Argentina, and other countries. Crisis-generated political-economic exigency is what really explains the wave of political repression throughout the Third World.

Delinking and Revolutionary Strategy[3]

The widely felt negative consequences of imperialism, colonialism, neocolonialism, and dependent capitalism generally, and now, the pressures and economic, political, and social costs of export promotion have led to numerous movements in the Third World that assume different forms and goals: national liberation, socialist revolution, African socialism, delinking, collective and national self-reliance, and so on. But as many revolutionaries have observed, if taking political power is difficult, its subsequent use in the pursuit of popular liberation is even more problematical. A review of some recent experience can provide a guide to some of the limitations and, perhaps through their better understanding, to the means to overcome them.

A revolutionary process implies an internal transfer of power and popular participation and the achievement of a greater degree of external independence. Attempts at transitions in the Third World have attempted either one or the other, or both. In some cases there has been no real attempt at either delinking or a redistribution of power and popular participation. I am thinking, for instance, of Indonesia under Sukarno, India, much of the so-called African socialism, and Brazil in the time of Goulart from 1961 to 1964. All of these attempts failed miserably. In some places, there was an attempt at external *delinking,* relative isolation from the world capitalist system, but without concomitant, simultaneous, far-reaching internal social and political changes, such as in Nasser's Egypt and Burma until recently. These regimes lasted a bit longer but in the medium run were substantial failures. The policies of subservient relinking undertaken by Sadat were in part attributable to the important failures of the Nasser regime. Burma also was relinking at a very rapid rate. In other attempts there have been not much external delinking but attempts of some kind of internal reorganization without the external delinking. I am thinking, for instance, of the Ghana of N'Krumah and in a certain sense of Allende's Chile. These were also disastrous failures.

One of the lessons of this experience is that to try neither delinking nor popular participation gets you nowhere. To try only external delinking without internal participation also gets you nowhere and leads back to rapid delinking. To try only internal participation without external delinking is extremely dangerous, very difficult to do, and likely to lead to a disaster. External delinking and internal participation, social and political mobilization, reinforce each other and are necessary in order to be able to pursue rapid structural change to a threshold from which one would not immediately slide backward. The only countries where this has been possible are those that we today call socialist. That is, external delinking and internal political change have been carried so far as to call them socialist. None of the other ways, the noncapitalist path, the popular-democracy path of African socialism, and so on, has produced results.

One of the paradoxes of these experiences and attempts at delinking, with or without internal political change, is that delinking is in essence voluntary; but it is immediately complemented and supplemented by involuntary delinking or "destabilization," the term Kissinger applied to this policy toward the Allende regime in Chile. That is, there are intentional attempts, (and of course the normal operation of the market system supports destabilization) to undermine this process of delinking and internal political change from the outside. With the assitance of a Quisling fifth column on the inside of the country there is pressure to delink the country even faster or farther than it would like to go, or at least to delink it under the control of the opposition to this process (externally and internally) rather than to delink it voluntarily under the control of the political forces that are carrying the process ahead. That in itself gives cause to ponder the real possibilities of delinking. The very fact that delinking is not only a policy that is attempted by progressive governments but is also an arm that is used against the progressive governments gives cause for reflection about the rational utility of delinking in the world today.

Two other recent developments give cause for considerable concern about the prospects for delinking and self-reliance in the immediate future. One of these is the apparent increasingly limited aspiration, let alone achievement, of delinking and self-reliance by recently independent and revolutionary regimes in the Third World. Thus, the newly independent ex-Portuguese territories in Guinea-Bissau, Angola, and Mozambique reached independence through prolonged revolutionary guerrilla struggle (and the 1974 revolution in Portugal). Yet none of them has sought to delink significantly from the world capitalist economy. Angola was enjoined by the Soviet Union not to become another Cuba, and the Cubans in Angola were guarding the Gulf oil installations that provide Angola's principal source of foreign exchange, the remainder of which comes from coffee and minerals that are also sold primarily to the West. Mozambique still depended on South Africa (and the decline in its supply of labor to the mines there was due less to Mozambican policy than to changes in the price and production of gold), and the FREILIMO regime had backtracked on its earlier policies and was again renewing Mozambican reliance on Western aid, trade, and private enterprise. Similar development marked neighboring Zimbabwe, whose Marxist ex-guerrilla leader Robert Mugabe was enjoined by Samora Machel to concede at the London Lancaster House negotiations on pain of losing Mozambique's support of his bases. Thereafter, Mugabe declared himself to be not only a practicing but also a practical Marxist, who acknowledged the need to maintain foreign capital, economic relations with South Africa, and Rhodesian white collaboration, and who could not deliver the previously promised land reform.

In Nicaragua, the Sandinistas agreed to repay the Somoza debt (much of it incurred in fighting against them) and with it to political strings attached to rolling over the debt and the economic and political costs of paying off the debt instead of importing investment and consumer goods with that money. The even more severe alternative, rejected by the Sandinistas, was to renounce the Somoza debt and thereby cut Nicaragua off from any further supplier credits and therefore from even more imports. At the same time, the Sandinistas sought to maintain the private sector in a mixed economy and avoided any declaration of socialism. The other development that gives increasing cause for concern is in those countries that have declared themselves to be Marxist and socialist, some of them over one and two generations ago.

The Relinking of the Socialist Countries[4]

The socialist East is also caught up in this world capitalist crisis, and provided another cause for concern. There is a process of increasing rapid reintegration or relinking into the capitalist international division of labor, not only through trade but also through production. There is also an increasing productive crisis throughout the Comecon countries in general; each of them separately and all of them together had achieved only half or less than half their growth targets for the 1976-1980 five-year plan.

In Poland production declined and "growth" was negative by 2 percent in 1979, 4 percent in 1980, and 14 percent in 1981. Poland is perhaps the most extreme crisis case in this regard, being caught between, on one hand, the increased oil prices the Soviet Union charges its partners in Eastern Europe and, on the other hand, the export difficulties they faced in the West because of recession. So they were caught in a "scissor's crisis" on an international level, reminiscent of the internal crisis during and after NEP in the Soviet Union. Inflation is increasing (as the papers say, inflation goes East), and they were unable to isolate themselves from the effects of this crisis. This is not unrelated to the Polish workers' revolt and deepening economic crisis of 1980 and 1981 and the subsequent repression.

In the major crisis of the depression and war, socialists and socialism welcomed capitalist crisis; they were in favor of the crisis and against capitalism. In the present crisis, it seems evident that the socialist world does not welcome the capitalist crisis at all—in fact, it is anti-crisis and pro-capitalist. That is, it is doing all it can to contribute to the recovery of capitalism and even to eliminate the effects of the crisis. The prime minister of Bulgaria, Theordore Zivkoff, put this very clearly, saying that "the crisis in the West affects us immediately and very deeply, because of our trade and other ties with the West. We hope that this crisis will pass as soon as possible." Socialism could then get back to business as usual. Deng Xiaoping in China spoke eloquently for himself and, at least for the time being, for many millions of Chinese, in his alliance with American imperialism and in the attempt to reintegrate China into the world capitalist economy as quickly as possible, with the preclaimed end of making China a world industrial power by the year 2000.

The economic and then political crisis in Poland and the growing economic crisis in Czechoslovakia and Romania, as well as the general economic difficulties in Eastern Europe and the Soviet Union, made clear that fundamental economic reoganization and concomitant political adjustment are becoming (in Poland, have already become) imperative. A major source of this impasse has been the attempt to graft extensive integration in the world capitalist economy (itself in crisis) onto inflexibility in economic and political organization in Comecon countries. One possible way out of the impasse might be a retreat and involution to delink again, but even if that were still possible, which is doubtful, it might require unacceptable economic and political readjustments at home. The other option is to remedy the impasse of capitalist integration and socialist inflexibility by (para-doxically) further relinking with the capitalist world economy and also following the politically (but perhaps ultimately less costly) complementary flexibility at home. That has been the option so far followed in China and Vietnam (not to mention Kampuchea, whose ousted Khmer Rouge now renounces communism and socialism for the rest of the century), and it is the policy of those in North Korea who seek to avoid the son of Kim II Sung as his successor and main-tainer of past policies.

All this is not to say that the attempts at socialism were mistaken or useless. The socialist countries all made significant advances of con-siderable benefit to their populations. What the World Bank now calls "basic needs" are met in the socialist countries; they have increased production, but they have not been very successful in increasing productivity. They have managed to produce an important expansion in production by mobilizing all inputs and therefore increas-ing outputs. Compare China with India, for instance, or Rumania, Bulgaria and so on with Turkey or Greece, or take the most obvious case of the Soviet Union: By having made a socialist revolution, they are now able to rejoin the world capitalist division of labor, but with an entirely different productive basis internally (in one word, industrialization) and an entirely different bargaining power externally.

This expansive growth approaches limits, however, which seem to have been reached in many socialist economies around 1970, unless and until they reorganize production to increase it intensively by raising productivity. Here the socialist economies have been much less able to show successes. The need for increased productivity is the major reason why they are now reverting to technology from the West and are trying to reorganize their economies internally. But productivity comes at the cost of the relative social equality that has been achieved during the earlier period, as experience in Eastern Europe and now China suggests.

Thus, these socialist experiences have been very important and very useful, but they have not produced precisely what was expected of them, either internally of externally. As the French Revolution did not bring the peasants to power, so the Soviet Revolution certainly did not bring the Russian proletariat to power, and internally they have not brought what we previously understood by socialism. Originally socialism was understood to be a process of transition to communism. It seems extremely difficult, if impossible, today to sustain the thesis that the "really existing socialist societies" in Eastern Europe are in any sense a transition to communism. On the contrary, if they are in transition to anything today, it is more likely a transition to capitalism.

But capitalism itself is undergoing another crisis-generated transition or transformation, of which the relinking of the socialist economies and the analogous reorganization of the Third World to participate in a new international division of labor through so-called export-led growth are integral elements. Both contribute to the necessary lowering of production costs and to capital's ability to reorganize the world economy during this period of crisis and to lay the basis for a possible subsequent period of renewed capitalist expansion. Whether these and other developments will fundamentally alter the structure and operation of the world capitalist system remains to be seen, but it seems unlikely for the foreseeable future.

Notes

1. This section is based largely on Frank (1980b, 1979).
2. This section is a summary of Frank (1980a, 1981).

3. This section is further elaborated in my contribution to *Dynamics of the Global Crisis* (Amin et al., 1982). See also my forthcoming paper for the August 1982 Congress of the International Political Science Association (Rio De Janiero).

4. This section is based on and further elaborated in the chapter devoted to socialist economies in *Crisis: In the World Economy* (Frank, 1980a) and in the section devoted to socialism in my contribution to *Dynamics of the Global Crisis.*

References

Amin, Samir, Giovanni Arrighi, André Gunder Frank, and Immanuel Wallerstein
   1982   Dynamics of the Global Crisis. New York: Monthly Review Press/London: Macmillan.

Frank, André Gunder
   1981   Crisis: In the Third World. New York: Holmes & Meier/London: Macmillan.
  1980a   Crisis: In the World Economy. New York: Holmes & Meier/London: Macmillan.
  1980b   World Accumulation 1492-1789. New York: Monthly Review Press/London: Macmillan.
   1979   Dependent Accumulation and Underdevelopment. New York: Monthly Review Press/London: Macmillan.

Henry Veltmeyer: Surplus Labor and Class Formation on the Latin American Periphery

There is little question about the centrality of class relations and class struggle in the development of capitalism or about the process of capital accumulation involved in class formation. Indeed, for Marxists both are axiomatic. However, when it comes to an analysis of these conditions in the contemporary era on what could be termed the "periphery" of the capitalist system, the matter is somewhat different—and more complicated. Here the relationship between capital accumulation and class formation is subject to considerable debate and even brought into question.[1] At issue in this debate are the conditions under which capitalism in its expansion penetrates, breaks down, and eventually transforms noncapitalist social formations. In its classical form, this problem has been generally posed in terms of a transition toward a system based on the productive relationship of wage labor, the free exchange of labor power for a wage. Although the theory of this transition allows for a number of divergent forms and a very uneven, protracted development,[2] there is no question about the fundamental process involved: dispossession of the direct producers from their means of production and the increasing dependence on conditions regulated by the expansion of capital, conditions that convert on an increasing scale direct producers into wage workers.[3]

With numerous qualifications (reference to variable, historically specific conditions in different social formations), studies of capitalist development and class formation have always revolved around variations of this proletarianization process. However, a number of more recent studies of peripheral capitalist development (for example, Meillasoux, 1972; Alavi, 1975; Amin, 1975; Bartra, 1974; Dietrich, 1978) have begun to question this traditional formulation of the transition problem. In fact, with respect to agriculture, historically the basis of capitalist development, these studies suggest that countries on the periphery have not generally taken the paths toward capitalism traced out in the classic works of Marx and Lenin. As Lehman (1980:9-10), among others, points out the classical model does not fit the reality of peripheral formations in the contemporary epoch of capitalist development. In particular, it does not explain some of the most characteristic features of peripheral social formations: the persistence, even growth, of peasant smallholding in agriculture, and a more general reproduction of precapitalist production relations in both the urban and rural economies.

There is some confusion as to how to best approach an analysis of this problem—to conceptualize class formation in this context. For one thing, it is surrounded by controversy over the nature of capitalism.[4] A major point at issue in this controversy is whether societies on the periphery are still at an early stage of capitalist development as formulated by Marx (and Lenin), or whether this development takes a specific, qualitatively distinct form with a concomitant class structure. On this question, several positions can be distinguished. First, a number of studies argue that capital accumulation on the periphery has a dynamic of its own which distorts the basic structure of capitalist productive class relations (see Marini, 1973; Murmis, 1973; Pucciarelli, 1978; Campaña and Rivera, 1978; Amin, 1975). Some go as far as to distinguish not only a distinct social formation but a new "mode of production" based on the economic structure and productive relations of colonialism (Cardoso, 1973, 1975; Banaji, 1972; Alavi, 1975). A second set of studies treats the structure of productive relations as secondary to the structure of economic dependence, and, on the basis of this dependence, conceptualizes classes in relation to, and in terms of, the capitalist market extended into a "world-system" (Frank, 1967; Wallerstein, 1974).[5] These "dependency" theorists do not visualize peripheral capitalism as a distinct economic dynamic. They see it, rather, as the working of a world market under conditions that block development of the productive forces on the periphery, or even, in Frank's formulation, "underdevelop" them. The operative assumption in this theory of underdevelopment is that the market works like a "surplus appropriation chain" to accumulate capital, drain it out of the periphery, and transfer it to the metropolitan center (core economies) of the system. Within this system, the underdeveloped peripheral economies of the Third World stand in the same relation to those at the center as agriculture has generally stood in relation to industry: as a source of an economic surplus, value that circulates in the world capitalist system in a commodity form of cheap raw materials and wage goods.

A third position traces back the conditions of economic backwardness, as well as the characteristic class structure of peripheral formations, to an "insufficiency of capitalist development" based on the general failure of capital to penetrate agriculture (Laclau, 1971; Fernández and Ocampo, 1974; Assadourian et al., 1971; Kay, 1975). These studies work more closely from traditional Marxist theory in their analysis of the barriers to capitalist development erected by feudal tenure, ground rent, merchant's capital, and so on. The persistence of these precapitalist relations and the prolongation of merchant's capital within peripheral social formations, it is argued (or assumed), places absolute limits on the production of surplus value and the accumulation of capital as well as more generally on the economic development of society. This position is clearly at odds with dependency theory, which generally holds that regardless of how production is organized within peripheral formations, these formations provide the ultimate and basic source of the capital accumulated at the center through the exploitive mechanisms of the world market. In contrast to this theory, exponents of a more traditional Marxist position argue that the relative economic backwardness of peripheral social formations is due not to the superexploitation of workers and producers, but, as Kay (1975:55) puts it, "because [capitalism] has not exploited them enough." In other words, development of the productive forces requires the destruction of precapitalist relations and the further extension of the real capitalist mode of production. And this, as Marx consistently argued, involves much more than the extension of commodity production and "mere commerce"; it requires the separation of the direct producers from their means of production (1967: Vol. I, 713-714).

Variations of these three positions on the nature of peripheral capitalist development lie behind most of the controversy as well as the little analysis actually conducted on class relations within peripheral social formations. More recently, however, this entire problem has been placed in a new perspective by studies that focus on structures that typically combine several modes of production within a given social formation (Bartra et al., 1976; Scott, 1976; Dietrich, 1978; Dietz, 1979; Taylor, 1979; Wolpe, 1980; Chinchilla and Dietz, 1981).[6] In these studies the "transition problem" is reformulated as a question of determining the conditions under which the process of capital accumulation is based on the complex articulation of the capitalist mode of production with noncapitalist ones. In this formulation of the problem quite new questions are raised about the class structure of peripheral social formations. For one thing, these questions are no longer displaced from the center of analysis, as with theories of dependency and underdevelopment. For another, there is no longer any question of two distinct modes of production, or of the dynamics of a distinct "colonial" mode of production. Analysis of class formation becomes a matter of sorting out specific combinations of various modes of production within a larger system dominated by capital, a system analyzed at a determinate phase of its worldwide development.[7] Within this context, characteristic features of peripheral social formation, such as the persistence of precapitalist modes of surplus extraction, the increased involvement of women in precapitalist relations, and the proliferation of petty production in its various forms, can be looked at in a new light. As with the social formations found at the center of the world capitalist system, class structures on the periphery can be analyzed in terms of forces released in the expanded reproduction by capital.

The many questions surrounding this problem of class formation and capitalist development are by no means settled, and this chapter will not contribute toward this end. What I will attempt, however, is to bring into sharper analytical focus elements of what could be termed a "modes of production" approach to class formation. Modifying the framework of this approach, this study suggests that peripheral societies share economic conditions not found to any significant extent at the center of the system; that in terms of these conditions it is possible to identify a class structure typical of peripheral formations; and that this structure is shaped by what Marx termed "the general law of capital accumulation." With reference to conditions specified by this law,[8] I argue that the class structure of peripheral formations revolves around the production of a relative surplus population and that certain characteristic features of this structure (persistence of precapitalist relations, active semiproletarianization, proliferation of petty production in its various forms, the sexual division of labor, and so on) serve to expand capital under conditions of superexploitation.

Accumulation and Peasantry

Notwithstanding the controversy over the nature of capitalism, the basic precondition for the emergence and development of the capitalist mode of production is an available supply of free wage labor.[10] The major source of this supply has always been agriculture, and the bulk of the world's agricultural producers is found and increasingly concentrated in the peripheral formations of the Third World.[11] Capitalist penetration of agriculture—and, by extension, peripheral social formations—generally yields necessary supplies of "free" wage labor by creating conditions that separate the direct producers from their means of production, contract the economic basis of independent production, and break down the extraeconomic mechanisms of precapitalist property relations. In advanced capitalist countries this process has long run its course, with the capitalist mode of production in each case holding sway over the entire economy.[12] As for the periphery, these same developments have involved an exceedingly slow, more contracted process, but there is no mistaking the same fundamental connection between capital accumulation and the progressive dispossession of direct producers from their means of production. Examination of structural and historical data on land tenure, rural emigration, and labor and employment patterns in Latin America demonstrates the scope of the problem. In each and every case, the conversion of farms into agroexport capitalist enterprises, and a more general conversion of land into a commodity, have resulted in a massive concentration of landownership and an equally massive expropriation by both economic and extraeconomic means of the peasantry.[13] Although, as we will see, many of these dispossessed peasants retain access to some land through family ties, sharecropping, or tenant farming, the capitalist development of agriculture over time has created an enormous surplus population "set free," in Marx's terms, "to provide a labour reserve available to be thrown into other sectors of production as required by capital accumulation" (1967: 632-633).

The accumulation of such a "relative surplus population" is, of course, a necessary condition of existence for the capitalist mode of production, and as such has always functioned as an industrial reserve army (Marx, 1967:632). However, with the worldwide extension of capitalism, this industrial reserve army is increasingly restricted to peripheral formations. While the "conjuctural" fluctuations of unemployment in the advanced capitalist formations at the center of the system remain significant, they are quite modest when compared to the steady growth of the industrial reserve army on the periphery. By conservative estimates, the industrial reserve army includes at least 25 percent of the economically active urban population in peripheral formations, and this does not take into account massive rural underemployment both overt (e.g., landless peasants who actively seek wage work) or "hidden" (e.g., *minifundistas*). Table 6.1 provides a brief glimpse of this problem as it relates to Latin America. As Amin (1980:14) notes, this structural development is inextricably linked to the new international division of labor created by the world imperialist system and the resulting internationalization of the supply of labor power.[14] Within this development, the industrial reserve army has taken forms in Latin America that establish the characteristic features of peripheral social formations.

The first such characteristic is the incomplete nature of rural proletarianization based on the maintenance and partial reproduction of precapitalist relations and modes of production in agriculture (Bettleheim, 1972; Meillasoux, 1972). Unlike the experience of advanced capitalist formations, the existence and growth of capitalist production in and around agriculture on the periphery has not meant the dissolution of subsistence agriculture or precapitalist forms of agriculture. What it has meant is the proliferation of petty commodity production and the persistence of smallholding subsistence production as well as various tenancy and sharecropping arrangments based on rent or payment in kind, and even some vestiges of feudalism and other precapitalist modes of surplus extraction. There have been numerous attempts to explain these phenomena and to categorize the forms and relations of agricultural production involved. Many anthropologists have followed Chayanov in conceptualizing household units of subsistence or petty production as part of a "peasant economy" and as such a system with its own internal logic and social formation. There is some question as to whether such an economy constitutes a distinct mode of production or merely a form of production,[15] but it is generally assumed that peasants constitute more of a community than a class (Lehman, 1980; Smith, 1979). Other studies focus instead on

TABLE 6.1 Underutilization of Labor (ca. 1970)

Country	EAP Agri-cultural	EAP Nonagri-cultural	Open Unem-ployment Rate[2]	Equivalent Unemployment in Agriculture[1] Rate[2]	Nonagricultural Underemployment Rate[2]	Equivalent Nonagricultural Employment Rate[2]	Total Under-utilization of Labor Rate[2]
Argentina	1,318	7,505	1.9	10	27.8	12.0	13.6
Brazil	11,965	16,709	6.9	35	43.5	21.8	34.3
Chile	665	2,056	5.0	20	37.9	17.3	22.8
Colombia	2,686	3,709	7.4	25	39.2	20.2	29.6
Mexico	5,293	7,180	3.8	40	27.9	11.8	29.2
Venezuela	714	2,301	6.2	19	42.9	20.5	24.2
Total % underutilized	22,614	38,830	5.5 / 18.9	34 / 42.7	36.8	17.6 / 38.4	28.4 / 100.0

1. The total underutilization has been calculated on the basis of the percentage difference between supply and demand of labor, thus including open unemployment. The methodologies used are not always the same, partly because of local features, so that the figures should not be taken at their absolute value—they only serve to estimate orders of magnitude.

2. The rates refer to the relevant economically active population.

SOURCE: ECLA-LTTP (Wilkie, 1980: 174).

the degree to which these peasant producers, regardless of their relationship to the means of production, are integrated into the market economy and subsumed by capital as a class of independent commodity producers—and consumers (Bernstein, 1979). Here it is argued that most agricultural producers, having for the most part entered the circuit of commodity exchange, are exploited by capital through the pricing mechanism of the capitalist market, and that in relation to this mechanism, they constitute a class within the broader capitalist system (Amin, 1980). A third set of studies recognizes the formal unity of a peasant economy but draws attention to the way it is of necessity always subordinated to the dominant mode of production (Díaz-Polanco, 1977). In the present context, these studies follow Lenin's analysis of the peasantry as a transitional heterogeneous grouping which tends to differentiate into the basic classes of capitalist system: a small group of large landholders becoming capitalist farmers; a larger group of medium-sized landholders converting to commodity production more generally; and the large mass of smallholders, falling into the proletariat or its reserve armies.[16] The determining factor in this class formation is the accumulation of capital in agriculture, a development directly reflected in the concentration of arable land, an increase in the intensity of cultivation, and the dissolution of precapitalist relations in agriculture.

It has to be said that each of these categorizations of agricultural production captures an aspect of class formation on the periphery. Some communities or household units of agricultural production undoubtedly do not owe their conditions of existence to the functioning of the capitalist mode of production and thus are insulated from the class relations and institutions of capitalist society. Strictly speaking, these are the only producers—and only small, isolated pockets remain—who can be properly termed "peasants." Other elements of the rural farm population are just as clearly integrated into some domestic or international market dominated by capital and can be usefully categorized as petty bourgeoisie. Again, as noted earlier, the dispossessed peasantry remains the chief source of the industrial reserve army in its latent form, and as such the basis for a slowly expanding but strictly limited urban and rural proletariat. However, together these various categorization account for but a small part of the population economically active in agriculture. They do not apply, for example, to all those who retain access to land through family ties, tenancy, sharecropping, or some other precapitalist arrangements

(Paré, 1977; Esteva, 1978; and Rello, 1976).[17] Nor do they properly apply to the vast bulk of minifundistas who regularly combine subsistence and/or petty production with wage labor contracted on a seasonal or casual basis (Bartra, 1974; Favre, 1977; Villarreal, 1978; Täussig, 1978; Moncayo and Rojas, 1979).[18] Those in this position, involving 60 percent or more of the economically active rural population in Central America and the Andean countries, cannot be properly or usefully regarded either as peasants or as representatives of an independent mode of production; nor, in class terms, can they be adequately conceived as members of the petty bourgeoisie or the proletariat. As suggested by Paré (1977) and Maffei (1979), among others, both the petty bourgeois and the proletarian character of agricultural production in peripheral formations have been much exaggerated. The large mass of dispossessed peasants, together with all those who combine subsistence/petty commodity production with seasonal or casual wage labor, are more correctly placed into the *semiproletariat.* Although this remains a controversial question, this categorization reflects the effective relationship of the vast bulk of small producers to the dominant capitalist mode of production: as a source of cheap surplus labor and as such a lever of capital accumulation.

There is, perhaps, nothing startling here. After all, the classical studies of primitive accumulation in European agriculture by Marx, Kautsky, and Lenin identified much the same phenomenon among the small landholders (on this point see Hussain and Tribe, 1981). However, what is different about this process of primitive accumulation in the contemporary context of Third World agriculture is that it is clearly not a transitory phenomenon; semiproletarianization (that is, the combination of wage labor and subsistence/commodity production based on the incomplete separation of direct producers from their means of production) is, in fact, an active process of class formation in most peripheral countries and regions, even at a relatively advanced stage of capitalist development.[19]

The economic conditions of this semiproletarianization are most easily established for those formations in Central America and the Andean states of South America where the massive production of a surplus population of landless peasants is a relatively recent phenomenon (Moncayo and Rojas, 1979; Täussig, 1978; Winson, 1978). In these countries, the production of a large surplus population is closely tied to the expansion of capitalist agroexport agriculture.

Take, for example, the haciendas organized around peasant communities in Columbia, Ecuador, and Peru. Typically, one-half of the workforce on these haciendas is made up of minifundistas, with the other half drawn from various sources, generally the coastal region (Rutledge, 1977; Favre, 1977; Täussig. 1978). The significant feature here is that whereas the coastal immigrants generally enter the workforce as *afiliados* (permanently employed), the poor local peasants do so as casual contract workers, working in small, unstable gangs at minimal wages and moving from one job and small contractor to another (Täussig, 1978:427). Like the many small producers hired on a seasonal basis, these casual contract workers rely for subsistence on their minifundios, which are generally worked in their absence by other members of the household, especially wives (Deere, 1977:61-63; Burbach and Flynn, 1980:140-150).

The connection between subsistence agriculture and the process of capital accumulation is reflected in the internal structure of peasant households and communities. As Deere (1977) has argued, the basic element in this structure is a division of labor by sex, characterized by the female production of subsistence foodstuffs and male semiproletarianization. In terms of this structure, whatever their mode of agricultural production—and it is even possible to detect vestiges of feudalism—small farm households are generally well adapted to the requirements of capital accumulation. Whenever the mass of functioning capital expands in agriculture, or, as we will see, in mining and industrial enclaves, the surplus labor of the peasant, family, and kin is released and made available under various conditions of wage labor. With each contraction of the system, whether seasonal or due to market fluctuations, these rural households and their communities either store this surplus labor or function as hospitals of capital accumulation, absorbing the dead weight of the industrial reserve army.

Accumulation and the Working Class

Semiproletarianization is one structural adaptation to the requirements of capital for cheap surplus labor. The maintenance of subsistence plots and precapitalist relations function as means of storing fluctuating reserves of surplus labor and of lowering the reproduction costs of this labor. However, capitalism on the periphery has developed other structural responses to the same problem. One such response is reflected in the formation of a class of casual day laborers in the agroexport sector of the most advanced capitalist economies on the periphery; the other is reflected more generally in the typical structure of the working class in the urban centers, especially those connected to the agroexport economy.

As for the first phenomenon, it is a highly visible product of a turn to more capital-intensive methods of production adopted in many coastal plantations (D'Incão e Mello, 1975; Scott, 1976; Saint, 1981:91*ff*). In those regions and countries where this development is most advanced (such as Brazil, Mexico, and Peru), the bulk of the workforce is still based on the underemployed or seasonally unemployed members of small farm families. However, the workforce on these plantations is increasingly drawn from the mass of unemployed in the urban periphery of nearby towns and cities. These unemployed are the social product of a process that bears close comparison with the English Enclosure Movement analyzed by Marx. In this process, segments of the agroexport bourgeoisie no longer find it necessary to bear the cost of maintaining a casual labor force on the land through the cession of subsistence plots, tenancy arrangements, and the like. With the adoption of more capital-intensive methods of production on the sugar, rice, and cotton plantations, it becomes more economical to expel these casual laborers and truck them back on a daily basis from the swelling urban slums (D'Incão e Mello, 1975; Gomes da Silva, 1975; Scott, 1976). In fact, it has been estimated (Saint, 1981:102) that the switch to casual wage labor trucked in from nearby towns and urban slums can result in savings to the employer of 10 to 30 percent.

A number of recent studies (especially D'Incão e Mello, 1975, and Gomes da Silva, 1975) bring out the significance of this development. During 1964-1975 in the not atypical case of Brazil, the absolute number of nonresident rural workers, the *boia fria,* increased by almost 44 percent while the overall rural population declined by one-third (Saint, 1981:93). By 1975, Gomes da Silva (1975:16) estimated that in the case of Brazil, up to 39 percent of the agricultural workforce, and 25 percent or so in the more developed areas like São Paulo, were involved in this highly exploitive and oppressive system of casual wage labor.[20] The demand for this labor in agriculture is highly seasonal, and when it peaks and wages rise the work groups expand to include persons normally underemployed in the urban economy, including women and children (Graziano de Silva, 1977). In fact, a significant and increasing proportion of this casual workforce is constituted by women (Guimarães, 1978; Martinez-Alier, 1977). In one particular study by Olivera (1978), it was found that 78 percent of 194 boia fria families interviewed had two or more working members, suggesting a different sexual division of labor (or family survival strategy) than the one found by Deere in Peru. Nevertheless, in both cases, the structural basis of the sexual division of labor is exploitation of a sizable floating reserve of surplus labor.

The mass of surplus labor retained in agriculture through the mechanisms of subsistence production, migration, and other forms of semi-proletarianization, is enormous. However, as capitalism advances an ever larger part of the active industrial reserve army can be found or is pushed into the urban centers, especially the coastal towns and cities connected to the agroexport or mining enclaves of the world economy. The largest part of this surplus population is generated by the capitalist development of agriculture. But the urban economy itself continually regenerates and replenishes this surplus, absorbing workers here and expelling them there. In every division of the urban economy, as in agriculture, there exists a large mass of unemployed or underemployed workers, which, as Bennholdt-Thomsen (1976) and Villarreal (1978) have shown, generally functions as a mechanism for holding down wages in the capitalist sector. In itself, there is nothing unqiue about this industrial reserve army. It is, after all, an integral feature of all capitalist economies. However, within peripheral formations it has a number of distinctive structural characteristics that have a direct bearing on class formation, as well as more generally the international division of labor within the capitalist system.

The first such characteristic is found in the structure of the urban working class. Available data and a number of recent studies (Bromley and Gerry, 1979; Portes, 1978) show that a large part of the surplus population released from agriculture surfaces in the "informal sector" of the urban economy composed of casual wage labor, disguised wage labor, self-employment in petty production and trade, and a host of petty services such as street vending, odd-jobbing, car washing and watching, and domestic service. Accounting for more than a third of the economically active population in major urban centers and in some countries up to one-half of the urban workforce, this surplus population has been studied for some time as a marginal phenomenon and thus fated to disappear with the advances of large-scale industrial capitalism. However, it is now clear that this is far from the case. As the major component of the industrial reserve army in its various forms, it is a structured and growing part of the urban economy in peripheral formations (Bromley and Gerry, 1979; Portes, 1980). One explanation for this fact that has been offered is that the uneven nature of industrial capitalism in its worldwide development tends to restrict the absorptive capacity of urban peripheral economies (Nun, 1969). However, this somewhat obvious explanation is inadequate at two levels. For one thing, it does not explain the way and the degree to which the labor employed in the informal sector of the urban economy is structured into the broader capitalist system. For another, it does not explain the growth of the informal sector in the face of an increasingly mobile international capital that seeks its reserves of cheap labor at the major point of its reproduction (the periphery) rather than drawing it toward the industrial heartland in the metropolitan centers of the world-system. A better explanation of these developments can be found in the general law of capital accumulation, according to which an expanding mass of functioning capital brings about a corresponding increase in surplus population at lower wage rates (Marx, 1967:637).[21] The operation of this law is expressed most generally in the fact that the industrial sectors in which employment has remained relatively stagnant or even declined are those with above-average wage rate, while sectors in which employment has tended to expand are those with lower-than-average wage rates.[22]

An even more dramatic expression of this law of capital accumulation can be found in the links between the informal and formal sectors of the urban economy. As in the rural economy, these links hinge on the existence of noncapitalist forms and relations of production, such as subsistence and networking obligations, petty commodity production and trade, informal land occupation, and unpaid family labor (Portes, 1980; Bromley and Gerry, 1979). On the basis of such non- and precapitalist institutions, and ready access to a highly elastic labor supply, the informal sector of the working class[23] is able to reduce the costs of capitalist production substantially. These savings (see Davies in Bromley and Gerry, 1979:98*ff*) occur at two levels. First, through a series of subcontracting relations with other firms, the informal sector provides capitalists a broad range of low-cost wage goods and services. A graphic illustration of this point is given by Bromley and Gerry (1979) with respect to "self-employed" garbage collectors who, like many petty producers in the informal sector, are integrated, via other levels and types of enterprise, into a multinational corporation or some other unit of large-scale capitalist production. In his intersectoral case study Bromley calculates that the inclusion of self-employed garbage collectors within Carton de Colombia would have increased the cost of wastepaper to the corporation by 300 percent. With savings in this order of magnitude it is little wonder that the various studies collected and edited by Bromley and Gerry (1979) suggest that rather than destroying petty production, peripheral capitalist development tends to increase the levels and incorporation of petty and small capitalist enterprise.[24] A second way in which the informal sector contributes to the process of capital accumulation is in the provision of a self-supporting reserve army of labor on which capitalists can draw without having to bear the full costs of its reproduction. Several studies have established that the wages of workers in the informal sector are not sufficient to cover more than their daily reproduction costs. The generational reproduction of these workers is generally covered by the extramarket mechanisms of the informal sector or the labor of family members that retain access to some land. In some cases, these workers are not forced to migrate with each contraction or expansion of capitalist production, but are able to stay on the farm, commuting to the city for wage work on a daily basis. In these cases, capitalists do not even have to fully bear the workers' daily reproduction costs.

Another expression of the law of capital accumulation can be found in the sexual composition of the working class and its reserve armies. Like dispossesed rural migrants, women are generally drawn into capitalist production under very specific conditions of low pay, marginal employment in low wage industrial enclaves, and a general intensification of precapitalist relations (Gardiner, 1975; Saffioti, 1977; Deere, 1977). Froebel, Heinrichs, and Kreye, in a series of case studies into the new international division of labor, found an increasing preference of multinational corporations for female labor (1980:348). In fact, the authors argue that this preference is so pronounced that when the supply of female labor is depleted, industries tend to relocate production to areas where young female labor is yet or easily available. This concentration of women in low-wage industries is, of course, also characteristic of advanced capitalist formations where other, more traditional sources of surplus labor, such as rural migrants have been largely exhausted. More characteristic of peripheral formations is a much greater reliance on female labor in meeting the reproduction costs, both daily and generational, of workers in general (Deere, 1977; Saffioti, 1977). While capitalism everywhere relies on the exploitation of female domestic labor,[25] the intensification of precapitalist relations in the organization of women's work serves to offset pressures on the production of surplus value. The widespread institution of domestic service serves a similar purpose with respect to the claims made against the existing mass of surplus value. With a third or so of the female labor force in Latin America employed as domestics,[26] the importance of such pockets of precapitalist relations in the reproduction of capital is clear. As Saffioti (1977:30) has argued, the magnitude of the exploitation rate very much depends on the relative weight of such pockets within the broader capitalist system.

Exploitation and Superexploitation

What has been suggested thus far is that there is an important structural difference between peripheral formations and those found at the center of the world capitalist system. Whereas class positions in the latter are overwhelmingly based on the productive relation of wage labor, those in the former derive from conditions of an industrial reserve army—a relative surplus population created by the accumulation and concentration of capital on a world scale. Under these conditions, various pockets of precapitalist relations are maintained, even reproduced, within a larger structure dominated by the capitalist mode of production. Within this structure, capitalists are able to dispose of a large mass of labor power without having to bear the full costs of its reproduction. These are largely assumed by women under some conditions, rural migrants and entire communities of small producers under others.

A close examination of these conditions—to quote Marx from a different context—"exposes the inner secret, the hidden basis of the entire social structure": a set of complex mechanisms for the extraction of surplus value under conditions of *superexploitation*—the forcible reduction of wages below the value of labor power.[27] The forms of this superexploitation are varied, but all of the mechanisms thus far identified—the capitalist labor market, contract labor, forced labor, rent, unpaid family labor, the product market, and so on—are based on conditions internal to peripheral social formations, especially the sexual division of labor and the domestic unit of subsistence production. While capitalism tends to destroy the family and the self-subsistent community as units of production, on the periphery they have been adapted to the very specific contemporary requirements of "primitive accumulation."[28] For one thing, the sexual division of labor not only absorbs the cost of ensuring a continued supply of labor power, but it regulates the supply of available male labor and the price of this labor in general (Deere, 1977; deLeal and Deere, 1979:104-106).[29] More generally, the domestic unit of subsistence production organized around family labor not only subsidizes the expansion of capitalist agriculture but forms the basis of a limited but growing industrial capitalism as well. On the one hand, communities or households of small producers provide a continual source of cheap surplus labor to agrarian and urban capitalist enterprises. On the other hand, the petty bourgeois element in both the rural and the urban economy is exploited at a different level though the mechanisms of the capitalist product market. Under the conditions of their insertion into this market, independent producers have little access to credit, are easily forced into a debt relationship, and, most important, have little control over the prices their products can bear. By paying them prices which are below the embodied value of their labor, selling them commodities at prices above their value, loaning them money at higher rates of interest, and renting them land in return for a substantial part of their produce or labor, agrarian capitalists manage to extract surplus value from these nominally independent commodity producers (Beaucage, 1975; Bartra, 1974; Vergopoulos, 1978; and Amin, 1975). As for the industrial bourgeoisie, the low costs of labor in agriculture allow them to lower the wages paid to the urban working class and thus further offset various class pressures on the production of surplus value.[30] In either case, the pricing system of the capitalist market, like the system of smallholding subsistence production and other conditions of cheap surplus labor, generally functions as a mechanism of surplus transfer and as a lever of capital accumulation—reducing the cost of reproducing labor power within the capitalist sector. As suggested above, the economic conditions of this dynamic defines the most characteristic features of peripheral class formation.

Concluding Remarks

this chapter has briefly explored various problems involved in a class analysis of peripheral social formations. It was suggested that this analysis is complicated by the economic conditions of a very uneven worldwide process of capital accumulation. Although these conditions affect the internal structure of both the capitalist class and the working class, they apply particularly to a complex of pre-capitalist relations reproduced within a larger structure dominated by capital (subject to the basic laws of capital accumulation). Within this structure, the family and self-subsistent/petty commodity production in its various forms have evolved as institutions that facilitate the creation and preservation of an industrial reserve army. The enormous size and various forms of this surplus population condition the basic class structure of peripheral formations. Not only does peripheral accumulation generate a large class of individuals and families caught up in a struggle for survival and independence on the one hand and higher wages and more stable employment on the other, but it creates major structural divisions within the proletariat. A preliminary analysis (see, for example, Cohen et al., 1979) of these divisions suggests that the semiproletarianized peasantry, rural migrants, women, and other forms of surplus population have no clear relationship to an organized class struggle based on the capitalist relation of wage labor. To bring this problem into a proper political or analytical focus requires a much closer look at the questions raised here.

Notes

1. The classical theory of this relationship is derived from Marx but is most clearly formulated by Lenin. In this form, the theory of capitalist development as class formation has been challenged on a number of levels. Those studies that deny the relevance of class to an analysis of contemporary social formations which are characterized by the persistence of a significant peasant economy either emphasize the role of the family and kinship structures in the social organization of production (Campaña and Rivera, 1978) or the isolation and relative independence of the peasant economy. On this basis, Lehman (1980) for one, argues the equal importance of the concept of "enterprise," the unit of peasant production, to that of productive class relations. More generally, this entire problem revolves around the question of whether most agricultural producers in peripheral formations represent a distinct mode of production (simple or petty commodity, independent, domestic, peasant, and so on) or merely a form of production. In the latter case, "peasants" are conceived in broad terms as a class of that dominant mode, a heterogeneous grouping composed of various classes and fractions, or a transitional formation of various classes ranged within the dominant mode. Besides the Latin American sources discussed or referenced in this chapter, important points in this debate on the nature of the peasantry in its more recent form can be found in the *Journal of Peasant Studies* (see in particular Duggett, 1975; Scott, 1976; Ennew et al., 1977; Friedmann, 1978, 1980).

2. The classical models of this transition, as formulated by Marx and Lenin, have been subject to a series of debates departing from the Dobb-Sweezy polemic in the 1950s. On the divergent contemporary forms of this transition in Latin America see in particular the studies edited by Duncan and Rutledge (1977) and those appearing in *Latin American Perspectives,* Vols. 18-19 (1978).

3. See Marx (1967: Vol. I. 613-614): "Accumulation, reproduces the capital-relation on a progressive scale, more capitalists or larger capitalists at this pole, more wage workers at that. The reproduction of a mass of labour-power, which must incessantly re-incorporate itself with capital for that capital's self-expansion, which cannot get free from capital, and whose enslavement to capital is only concealed by the variety of individual capitalists to whom it sells itself, this reproduction of labour-power forms, in fact, an essential of the reproduction of capital itself. Accumulation of capital is, therefore, increases of the proletariat."

4. See Foster-Carter (1978) and Veltmeyer (1980) for reviews of this controversy, which dates to the mid-1960s, when certain texts by Frank (1967) and Vitale (1971) triggered an extended polemic on the feudal or capitalist character of Latin America (see in particular the essays in Assadourian et al., 1973). At issue in this polemic are two conflicting concepts of the capitalist mode of production, the one based on market orientation, the other on the productive relation of wage labor. As Cueva (1978) points out, a major result of defining capitalism loosely in terms of a connection to the "world market" is that the entire problem of capitalist development as a transition between, or the complex articulation of, different modes of production disappears or cannot even arise.

5. Formulation of this dependency theory are legion. On its Latin American origins and expressions see in particular the reviews by Chilcote (1974, 1981) and various assessments in issues 1, 11, 21, and 30-31 of *Latin American Perspectives.* As for the lack of internal class analysis by dependency theorists, the point is well established by a long series of critiques. As Henfrey (1981:35) notes with respect to Frank, the only class brought into any analytical focus is the dependent (or *comprador* or lumpen) bourgeoisie. However, Henfry observes, even here what is provided is no analysis of class formation, relations, or struggles, "merely the reiteration of this bourgeoisie's standard, merely economic, and inexorably subordinate external relations."

6. The point of departure for this approach is Marx's concept of the mode of production, formulated by Laclau (1971:33) as follows: "the logical and mutually coordinated articulation of: 1. a determinate type of ownership of the means of production; 2. a determinate form of appropriation of the economic surplus; 3. a determinate degree of development of the division of labour; 4. a determinate level of development of the productive forces." On the basis of this concept, it is, as Cueva (1978:15) points out, "difficult to find in America after Columbus any *basic* productive relations other than slavery, servitide [feudalism] and paid labor [capitalism]."

7. There is some question as to the basic unit of analysis in the modes of production approach. On the basis of principles established by Godelier (1974, 1977) and Rey (1976), analysis is usually confined to the relations and structures internal to a given social formation. However, as Barkin (1981:156*ff*) points out, a modes of production approach to the analysis of a given social formation is best placed in the wider context of a worldwide process of capital accumulation. Such an analysis should not be confused with the "world-systems" approach popularized by Hopkins and Wallerstein in an extension of dependency theory.

8. "Law" in this usage specifies a set of objective conditions that people do not freely choose but contract by virtue of their position in the social organization of

production. In the present context it refers to certain tendencies rooted in the basic structures of the capitalist mode of production. To focus on this economic dynamic underlying the process of class formation is not to deny the working of political and ideological factors, or more generally the role of the class struggle in capitalist development. As a matter of principle, it can, however, be generally assumed that the conditions of this struggle are rooted in the economic dynamic of capitalist development. In effect, it is not possible to speak of a political dynamic distinct from conditions arising from a given combination of productive forces and relations of production. In any case, the focus of this chapter is restricted to the economic dynamic of class formation specified by references to "laws of capital accumulation." These laws, as Marx was careful to point out, are modified in practice by a host of variable historical circumstances and should be conceived of as general tendencies only (1967: Vol III, 173-175, 232).

9. See Bartra (1974: Bartra 1976), Bennholdt-Thomsen (1976), Saffioti (1977), and Dietrich (1978) for other formulations of this argument.

10. Marx himself was very clear and insistent on this point. Unlike Frank, Wallerstein, and other exponents of dependency theory or a more generalized world-systems approach, Marx did not define capitalism in terms of the presence of commercial capital. Belonging to the sphere of circulation, this form of capital has the exclusive function of acting as a vehicle for exchanging goods, and as such it exists regardless of the mode of production involved. For Marx, one can only speak of the CMP with the generalized existence of free wage labor (1967: Vol. I, 169).

11. In this connection, a recent study by Amin (1980) on the class structure of the world imperialist system is illuminating. Amin estimates that the population of the periphery is still four-fifths rural, with 75 percent of the peasantry poor and/or exploited (p. 10). In contrast, the active population in capitalist centers is overwhelmingly composed of urban wage earners. All of this peasantry (with the exception of a few insignificant groups), according to Amin, is either exploited directly by agrocapitalists or formally subjected to the dominion of capital via the laws of commodity production and vertical integration into the agroindustrial complex (pp. 17-23). Latin America is somewhat exceptional in terms of these generalizations, given its relatively high levels of urbanization. However, as we will see, the same processes that generate various forms of an industrial reserve army are very much at work in the urban economies of peripheral formations.

12. The apparent exception to this rule is agriculture, where the bulk of production in each case, incuding the most advanced capitalist countries like the United States and Canada, is based on owner-operated farms organized lagely around family labor, with quite residual use of sharecropping and tenancy (Bernier, 1976). A useful perspective on this phenomenon is provided by Mann and Dickinson (1978). What they argue is that it is not in the interest of capital to directly intervene in the process of agricultural production because of the structural discrepancy between production time and actual labor time. In this connection, they point out, in defining the capitalist sector in agriculture it is not enough to determine the ratio of wage labor to family labor. Taking into account the actual labor time expended in agricultural production, as opposed to the longer production time, wage labor appears as a critical factor in the operation of many farms formally classified as noncapitalist (based on family labor) but relying heavily on seasonal wage labor as well as unpaid family labor.

It is also possible to speak more generally of units of agricultural production in advanced capitalist societies as capitalist enterprises. As Friedmann (1980) argues, it is a mistake to see in these enterprises a distinct mode of production—independent, petty, domestic, and so on. At most one can speak of "independent commodity production" as a form of production (specifying the unit of production and the social formation of which it is a part). Generally speaking, in advanced capitalist societies household units of agricultural production are dependent on the CMP for their conditions of existence and are surrounded by capitalist institutions that reduce the independent operator to a nominal but not effective owner to his means of production. Moreover, in all respects except the need to hire much wage labor, the farm functions as a capitalist enterprise, with the farmer compelled to behave as a capitalist as a condition of survival.

What remains unsettled in the various ongoing debates on this question is the degree to which these considerations apply to peripheral Third World societies. Amin (1980) for one, argues that almost all so-called peasants are subordinated to the CMP either directly, via vertical integration into an agroindustrial complex, or indirectly, via what Bernstein (1979) terms "commoditization"—dependence on commodity relations for reproduction of their conditions of existence. Friedmann (1980) provides a valuable theoretical extension of this concept, although the point of reference for her argument is the household unit of agricultural production in advanced socities. Its application to agricultural formations on the periphery is much more debatable. However, this entire question will not be directly addressed here.

13. The data on this concentration are staggering, particularly so with respect to Latin America, where large holdings, with an average size of 514 hectares, account for 7.9 percent of the total units but 80.3 percent of the total land, and small holdings, with an average size of 2.7 hectares, account for 66 percent of the total units but only 3.7 percent of the total land (Ceres no. 81). As for the mass of peasants dispossessed in this process, data on open unemployment in Latin American agriculture (an average rate of 18.9 percent for the six largest countries) and an "equivalent unemployment" (including forms of underemployment) of an average rate of 42.7 percent for these same countries are revealing even without any further analysis (see Wilkie, 1980:174). More generally, the much higher rates of concentration for Latin America compared to Asia and Africa are reflected in higher levels of urbanization and its associated class formation.

14. The tendency for international capital to increasingly shift production to the periphery and its large reservoirs of surplus labor is a characteristic feature of the capitalist system in its present phase of worldwide development. The effects of this peripherisalization on the international structure of industrial capitalism have been explored in a number of recent studies. The new international division of labor associated with this development has been explored in three recent studies (Bromley and Gerry, 1979; Seers et al., 1979; and Froebel et al., 1980). I will draw on these studies below. One major effect of the internationalization of the supply of labor power is the beginnings of an involution in the role of immigrant Third World labor as the reserve army of Western European and North American capitalist industries (see Castells, 1975; Nikolinokos, 1975; Buroway, 1976; Portes, 1978; Centro de Estudios Puertoriquenos, 1979). Before this new development in world capitalism, migration worked as a mechanism that enabled large numbers of inactive members of the industrial reserve army to recover their status as a reserve at the international level.

15. See the useful distinction on this point made by Díaz Polanco (1977) and Friedmann (1980).

16. This is essentially Lenin's position. See the exposition on this position by Hussain and Tribe (1980: Vol. II) and Lehman (1980).

17. This is the point at issue in Esteva's (1978:709) and Rello's (1976:102-103) dispute of Bartra's (1974:171) characterization of at least 60 percent of the rural population in Mexico as proletarians. As Esteva sees it, much of this population is impoverished, but its members are by no means effectively part of the rural proletariat. In fact, Esteva goes so far as to see in the rural peasantry, despite the complexity of the productive relations involved, a distinct social class. I will speak to this issue below.

18. This concept of "semi-proletarianization" as an active process of peripheral capitalist development has been advanced and elaborated by Sacouman (1980) in a series of illuminating studies on rural Atlantic Canada.

19. A wide range of studies has established that the great majority of smallholders (less than 5 hectares) who, at the latest respective censuses, comprise more than 80 percent of total holders in some countries (El Salvador, Guatamala) and well over 60 percent in most others, derive more than 50 percent of their income from wage labor. On this distribution of landholdings see Wilkie (1980:46-47). On the generalized dependence on wage labor see various case studies in Duncan and Rutledge (1977) and issues 18, 19, and 27 of *Latin American Perspectives.*

20. See D'Incão e Mello (1975) on the conditions of exploitation and oppression involved in this system of casual day labor. With payment generally made on a daily piecework basis and with an average working day of twelve to fourteen hours, including a lunch break and transportation time of two to three hours, this form of agrarian capitalism is highly exploitive at the levels of both absolute and relative surplus value.

21. Marx (1967: Vol. 637) formulates this law as follows: "Taking them as a whole, the general movements of wages are exclusively regulated by the expansion and contraction of the industrial reserve army, and these correspond to the periodic changes in the industrial cycle. They are, therefore, not determined by the variations in the absolute numbers of the working population, but by the varying proportions in which the working class is divided into active and reserve army, by the increase or diminution in the relative amount of the surplus population, by the extent to which it is now absorbed, now set free."

23. Klein's (1979:312) analysis of labor market data shows that of the mass of rural migrants (4.5 million) absorbed by the urban centers of Latin America from 1950 to 1960, the rate of expansion for the so-called informal market was twice that of the economically active population as a whole. Recent studies of available labor force data show that the "informal urban sector" is largely associated with the category of petty services and production registered as "self-employed." In many countries this category of workers accounts for at least a third of the economically active population (Buttari, 1979:208-210), and this excludes the large category of live-in female servants.

22. This development is most clearly expressed in the process of tertiarization experienced in every country in Latin America—namely, the dramatic expansion of employment in industries based on unproductive labor, particularly commerce and low-wage service industries (Schmink, 1977; Buttari, 1979:idem). Underlying this process is an expanding system of urban "self-employed" where over 30 percent earn

less than half the minimum wage. Recent developments in the international distribution of industrial production have introduced relatively high-wage industrial enclaves based on parts assembly and subcontracting. However, the general law referred to still holds; it operates under these conditions on an international scale.

24. De Wind (1979:144*ff*) provides an illuminating case study of this process in Peru. He found that Cerro de Pasco, a giant multinational in the mining sector, through an annual turnover of 20 percent created or recreated every five years as many petty producers as its total workforce. Various studies in Bromley and Gerry (1979) point to different aspects of this same process of deproletarianization.

25. This point, although well established, is still subject to debate with respect to the questions of whether women's domestic labor is productive of surplus value and whether it can be conceived of in terms of a distinct, albeit subordinate, mode of production. On these questions see Seacombe (1974) and Jean Gardiner (1975). Saffiotti (1976, 1977, 1979) has posed this problem in the Latin American context.

26. According to the 1970 census analyzed by Filet-Abreu de Souza (1980:41), 32 percent of the female workforce in the case of Brazil (which is typical in this respect) is made up of domestic servants, and this does not include the *diaristas* (live-out servants), as these are generally registered as *autonomas* (self-employed). Studies by Smith (1973) and Schmink (1977) point to a similar situation for Peru and Venezuela.

27. This concept of "superexploitation" has two conflicting points of reference. The first is expressed most clearly by Amin (1977:186*ff*) in support of Emmanuel's proposition that the law of value operates across national boundaries on a global scale—that is, that there are "world values" which take the form of commodities that circulate throughout the world system (e.g., one labor hour of a European or American worker is equal in value to one labor hour of an African worker because the product of labor in each case becomes an international commodity). The assumption made by Emmanuel and shared by Amin is that capital is mobile but labor is immobile. Under these conditions capital mobility shows a tendency toward an equalizing rate of profit throughout the world, while remuneration to labor, which is immobile, varies from one country to another according to historical conditions. Hence the transformation of values into international prices (via trade) implies a transfer of value; and in relation to this value, a discrepancy of wage rates in the order of six to one (twenty to one in agriculture) from one country to another represents an extraordinary variation in the rate of exploitation (1980:12-19). Strictly speaking, however, we cannot speak here of "superexploitation," which implies more than a magnitude of unpaid labor; it implies the forced reduction of the value of labor power (which is, in any case, lower in peripheral regions for historical reasons). This reproduction can occur only by the refusal of capital to fully cover the reproduction costs of this labor power. This concept of superexploitation (see Marini, 1973; Osorio Urbina, 1975; and even Frank, 1978) can be traced back to Marx in his brief reference to "the circumstances that . . . determine the amount of accumulation." In this connection, Marx wrote: "In the chapters on the production of surplus value, it was constantly pre-supposed that wages are at least equal to the value of labour-power. Forcible reduction of wages below this value plays, however, in practice too important a part, for us not to pause upon it for a moment. It, in fact, transforms, within certain limits the labourer's necessary consumption-fund into a fund for the accumulation of capital" (1967: Vol. I, 599). A connection between this extraction of excess surplus value and the partial reproduction of labor power on a noncapitalist basis was made by Marx as follows: "The part played in our days by the direct robbery from the labourer's necessary consumption fund in the

formation of surplus value, and therefore, of the accumulation fund of capital, the so-called domestic industry has served to show" (p. 602).

28. See Meillasoux (1972) on the analysis of "primitive accumulation" as "a transfer from one mode of production to another." So formulated, the "so-called primitive accumulation" as discussed by Marx is converted from a question involving the original formation of capitalism to one involving its expanded reproduction on the periphery of a worldwide system. Amin (1975, 1977) has expanded on this contemporary form of primitive accumulation, as has Bartra (1982) in his Luxembourgian concept of "permanent primitive accumulation."

29. This regulatory function is clearly expressed in the increased demand for female labor with the extension of capitalist agriculture (Deere, 1977:60). As we have already observed, Froebel et al. (1980) identified a similar demand for female labor by multinational corporations that operate in the industrial sector.

29. The connection made here between the conditions that lower the value of labor power and exploitation is disputed by Friedmann (1980) in a critique of Vergopoulos's formulation of this argument. "It is true," Friedmann notes, "that lower prices of agricultural commodities make an important contribution to capitalist accumulation through lowering the value of labour power." But, she continues, "to benefit from lower prices is not the same as to exploit" (1980:169). I cannot in this brief space engage this argument, but the crux of it (and this argument can be generally extended to the question of unequal exchange between regions and countries) is that unless it can be shown that the reduction in the embodied value of labor power results from specific actions of the beneficiary class, then we cannot speak of "exploitation" as such (p. 171). A similar position is taken by Margulis with respect to a general argument formulated in different ways by Amin (1975), Bartra (1974), Vergopoulos (1978), and Zamosc (1979), among many others. In terms of Marx's theoretical formulations, Margulis (1978:13-15) argues that the various appropriating mechanisms based on precapitalist modes of production, extraeconomic conditions, or unequal exchange involve not the extraction of surplus value but merely lost labor time. Although the peasantry is exploited at a number of different levels, any transfer of surplus value, Margulis adds, is based on conditions of proletarianization—namely, the provision to industrial and agrarian capitalists of cheap labor.

It is not possible in the context of this chapter to take up this issue raised by Friedmann and Margulis. However, in provisional defense of the position taken—that appropriation of value, whether embodied in the price of directly purchased labor power or in the form of wage goods, involves exploitation (and under some conditions, superexploitation)—it is suggested that the mechanisms of class exploitation can be and generally are embodied in certain structural arrangements rather than a direct social relationship between two classes of individuals. At a structural level, the mechanisms and social relations sought by Friedmann, although not generally specified, can, I submit, be identified. This whole question, however, requires a great deal more attention.

References

Alavi, Hamza
    1975   "India and the colonial mode of production," pp. 160-197 in Ralph Miliband and John Saville (eds.) Socialist Register. London.

Amin, Samir
  1977   Imperialism and Unequal Development. New York: Monthly Review Press.
  1980   "The class structure of the contemporary imperialist system." Monthly
         Review 32 (January), 9-26.
Amin, S. and K. Vergopoulos
  1975   La cuestión campesina y el capitalismo. Mexico: Nuestro Tiempo.
         Assadourian, Carlos Sempat et al.
  1971   "Modos de producción, capitalismo y subdesarrolo en América Latina."
         Cuadernos de la Realidad National (Santiago, Chile). Also in English in
         Two Thirds, 1 (1978): 20-33.
  1973   Modos de producción en América Latina. Córdoba, Argentina: Pasado y
         Presente (40).
Banaji, Jairus
  1972   "For a theory of colonial modes of production." Economic and Political
         Weekly 7 (December 23): 2408-2502.
Barkin, David
  1981   "Internationalization of capital: an alternative approach." Latin America
         Perspectives 8 (Summer-Fall): 156-161.
Bartra, Roger
  1974   Estructura agraria y clases sociales en México. Mexico City: Ediciones
         Era.
  1975   "Sobre la articulación de modos de producción en América Latina." His-
         toria y Sociedad (Mexico City) 5 (Spring): 5-19.
  1982   "Capitalism and the peasantry in Mexico." Latin American Perspectives 9
         (Winter): 36-47.
Bartra, Roger et al.
  1976   Modos de producción en América Latina. Lima: Delva Editores.
Beaucage, Pierre
  1975   "Modos de producción articulados o lucha de clases?" Historia y Sociedad
         5 (Spring): 37-58.
Bennholdt-Thomsen, Veronica
  1976   "Los campesinos en las relaciones de producción del capitalismo periférico."
         Historia y Sociedad 6: 29-37.
Bernier, B.
  1976   "Capitalism in Quebec agriculture." Canadian Review of Sociology and
         Anthropology 13 (November): 422-434.
Bernstein, Henry
  1979   "Concepts for the analysis of contemporary peasantries." Journal of Peas-
         ant Studies 6 (July): 421-443.
Bettleheim, Charles
  1972   "Theoretical comments," in Arghiri Emmanual, Unequal Exchange: A
         Study of the Imperialism of Trade (B. Pearce, trans.). New York: Monthly
         Review Press.
Bromley, Ray and Chris Gerry (eds.)
  1979   Casual Work and Poverty in Third World Cities. New York: John Wiley.
Buroway, Michael
  1976   "The functions and reproduction of migrant labor: comparative material
         from Southern Africa and the United States." American Journal of Sociol-
         ogy 81 (March): 1050-1087.

Burbach, Roger and Patrica Flynn
1980   Agribusiness in the Americas. New York: Monthly Review Press.
Buttari, Juan J.
1979   Employment and Labor in Latin America: A Review at National and Regional
        Levels. Estudios Conjuntos Sobre Integración Económica Latinoamericana
        (ECIEL), O.A.S.
Campaña, Pilar and Gigoberto Rivera
1978   "El proceso de descampesinizacion en la Sierra Central del Perú." Estudios
        Rurales Latinoamericanos 1 (May-August): 71-100.
Cardoso, Ciro
1973   "Sobre los modos de producción colonial de América," in Carlos Sempat
        Assadourian et al. (eds.) Modos de producción in América Latina. Cór-
        doba: Pasado y Presente (40). Also in English in Critique of Anthropology
        (4-5).
Cardoso, Fernando Henrique
1975   "Los modos de produccion coloniales: estado de la cuestión y perspectiva
        teórica." Historia y Sociedad 5 (Spring): 107-126.
Castells, Manuel
1975   "Immigrant workers and class struggles in advanced capitalism." Politics
        and Society 5, 1: 33-66).
Centro de Estudios Puertorriquenos
1979   Labor Migration Under Capitalism: The Puerto Rican Experience. New
        York: Monthly Review Press.
Chilcote, Ronald H.
1974   "Dependency: a critical synthesis of the literature." Latin America Perspec-
        tives 1 (Spring): 4-29.
1981   "Issues of theory in dependency and Marxism." Latin American Perspec-
        tives 8 (Summer-Fall): 3-16.
Chinchilla, Norma and James Dietz
1981   "Toward a new understanding of development and underdevelopment."
        Latin American Perspectives 8 (Summer-Fall): 138-147.
Cohen, Robin et al. (eds.)
1979   Peasants and Proletarians. London: Hutchinson.
Cueva, Agustin
1978   "The mode of production concept in Latin America." Two Thirds 1 (first
        quarter): 13-20.
De Leal, Magdalena and Carmen Deere
1979   "La mujer rural y el desarrollo del capitalismo."
De Wind, Josh
1979   "From peasants to miners: the background to strikes in the mines of Peru,"
        pp. 149-172 in Robin Cohen et al. (eds.) Peasants and Proletarians. Lon-
        don: Hutchinson.
Deere, Carmen Diana
1977   "Changing social relations of production and Peruvian peasant women's
        work." Latin American Perspectives 4 (Winter-Spring): 48-69.
Dietrich, Heinz
1978   Relaciones de producción en América Latina. Mexico: Ediciones Cultura
        Popular.

Dietz, James
  1979   "Imperialism and underdevelopment: a theoretical perspective and a case
          study of Puerto Rico." Review of Radical Political Economics 11 (Winter):
          16-32.
D'Incão e Mello, Maria C.
  1975   O boia fria: accumulação e miseria. Petrópolis: Editora Vozes.
Díaz Polanco, Hector
  1977   Teoria marxista de la economia campesina. Mexico: Juan Pablos.
Duggett, Michael
  1975   "Marx on peasants." Journal of Peasant Studies 2 (January): 159-182.
Duncan, Kenneth and Ian Rutledge
  1977   Land and Labour in Latin America. Cambridge: Cambridge University
          Press.
Emmanuel, Arghiri
  1974   "Myths of development versus myths of underdevelopment." New Left
          Review 85 (May-June): 61-82.
Ennew, Judith, Paul Hirst, and Keith Tribe
  1977   " 'Peasantry' as an economic category." Journal of Peasant Studies 4 (July):
          295-322.
Esteva, Gustavo
  1978   "Y si los campesinos existen?" Comercio Exterior (Mexico) 28 (June):
          699-732.
Favre, Henri
  1977   "The dynamics of Indian peasant society and migration to coastal plan-
          tations in central Peru," pp. 253-268 in K. Duncan and I. Rutledge. Land
          and Labour in Latin America. Cambridge: Cambridge University Press.
Fernández, Raúl A. and José F. Ocampo
  1974   "The Latin American Revolution: a theory of imperialism, not depend-
          ence." Latin America Perspectives 1 (Spring): 30-61.
Filet-Abreau de Souza, Julia
  1980   "Paid domestic service in Brazil." Latin American Perspectives 7 (Spring):
          35-63.
Foster-Carter, Aidan
  1978   "The modes of production controversy." New Left Review 107 (January-
          February): 47-78.
Frank, André Gunder
  1967   Capitalism and Underdevelopment in Latin America: Historical Studies of
          Chile and Brazil. New York: Monthly Review Press.
  1978   "Super exploitation in the Third World." Two Thirds 1 (Fall): 15-28.
Friedmann, Harriet
  1978   "Simple commodity production and wage labour in the American plains."
          Journal of Peasant Studies 6 (October): 71-100.
  1980   "Household production and the national economy: concepts for the analysis
          of agrarian formations." Journal of Peasant Studies 7 (January): 158-
          184.
Froebel, F., J. Heinrichs, and O. Kreye
  1980   The New International Division of Labour. London: Cambridge Univer-
          sity Press.

Gardiner, Jean
1975 "Women's domestic labour." New Left Review 89 (January-February): 47-58.

Godelier, Maurice
1974 "On the definition of a social formation." Critique of Anthropology 1.
1977 Perspectives in Marxist Anthropology. London: Cambridge University Press.

Gomes da Silva, José
1975 O boia fria: contradicão de uma agricultura em tentativa de desenvolvimento." Reforma Agraria 5 (September-October): 2-44.

Graziano de Silva, José
1977 "O boia fria: entre aspas e com pingos nos I's," in MOVA:III Reunião Nacional. Botucatu, São Paulo: Departmento de Economía Rural, UEPJMF.

Guimarães, Sergio Pires
1979 "A mulher como força de trabalho na agricultura," in MOVA: IV Reuniao Nacional. Botucatu, São Paulo: Departamento de Economía Rural, UEPJMF.

Henfrey, Colin
1981 "Dependency, modes of production and the class analysis of Latin America." Latin American Perspectives 8 (Summer-Fall): 17-54.

Hussain, Athan and Keith Tribe
1981 Marxism and the Agrarian Question (2 vols). London: Macmillan.

Kay, Geoffrey
1975 Development and Underdevelopment: A Marxist Analysis. London: Macmillan.

Klein, Emilio
1979 "Empleo en economías campesinas de América Latina." Estudios Rurales Latinoamericanos 2 (September-December): 306-321.

Laclau, Ernest
1971 "Feudalism and capitalism in Latin America." New Left Review 67 (May-June): 19-38.

Lehman, David
1980 "Ni Chayanov ni Lenin: Apuntes sobre la teoría de la economía campesina." Estudios Rurales Latinoamericanos 3 (January-April): 5-23.

Maffei, Eugenio
1979 "Algunas consideraciones sobre el campesinado minifundista latinoamericano, la agricultura de subsistencia y el concepto de economía campesina." Estudios Rurales Latinoamericanos 2 (January-April): 122-128.

Mann, S. A. and J. M. Dickinson
1978 "Obstacles to the development of a capitalist agriculture." Journal of Peasant Studies 5 (July): 466-81.

Margulis, Mario
1978 "Acerca del valor en la estructura agraria." Cuadernos Agrarios 1 (May): 3-23.

Marini, Ruy Mauro
1973 Dialéctica de la dependencia. Mexico: Ediciones Era.

Martinez-Alier-Verena
1977 "As mulheres do caminhao da Turma," in Jaime Pinsky (ed.) Capital e trabalho no campo. São Paulo: Editora Hucitez.

Marx, Karl
1967   Capital (3 vols). New York: International Publishers.
Meillasoux, Claude
1972   "From reproduction to production." Economy and Society 1 (February): 93-105.
1979   "Modalidades históricas de la explotatión y la sobre-explotación de trabajo." Estudios Rurales Latinoamericanos 2 (May-August): 147-172.
Moncayo, Victor and Fernando Rojas
1979   "Producción campesina y capitalismo." Bogotá: CINEP (Centro de Investigación y Educación Popular).
Murmis, Miquel
1973   Tipos de capitalismo y estructura de clases: Elementos para el analysis de la estructura social de la Argentina. Buenos Aires: CICSO.
Nikolinokos, M.
1975   "Toward a general theory of migration under late capitalism." Race and Class 17 (July): 5-18.
Nun, José
1969   "Superpoblación relativa, ejército industrial de reserva y masa marginal." Revista Mexicana de Sociología 5, 2: 174-236.
Oliveira, Maria Coleta de
1978   Classe Social, Família e Fecundidade: Um Estado Sobre as Estrategias de Reprodução de Trabalhadores Rurais. Report for PISPAL. São Paulo: Faculdade de Arquitetura, Universidade de São Paulo.
Osorio Urbina, Jaime
1975   "Superexplotación y clase obrera: el caso mexicano." Cuadernos Políticos, (Mexico), 6 (October-December). Republished in Two Thirds 1 (Fall, 1978): 5-14.
Paré, Luisa
1977   El proletariado agrícola en México. México: Siglo XXI.
Portes, Alejandro
1978   "Migration and underdevelopment." Politics and Society 8, 1: 1-48.
1980   "The informal sector and the capital accumulation process in Latin America." Prepared for the second seminar of the Working Group on Latin American Urbanization, Carmel, California, April 2-March 31. Report by William Canak in Latin American Research Review 16, 3: 152-153.
Pucciarelli, Alfredo
1978   "La estructura de clases del capitalismo dependiente: El caso argentino." Estudios Rurales Latinoamericanos 1 (May-August): 7-58.
Rello, Fernando
1976   "Modo de producción y clases sociales." Cuadernos Políticos (Mexico) 8 (April-June): 100-105.
Rey, Pierre Phillipe
1976   Las alianzas de clases. Mexico: Siglo XXI.
Rutledge, Ian
1977   "The integration of the highland peasantry into the sugar cane economy of Northern Argentina, 1930-1943," pp. 205-228 in K. Duncan and I. Rutledge, Land and Labour in Latin America. Cambridge: Cambridge University Press.

Sacouman, James
    1980   "Semi-proletarianization and rural underdevelopment in the Maritimes."
            Canadian Review of Sociology and Anthropology 17 (August): 232-45.
Saffioti, Heleieth
    1976   A mulher na sociedade de classes: mito e realidade. Petrópolis: Editora
            Vozes. (Translated as Women in Class Society. New York: Monthly Review
            Press, 1978.)
    1977   "Women, mode of production, and social formations." Latin American
            Perspectives 4 (Winter-Spring): 27-37.
    1978   Emprego doméstico e capitalismo. Petrópolis: Editora Vozes.
Saint, William
    1981   "The wages of modernization: a review of the literature on temporary labor
            arrangements in Brazilian agriculture." Latin American Research Review
            16, 3: 91-110.
Scott, C. D.
    1976   "Peasants, proletarianization and the articulation of modes of production:
            the case of sugar cane cutters in Northern Peru 1940-69." Journal of Peas-
            ant Studies 3 (April): 321-41.
Seacombe, Wally
    1974   "Domestic labour: a reply." New Left Review 94 (November-December):
            85-96.
Seers, Dudley et al. (eds.)
    1979   Underdeveloped Europe: Studies in Core-Periphery Relations. Sussex:
            Harvester Press.
Schmink, Marianne
    1977   "Dependent development and the division of labor by sex: Venezuela."
            Latin American Perspectives 4 (Winter-Spring): 153-179.
Smith, Margo
    1973   "Institutionalized servitude: the female domestic servant in Lima, Peru,"
            pp. 192-206 in Ann Pescatello (ed.) Male and Female in Latin America.
            Pittsburgh: University of Pittsburgh Press.
Smith, Gavin
    1979   "Socio-economic differentiation and relations of production among rural-
            based petty producers in Central Peru, 1880 to 1970." Journal of Peasant
            Studies 7 (April): 286-310.
Taussig, Michael
    1978   "Peasant economics and the development of capitalist agriculture in the
            Cauca Valley, Colombia." Latin American Perspectives 5 (Summer): 62-
            90.
    1979   "The evolution of rural wage labour in the Cauca Valley of Colombia, 1700-
            1970," pp. 397-434 in K. Duncan and I. Rutledge, Land and Labour in
            Latin America. Cambridge: Cambridge University Press.
Taylor, John
    1979   From Modernisation to Modes of Production: A Critique of the Sociologies
            of Development and Underdevelopment. London: Macmillan.
Veltmeyer, H.
    1980   "A central issue in dependency theory." Canadian Review of Sociology and
            Anthropology 17 (August): 198-213.

Vergopoulos, Kostos
  1978   "Capitalism and peasant production." Journal of Peasant Studies 5 (July):
          446-465.
Villarreal, Juan
  1978   El capitalismo dependiente: estudio sobre la estructura de clases en Argen-
          tina. Mexico: Siglo XXI.
Vitale, Luis
  1971   Feudalismo, capitalismo y subdesarrollo. Universidad de Tolima.
Wallerstein, Immanuel
  1974   The Origin of the Modern World Systems. New York: Academic Press.
Wilkie, James
  1980   Statistical Abstract of Latin America, Vol. 20. Los Angeles: UCLA Latin
          American Centre.
Winson, Anthony
  1978   "Class structure and agrarian transition in Central America." Latin American
          Perspectives 5 (Fall): 27-48.
Wolpe, M. (ed.)
  1980   The Articulation of Modes of Production. London: Routledge & Kegan
          Paul.
Zamosc, León
  1979   "Notes teóricas sobre la subordinación de la producción mercantil cam-
          pesina al capital." Estudios Rurales Latinoamericanos 2, 3: 296-305.

Dale L. Johnson: Class Analysis

and Dependency

The limits of the dependency perspective, if not fully established, are at least reasonably argued: "The striking features of dependency writing . . . are its overemphasis on the external, its economism
at the expense of an undersatnding of the *social* relations of production, and its repetitive generality, with the lasting dearth of substantive
case studies" (Henfrey, 1981:27). A modes of production framework
currently is being presented as an alternative that gives due recognition to the "internal" of specific social formations by focusing on the
varied forms of production relations. But this alternative framework
overemphasizes the internal and formalizes social relations. Modes
of production offers a reasonably coherent analytic framework, but
there are few substantive case studies.

Modes of productionists attempt to distinguish the diverse social
forms in which production is carried out. This sets them off from
dependentistas, who too often close their eyes to the variable character
and dynamic quality of class relations in different national settings.
In their enthusiasm to attribute all to capitalism, some dependentistas[1]
have treated the Latin American region as a species of capitalism so
uniformly deformed and lacking in dynamism that it constitutes a distinct mode of production.

While dependent, underdeveloped capitalism is not a mode of production, it is a distinct historical-structural condition. What is debat-

able is, first, conceptualizing this condition as structured by modes of production in articulation and, second, attributing the status of pre-capitalist modes to relations of production that do not involve wage labor. Underdevelopment has its own morphology, which is formed within the history of relations of dependency imposed by the internationalization of capital on indigenous structures. Structures internal to regions and nations are continuously modified as they in turn guide, limit, and give form to world-system-level forces. Dependency, therefore, is more than a condition; it is a relationship or, more precisely, a series of relationships among classes of unequal power.

There obviously are great variations in the concrete manifestations of this condition and the ways in which the "external" and "internal" class forces mesh. This is so historically within regions or among nations, cross-regionally between Asia, Africa, and Middle East and Latin America, and among the world-system categories of periphery and semi-periphery. Since dependent and underdeveloped capitalism is a distinct historical-structural condition of unequal power relationships but not a mode of production, a condition that shows considerable empirical variation in time and space, it follows that there are no general "laws" specific to its functioning. What is general is only dependency itself, a situation that weakens and limits the autonomous actions of indigenous classes, and this takes many specific forms. The "laws" (I prefer the terms "structural tendencies" and "historical processes") that shape the dependency are, in the ultimate instance, those that impel the internationalization of capital, primarily those governing capital accumulation and class formation, two processes that, in my view, are distinguishable only by academic convention (economic and sociological analysis).

The idea of dependent underdevelopment as a distinct historical condition, formed by the interpenetration of the outward expansion of capital from the center and the political economies and class structures of regional and national societies is an indispensable starting point in any analysis of Asia, Africa, the Middle East, and Latin America. It is not clear that mode of productionists accept this point of departure, but it remains the intent, if not usually the practice, of dependentistas to analyze development and underdevelopment on this basis.

In this concluding chapter I direct attention to two very real shortcomings of the dependency perspective: its underemphasis on class analysis and its overemphasis on external determination. An analytic eye is cast on class relations; an analysis of class formations in the Latin American region is sketched; and an attempt is made to pose a dialectic of "general" and "proximate" determinants of the ills associated with dependent underdevelopment. While critical attention is given to aspects of the modes of production approach that relate to these shortcomings, it is not my intention to fully appraise modes of production as an alternative framework.

A preliminary comment on class and determinism is in order. McDaniel probably overstates the case when he says: "Dependency theory has generally been identified as an economic determinist theory of imperialism when in fact it is primarily a theory of Latin American social structures as shaped by relationships with the central capitalist countries" (1976:51-52). He notes several areas in need of elaboration, including a sharper mode of class analysis, and concludes that "these extensions can be carried out within the same basic conceptual framework (indicating) dependency theory's soundness and viability" (1976:53). This represents my own conviction.

To begin with, it is simply not accurate, as mode of productionists and others so often repeat, that the dependency perspective excludes class analysis. Consider only the most frequently cited authors: Quijano's work through a long and provocative trajectory has examined the interrelation between the historical forms of imperialist intrusion into dependent societies, the formation of national classes, the interests, activities, and struggles of these classes, and the class bases of national states. His chapter in this volume exemplifies this approach. Cardoso explicitly begins with class and a focus on the internal: "The questions, 'How does the *transition* from one situation of dependency to another occur?' or 'How can situations of dependency be eliminated?' ought to be asked in terms of 'Who are the classes and groups which, in the struggle for control or for the reformulation of the existing order (through parties, movements, ideologies, the state, etc.), are making a given structure of domination historically viable or are transforming it?' " (1977:16). Frank has focused extensively on formulations like "lumpen bourgeoisie." There are scores of books and countless articles on general and specific questions guided by the perspective of dependency that fall generally within a class analysis framework. Moreover, all dependentistas of Marxist persuasion at least aim toward a method of class analysis in attempting to construct a theory of capitalist development that takes account of the specificities of dependent and underdeveloped regions and nations. What, then, is the problem?

It begins, undoubtedly, with the central distinctions center/periphery, first world/third world, and similar heuristic dichotomies. These are indispensable constructs useful on a global scale for appreciating the main features of development, underdevelopment, and dependency, but they conceal enormously disparate regional and national variations. Overgeneralization is endemic to global concepts. These world-system departures predominantly pose dependency and underdevelopment in regional rather than class terms.[2] In attempting to connect regional political economy to class analysis, authors frequently have fallen short. Frank's "lumpen bourgeoisie" is more or less a puppet (the one product long ago manufactured locally by foreign investors) whose performance is orchestrated from abroad. In Frank's chapter in this volume on crisis and the state in the Third World he states: "The exigencies of the process of capital accumulation and the international division of labor, worldwide and in the underdeveloped countries themselves, thus become the principal determinants of the role and the form of the state in the Third World." This statement, like his characterization of local bourgeoisies as "lumpen," is accurate, but it also has a certain undialectical quality. I will explore the problem of trying to formulate a dialectical conception of the external-internal nexus, of the general and proximate, or specific, determinants, without singling out Frank for special attention. His work remains among the most fundamental and provocative in the field.

The problem of dialectical conceptions is basic to dependency theory. Cardoso, for example, errs on the side of internal determination. The main thrust of his work is comparative analysis of variations in the political activities of local classes in different historical periods and countries. But there is insufficient attention to the internationalized processes that form these classes and yield content and context to their locally rooted struggles. The method has to be one of addressing, as Petras puts it, the "reciprocating interplay between conflicting and collaborating classes which reproduce or refashion the economy and state structures through which they operate" (1981:154).

Quijano's contributions are much more balanced. First, he rarely overgeneralizes. His studies are specific to structural histories of national societies or to particular classes or processes. Second, he is careful to examine the specific forms of articulation between imperialist expansion and local class formation in which dependency is crystallized. Quijano analyzes international capitalism by its stage of development and the character of its interpenetration with the social structure of peripheral societies at different historical periods of national development. Still, I judge that his work often comes down too heavily on the side of external determination. Quijano precisely and Frank more generally imply that an expanded penetration of imperialism depends on the existence of local classes whose own position and interests can be enhanced by this penetration. But there is nothing automatic about the formation of "comprador" classes that can exploit labor internally and profit by external exchange.

As a "Marxist" alternative to dependency, mode of production argues the existence of a class framework and a proper balance of external and internal factors. We shall weigh the argument.

Modes of Production

Undoubtedly, the theoretical challenge to dependency formulated by mode of productionists has pointed to several problems that need reevaluation from the point of view of theory adequate to the object of analysis: the particular forms that the historical condition of underdevelopment and dependency have assumed in different parts of the world. However, there is no need to extend the mainly theoretical criticisms of the mode of production approach that are well-stated elsewhere (see especially Foster-Carter, 1978, and Henfrey, 1981). I have commented on modes of production as a "Marxist" alternative to dependency formulations (Johnson, 1981) and as a means of conceptualizing rural class relations (Johnson, 1982). Most of my comments are more in the way of general observations on issues of concern here rather than a theoretical statement.

Initially it strikes me that the great "capitalism versus feudalism" debate of the late 1960s, while it demolished the "dual society" thesis of modernization theory, was not resolved with respect to a sensible accounting for the existence of seemingly precapitalist relations of production. Below I enter some elementary arguments. First, where today (and for a long time back) can a feudal or any other precapitalist mode of production accurately be said to exist? Second, capitalism is not exclusively defined by either commodity markets or free wage labor. Third, nonwage labor forms of labor subjugation are indeed widespread and persistent in the Third World; these relations of production are best understood not as modes of production in articulation but in their linkages with the capital accumulation process and the reproduction of cheap labor power. Fourth, production relations that do not meet the purely capitalist criteria are not, by and large, impediments to unfettered capitalist development.

(1) If, somewhere in the world, a feudal mode of production empirically exists in the countryside while a mercantile bourgeoisie in the cities is enriched by traffic in commodities, there obviously would be real obstacles to a transition to capitalism, just as there were in the European transition. Feudal lords have no great interest in capitalization of agriculture when they have an enserfed peasantry to exploit; serfs have no interest in wage labor when they have rights to land, animals, and tools. Merchant capital has a primary interest in promoting trade, not industry. Correspondingly, in its outward expansion from its center, the capitalist mode of production must articulate with this feudalism. In class terms, the bourgeoisie of the center has to deal with and confront feudal lords and merchants if it is to spearhead capitalist development.

Surely there is no social system in the Third World today that remotely resembles this backward feudalism and forward capitalism. Nor has one existed since the early period of European colonization of the world, and then only in forms distinct from European feudalism. The Spanish and Portuguese obviously transplanted feudal-type institutions to America after the conquest. They did so for merchantilist ends of accumulation. This facade of feudalism persisted as a legacy limiting the development of the post-revolutionary war period and shaping how the region related to nineteenth-century British and twentieth-century American intrusions. What can be observed everywhere, even today, are production relations which are not based on wage labor. These relations have dual roots in preexisting, noncapitalist relations indigenous to areas of the globe and in the *historical bending* of these relations to serve colonial and imperial ends. These relations are no less exploitive than wage labor, and they inevitably articulate, often extremely well, with the accumulation process.

In short, where preexisting, noncapitalist relations exist, they are bent to serve the ends of accumulation. Often in Latin America and even in Asia these are not preexisting indigenous modes of production but forms of production invented by imperial interests. In his discourse on modes of production, Laclau (1977) analyzed the process of bending precapitalism and of "refeudalization." It is unfortunate that the mode of productionists have not pursued this idea, for it puts the historical course of underdevelopment and dependency in a quite different light from their approach and avoids the absurdity of the notion that imperialism, which has so painfully perverted all that is civilized, is a progressive force. I will return below to the theme of seemingly precapitalist relations in articulation with the accumulation process and relate this to the reproduction of the labor force under conditions of "super-exploitation" (see also Johnson, 1982).

(2) Mode of productionists reproduce the error of those they criticize—a narrow conception of capitalism. Frank and other dependentistas are routinely attacked for equating capitalism with the existence of commodity markets, while in the same stroke capitalism is defined by the criterion of the existence of free wage labor. Productionists say: If no exploitation of proletarianized labor, then no capitalism. Even less than dependentistas do they recognize the historically unique features of capitalism at different stages of its development, each stage marked by different sources of accumulation. Free wage labor became generalized late in the process of development, and then only in Europe and North America.

There is no need to enter this terrain with a lengthy analytic discourse on modes of production. It will suffice to note the following: If there is any single overriding feature of the capitalist mode of production, it is neither commodity markets nor wage labor; rather, it is the appropriation of value wherever and however it is produced for purposes of accumulation. If wealth is accessible, it is plundered and used to facilitate capitalist development; if goods can be commodified, bought cheaply and sold dear, and merchant profits added to the stock of capital, they are so treated; if plantations producing sugar or cotton require a labor force, slaves are captured and production for expanding capitalist markets engenders the establishment of a slave mode of production; if the economies of entire regions of the world can be geared to producing cheap primary products and importing expensive manufactures, colonization or other more subtle mechanisms are evolved to facilitate this form of accumulation; if, through technological and organizational innovation, there comes a moment when servile labor and independent producers can be more intensely exploited through wage labor than by servitude or unequal exchange, then peasants are "freed" and artisans are dispossessed of productive property and proletarianized. Of course, capitalist development has moved through different stages, from primitive accumulation, mercantilism, and manufacturing to the export of industrial capital, and, generally, the accumulation process deepens and widens as these stages unfold. The condition of dependent underdevelopment has been "produced" by these historical processes of accumulation. I do not mean this in an overly deterministic sense, as I will elaborate below. Obviously, an internationalized accumulation process always "articulates" with the class forces and economic conditions where it is implanted.

Today in the dependent periphery there is little left to plunder; agribusiness has displaced slave plantations; the classical international division of labor between primary producers and the industrializing center is being superseded, gradually and unevenly, by a new division of labor that shifts labor-intensive industrial processes to the periphery; dependent producers are being dispossessed of productive property (though no necessarily recruited as wage laborers); seemingly precapitalist forms of labor subjugation are declining in favor of wage or, more widely, in favor of a combination of wage labor and a variety of novel forms of labor servitude.

It is obvious that Asian, African, and Middle Eastern civilizations had advanced on the basis of noncapitalist modes of production prior to European colonization and that elements (or at least the effects) of these noncapitalist modes have persisted to some degree to this day. But it is a serious theoretical error to weave what remains of precapitalism and precolonialism, with legacies of prior historical forms of capital accumulation and a now-growing incidence of wage labor, into a new synthetic fabric labeled "articulation of modes of production," wherein a dominant capitalist mode is hemmed in and constrained by precapitalist modes.

(3) In Latin America, and even more so in Asia and Africa, nonwage labor relations of production remain evident to this day. Even Frank (Chapter 5), who in general sees development fettered by capitalism, not precapitalism, affirms widespread and persistent precapitalist relations. He accounts for this in historical terms by the divergent paths of primitive accumulation in the West and in the colonial and underdeveloping areas. In the West the process of primitive accumulation dispossessed peasants and artisans of their means of production but reabsorbed them as wage laborers. In the periphery, first plunder and raw exploitation and, later, the development of underdevelopment led to vast dispossessions, but there was only limited absorption of labor into the proletarian condition, leaving vast numbers of people grasping for subsistence outside purely capitalist relations of production.

Pointing to nineteenth- and early twentieth-century Latin American (specifically Peruvian) history, Quijano (Chapter 3) assesses the significance of precapitalism and its articulation with imperialism at different stages of development in the imperial center and within Peruvian national society. He examines the structure of precapitalist relations of production, the classes formed by that structure, and the nature of the state in interpenetration with the changing basis of imperialist intrusion into Peruvian society. The effects of these intrusions were to gradually remold precapitalist relations in the direction of facilitating capitalist accumulation, to restructure Peruvian classes, and to warp the character of the state as a nation-state.

(4) Implicit in Quijano's analysis is the idea that precapitalism is not a deterrent or obstacle to capitalist development induced by international forces. On the contrary, indigenous classes and weak nation-states facilitate foreign capital's penetration. Mode of productionists take a contrary view. What the few concrete applications of a mode of production framework to Latin America seem to come down to is the obstruction of capitalist development by the persistence of feudal relations of production in the countryside and, perhaps, the mercantile mentality of the dominant class. This is Taylor's position (1979). This also seems to be Chinchilla's view. In a prior work (Chinchilla and Dietz, 1981:145) it is asserted: "The stagnation which dependency theorists observed was not caused by external dependency but by the internal dynamic between production and reproduction of different modes of production at different stages within the social formation." Unfortunately, correlated with this position is the "capitalism is progress" and "imperialism is the vehicle of that progress" theses that Ahmad (Chapter 1) sharply criticizes. This is shamelessly explicit in Warren (1980) but implicit in mode of production work in general. "The current situation of economic growth in these social formations is the result of changes in the nature of the articulation of the various modes and the power of the classes in the social formation; it reflects the increasing strength of the capitalist mode and classes *vis a vis* the precapitalist" (Chinchilla and Dietz, 1981:145). This strikes me as a very different position from that of dos Santos's "new dependency" or Cardoso's "associated dependent development," where growth is recognized without equating it with either the withering away of feudalism or the progress of capitalist civilization.

In her chapter in this volume, Chinchilla makes a real contribution by examining the consequences of adopting one or another theoretical stance (modernization, dependency, evolutionary Marxism, or mode of production) in the study of a concrete historical case, Guatemala. The "capitalism is progress" assumption is not invoked, and her approach is more or less consistent with that advocated here: The proper method is one of historical/empirical examination that attempts to sort out and weigh the general and specific, the external and internal, determinants of particular processes or of the development/ underdevelopment of specific social formations.

Finally, a note should be added about mode of production and class analysis. Mode of production thinking has tended to be rather formalistic, concerned with the structural features of distinct modes rather than with structural movement. Modes articulate with each other rather than with the dynamic factor of the accumulation process and the course of class struggle, which, at the very least, should be seen as molding how modes blend together. There also seems to be a tendency to confuse a theoretical construct with empirical objects to be sought out in concrete social formations. At the extreme, each distinct relation of production can be mistaken for a different mode of production. Long (1975), for example, discovered a wide range of modes coexisting in the Andean countryside. This formalism and confusion of constructs with empirical objects seems to apply also the otherwise commendable efforts of those productionists who try to fine-tune the intricacies of class relations. This is the concern of Rey (1973), whose focus on modes of production is explicitly to understand the bases and strategic prospects of class alliances. At the theoretical level, Resnick and Wolff (1979) designate the "fundamental" and "subsumed" classes unique to different modes of production and center their analysis of articulation on class relations. They then appply their conceptual apparatus to the transition to capitalism in Western Europe. A variant of this approach is Bluestein (1982), who empirically designates four different modes of production (ancient, feudal, communal, and capitalist) in prerevolutionary Morelos, Mexico and the "class processes" that are associated with each mode. Effectively, these authors ignore the dominance of the capitalist mode of production and how it has shaped ("bent," or even created) production relations not based on wage labor. The one study of modes of production and class relations (apart from Chinchilla's in this volume) that does not fall into formalism is Ken Post's fascinating book (1978) on slavery, petty commodity production, capitalism, and the formation and struggles of the Jamaican working class.

The approach to class analysis developed here is quite distinct from that employed by mode of productionists. To begin, I pose class in relation to the problem of determinism.

General and Proximate Determinants

Moving toward a less deterministic, more dialectical method and a noneconomistic, class analysis approach would seem to require an adequate theoretical posturing of the articulation of forces emanating from the world-system level with the territorially based class forces in the periphery. "The transformation wrought within societies by their insertion in the world market must be seen as an ongoing reciprocal relationship: between the forces and relations of production within a social formation and those that operate through the world market" (Petras, 1981:150).

The problem is how to theorize and methodologically pose the general and specific determinants of the historical process in areas of the world that are in a condition of underdevelopment and dependency. These areas are recognizably parts of a larger world-system, and impulses from world-system centers undeniably exert powerful structuring effects throughout the periphery. At the same time, the world-system is organized by territory, by nation-states, and no matter how subordinated within internationalized relations of dependency, these states are repositories of power. Further, territorial states are expressions of class relations, and classes socially coalesce, form their consciousness and interests, and carry on struggles within territories. If historical movement is analyzed first as a process of class struggle, then it is methodologically wrong to ascribe causality to primarily economic impulses proceeding from the world-system level. However, the political economy of the world-system exercises a general causality insofar as territorial classes are structured by international forces and these classes are locked into relationships of subordinated dependency that extend beyond national frontiers.

The "general determinants" of the historical process are those forces that emanate from the world-system level. These imperative forces are primarily the internationalized accumulation and the class formation and class polarization processes. These processes are actualized in the class practices of center bourgeoisies, in the decisions of transnational corporations, in the international policies of center governments, and in the activities of international financial institutions. This implies a different concept of "world-system" than is current in the rather functionalist notions now gaining prominence. As Petras notes, "The conception of world system remains a static description of national features abstracted from the class realities which produce it" (1981:151).

"Proximate determinants" are those class relations (including the activitites of the state viewed as an expression of class relations) that are rooted in territorial units of the world-system. Although the relation between general and proximate determinants is asymmetrical, it is conceived dialectically, not as a one-way determinism. Depending on the particular object of analysis, it may be appropriate to emphasize one level of the analysis or the other. Structural analysis of the main features of underdevelopment would emphasize primarily general and conjunctural analysis mainly proximate determinants, but it would be seriously misleading to exclude either from any level of analysis. The problem with the main thrust of dependency analysis is that it sometimes disproportionately emphasizes the general determinants (or treats conjunctural analysis as structural), while a mode of production focus (in those too few instances where it is applied to concrete situations) isolates proximate from general determinants.

Dependency analysts have always insisted on the primacy of the internationalization of capital as the source of dependent underdevelopment: first the conquest and plunder of primitive accumulation, then colonization and the impositon of mono-export economies, and, now, the irresistable, multifaceted penetration of multinational corporations. Some dependentistas have not moved beyond this. On the other hand, Quijano, Cardoso, and others working within a dependency perspective consistently have analyzed how, in its international expansion, capital encounters economic conditions and sociopolitical forces that are specific to localities, nations, and regions. These conditions and forces leave their peculiar stamp; they facilitate and hinder, foment and deform, and give specific limits and many twists to the process of capitalist development. The external/internal nexus is unraveled if it is viewed as a dialectic of asymmetrical process. The structuring impulses are international in scope, but the actual outcomes are the result of localized conditions and struggles. The method is historical-structural,[3] involving analysis of political economy and class relations under conditions of dependency, where dependency itself is a class relationship among parties of unequal power.

In all but the most general studies of underdevelopment and dependency, the outcomes of historical processes are of first concern. Ascribing outcomes of territorial class struggles to world-system-level forces (the power of multinational corporations or the imperial state, the crises of accumulation stemming outward from the center, the machinations of the CIA, etc.) suppresses the dialectic of the external/internal. As I noted elsewhere:

> The problem is that much of the work by those utilizing the dependency framework has focused on external economic constraints and impulses and proceeded to view internal social struggle as a kind of dramatic production with a certain amount of improvisional theatre perhaps, but somehow not a real existence. The main actors in the Latin American Theatre—military officers, local businessmen, and suffering masses—may believe their drama is real life, it is implied, but the roles they play are written abroad and transmitted to them by the latest Madison Avenue technique and by covert imperial agents, backed up by explicit pressures from international lenders and Washington and sweetned with junior partner contracts with international capital. There is of course a certain descriptive validity and ideological appeal to this characterization of local actors as puppets. But a dialectical science of society cannot assume that the life of any nation is an orchestrated production computer programmed by the powerful of another nation.
>
> Imperialism and dependency are not a theatre of the absurd; the forms of international domination do not ordain overwhelming structures (even if, as in the Altusserian formulation, they are "relatively autonomous"); nor are events determined by the inexorable working out of imminant laws of motion of the capitalist mode of production. Ruling classes do not write history—their experience is a never-ending and largely failing struggle to achieve a workable hegemony. People make history by struggling against oppressive social realities and their oppressors; and this is nowhere more vivid today than in the dependent regions [Johnson, 1981:113-114].

At the same time, taking the general determinants of class formation into account, local actors are properly seen as trained and schooled in the academy of imperialism; they are not free agents. The character of a local bourgeoisie is shaped by the deformations and limitations imposed by the condition of dependency; a territorial working class is structured in the first instance by extraterritorial patterns of accumulation; intermediate groups, though proportionately smaller than in the center countries, have a disproportionate social weight due to the deformations and relative weaknesses of the polar classes; a surplus population of such magnitude is generated that it is beyond the capacity of any nation to even slightly ameliorate its condition, much less foster genuine social and economic development by absorbing the creative and productive energies of this multitude.

Thus, while territorial class struggles are the proximate causes of events, the forces forming classes and providing a context for their clashes are international in scope.

The Class Polarization Process in the Latin American Region

In most of the nations of Latin America today, the center of wealth and power is a grouping of big corporate-financial interests. Empirical studies of this grouping have tended to be descriptive and static,[4] but they do reveal that capital is highly concentrated in large-scale corporate enterprise, centralized in the activities of financial institutions, and organized through a series of tightknit, often family-based "interest groups." Each interest group operates as a conglomerate, extending control into diverse economic sectors. These groups are best termed the "finance capital fraction of the local bourgeoisie." This fraction has its historical origins in the oligarchic clans of earlier periods. In the recent stage of dependent development the economic base of these groups have been diversified and modernized, and they scramble to associate themselves with transnational capital in the more dynamic sectors of the economy. Transnational capital establishes a multisectoral direct presence, relating ever more intimately to local business, to a working class being formed under its overall sway, and to national states.

At the bottom of a rigidifying class structure are an expanding industrial working class and a vast array of immiserated peoples ("surplus population" or "marginalized classes"). The working class, understood as laborers totally dependent on wages, is a relatively small proportion of the population (10 to 30 percent depending on the country). The mass of immiserated rural and urban peoples is a much more substantial formation. The region contains millions who have been dispossessed of traditional means of existence, primarily agricultural, yet who are unable to obtain regular employment at wages that provide subsistence.

The process in Latin America, therefore, is not simply one in which capitalist development counterposes a growing industrial working class against a consolidating industrial capital in ever more polarized form. Under conditions of dependency, capitalist development forms a historically unprecedented surplus population that is dispossessed of property rights and subsistence but is not proletarianized.

This form of polarization, concentrated national and foreign finance-capital against a laboring population in quite distinct class situations, presents the central antagonism of Latin American societies. At the same time, the class relation capital-to-labor is set within a panoply of complimentary social relations: mediating relations that form intermediate groupings in the social structure; relations of exploitation that do not involve wage labor; and social relations that reproduce cheap labor power, a marked sexual division of labor, and, ultimately, the polarization process. These are discussed below.

A historical-structural method proceeds on the basis of understanding existing realities as a construction on what was and what is in the making. Within a perspective of uneven development class formations are of two types: those whose social existence is owed to preceding developmental stages and those that are primarily products of the economic and social transformations of the present, ongoing stage of dependent development. These class formations are highly conditioned by transformations in the relations of dependency, and it is the complex of antagonisms and accommodations among them, in the context of the basic polarization, that marks the intricate and unstable social fabric of Latin American societies.

The most important formations tied to the old order of classic underdevelopment and, where it has come about, as in the Southern Cone, national import-substitution industrialization include national capital in the competitive sectors of production for domestic markets, the petty bourgeoisie, and landowners and agricultural laborers engaged in production for export (in some countries *latifundistas* and enserfed peasants are still important). Class groupings formed or considerably augmented by the more recent process of dependent development include a maturing industrial working class, a managerial bourgeoisie and technocratic staff, the salaried middle class, the diverse rural and urban groupings among the surplus population, and various social or institutional forces such as the military, the church, intellectuals, and students. The superimposition of newer formations on a preexisting structure presents an extraordinary complex social structure and field of social struggle, especially in the more industrially advanced countries like Brazil, Argentina, Chile, and Mexico.

The highly uneven development that has formed this complex social structure is not a hybrid of modes of production. It is viewed more appropriately as a telescoping of one historical stage of capitalist development on another. Since the 1950s, the new forms of the internationalization of capital, as general determinants, have affected the indigenous structures of nineteenth-century classic underdevelopment and the national development of the 1930s and 1940s. This has created sharp transitional crises, not only of economic development but of the social fabric, which has bifurcated along the polar axis and fractionalized other class formations. These crises of transition, not the penetration of transnational corporations or the machinations of the CIA, are the specific determinants of the most salient events of the 1970s including the imposition of military dictatorships.

Space does not permit analysis of the range of class formatons identified above. Sketches of the structure of local bourgeoisies and of intermediate formations are presented below, and I comment on one issue—the reproduction of the labor force under conditions of below-subsistence wages—that relates most directly to the theoretical and methodological concerns raised here.

Local Bourgeoisies

The character of a local bourgeoisie is given by its roots in prior stages of development, by the transformation of its economic base in the stage of dependent development, by the divisions within it, by its relations with other classes, and by the expression of its interests within the state.

Today's banker-industrialist of industrial Buenos Aires is yesterday's gentleman-rancher of the rich, flat lands that stretch out from the port city. So it is also in most of Latin America.[5] The primary export producers and big export-import merchants of classic underdevelopment that formed genuine oligarchies survived the calamities of world wars and depression, withstood the threat of being eclipsed by emerging nationally based industrial bourgeoisies during the period of national development, and weathered populist and reformist challenges by multiclass political coalitions into the 1960s and early 1970s. The finance-capital fractions of local bourgeoisies are modernized oligarchies now resting on a firmer, transnationalized economic base.

In the countries of the Southern Cone over the last twenty to thirty years, the major sources of capital accumulation have shifted from primary production and import substitution industry to heavy industry (often state-initiated), intermediate goods production, consumer durables, and, increasingly, manufactured exports. The internal accumulation process moves in response to the activities of transnational corporations, international markets for nontraditional exports, and state activity. Modern capitals, foreign and local, conquer the internal markets once served by smaller-scale national industry, while they expand to supply the accoutrements of civilized life to a growing segment of high-income consumers produced by the formation of salaried intermediate strata and increasingly regressive income distribution.

As Quijano points out in Chapter 3, dominant classes in Latin America have always been sharply divided. While dependent development since the 1950s has greatly strengthened the finance-industrial segment and cemented its powerful alliance with transnational capital, its power as a class should not be exaggerated. Moreover, the shift in accumulation sources more than ever has fragmented and divided the local bourgeoisie as a whole. This presents a situation in which intraclass relations take on much economic and social-political significance. There is, first, a fierce competition of capitals among the large economic groups. Second, the important fraction (at least in Argentina, Brazil and Chile) of medium-sized and larger national capital located in consumer goods production and other long-established sectors of industry is threatened with bankruptcy, takeover by foreign firms or local interest groups, and political subordination. Third, small-scale capital and the petty bourgeoisie are being rapidly eliminated by concentration of production and market competition. Fourth, traditional landowners are marginalized more than ever from the mainstream of economic activity and political clout; in export agriculture and some basic food products, modern agribusiness, directed from abroad or from local corporate board rooms, displaces the latifundia and forces the peasantry to scramble for new sources of subsistence. Fifth, a professionalized managerial cadre, trained in schools of business abroad, ascends; a technocratic staff of engineers, lawyers, and systems analysts, together with a large group of politically skilled civilian and military technocrats located in agencies of state, comes into being. Thus, the new, transnationalized locus of accumulation constituently involves the restructuring of the local bourgeoisie. It obviously undermines the possibility of the emergence of any genuine "national bourgeoisie." Equally significant, a fractionalized local bourgeoisie creates a strong imperative for the behemoth of state power to assert its function of managing the affairs of civil society by dictating to the conflicting elements of that society. A divided and relatively feeble bourgeoisie, one that cannot aspire to be an instrument of the nation, one that cannot forge hegemony, needs a strong, decisive state. In these circumstances the way is open for the military to steward a political directorship. Under this directorship, the national industrial bourgeoisie of Argentina, the most important of the region, has been all but wiped out since the military intervention of 1976, while national industry in Chile is being sacrificed to the doctrines of the junta.

Of course, this directorship is assumed not only in the absence of an effective bourgeois class hegemony, but in the face of acute economic exigencies and, most of all, the assertions of other social forces in the polarizing and fragmenting social fabric. Among these important social forces in Latin America are the *capas medias*.

Intermediate Formations

Throughout the Third World, "middle classes" figure among the most important social forces moving events. Colonial authorities in Asia and Africa educated and yielded a place to an indigenous group of administrators who, in the period of independence struggles, turned on their masters. To this day, this class, aspiring to use the vehicle of the state to advance itself toward the status of bourgeoisie, holds a fairly firm grasp on state power. In Latin America, in the face of oligarchic and bourgeois class power, this group has never ruled; it nevertheless formed early and substantially, with a diverse base in the occupational structure. Its character is more clearly that that of an intermediate rather than "elite" formation of Africa or Asia; it stands between the bourgeoisies of the region (classes very weakly developed in colonized areas) and the working class and subsisting urban and rural masses. "Capas medias" (middle strata) is the term used in Latin America.

Capas medias became particularly prominent in those countries (Mexico, Brazil, Argentina, Chile, and Uruguay) that experienced a degree of national industrial development since World War I. Programs of state-sponsored industrialization and social-political reform were vigorously supported by the capas medias. The successes of these programs served to greatly expand the bases for the ample for-